The Evangelicals

The Evangelicals

What They Believe, Who They Are, Where They Are Changing

edited by

David F. Wells and John D. Woodbridge

Abingdon Press

Nashville   New York

THE EVANGELICALS

Library of Congress Cataloging in Publication Data

The Evangelicals.
  Bibliography: p.
  Includes index.
  1. Evangelicalism. I. Wells, David F.
II. Woodbridge, John D., 1941-
BR1640.E9   280'.4'0973   75-15574

ISBN 0-687-12181-7

Quote appearing in the chapter by V. Elving Anderson is "Creation and Evolution in Science Education," by Dr. Richard H. Bube, *Journal of the American Scientific Affiliation*, (1973), pp. 69-70, and is used by permission.

MANUFACTURED BY THE PARTHENON PRESS AT
NASHVILLE, TENNESSEE, UNITED STATES OF AMERICA

Truth is so obscure in these times, and falsehood so established, that unless we love the truth, we cannot know it.—Blaise Pascal, *Pensées*

Contents

Introduction

The current resurgence of evangelical Protestantism, coming as it does after an era of painful eclipse and emerging under the high noon of secularism, constitutes a remarkable historical development. The development seems particularly notable because the demise of evangelical Protestantism, both in the popular imagination and the academic mind, had appeared so complete. Even the major role that evangelicalism had played in shaping American culture in the nineteenth century seemed generally forgotten, and progressive views of historical development assumed that once the pattern of twentieth-century evangelical decline was established it could not be substantially reversed. The fact that the movement now can no longer be regarded as simply reactionary, but is vigorously and sometimes creatively speaking to the needs of the contemporary world is a phenomenon that has already brought considerable comment and which deserves further analysis. In order to gauge the significance of this resurgence and at the same time to provide a loose framework for some of the essays which follow, it is worth recalling how evangelical fortunes have undulated, especially during the last one hundred and fifty years.

By the middle third of the nineteenth century, evangelical Protestantism, led principally by theological conservatives, dominated American religion. It received its life impulse from the periodic revivals which coursed through

9

the land and forced into retreat both deism and skepticism, those children of the Enlightenment. According to Robert Baird, the evangelical phalanx in 1843 when his book *Religion in America* was published, included nearly all Protestants. Although his analysis may have been somewhat simplistic, and was definitely shortsighted concerning the growing strength of the Roman Catholic Church, it nevertheless does give some indication of the considerable influence wielded by evangelicals at the time. Convinced that the propagation and implementation of evangelical faith were the most effective means of civilizing the world, restraining vice, and making America a decent place to live, these evangelicals sponsored a vast range of missionary and social relief programs through their voluntary organizations. The passion of the land, Timothy Smith has rightly said, became "Christian liberty, Christian equality, Christian fraternity." A working relationship emerged between the politicians who guided the republic's fortunes and the evangelical clergymen who guarded its morals. Who could doubt that God had peculiarly blessed this nation with limitless material resources and its people with limitless spiritual energies? Disputes in the ranks concerning interpretations of Calvinism, millennial thought, and the enslaving of the black man notwithstanding, evangelicals were effectively shaping American culture.

The Civil War marked a watershed in American church history. Existing ecclesiastical divisions among evangelicals over the slavery issue were dramatically reinforced by the north-south split. Christians in the north and the south were no longer quite as confident that God's blessing was upon them and their land. Moreover black evangelicals and white evangelicals went their separate ways as the country moved through the Reconstruction Era (1865-1877) and beyond into the ignominious period of "Jim Crow" legislation.

In the closing decades of the last century the fact that the evangelical heyday might be ending was signaled in many other ways, not least of all in the educational realm. Institutions of higher learning were now assaulted by a barrage of bewildering ideas of a philosophical and scientific nature. Biblical criticism, basically a German import, eroded confidence in the integrity of the biblical text; notable Protestant figures such as President James McCosh of Princeton University capitulated to the new teachings about evolution and natural selection. The whole tenor of the Protestant community began to change. Assorted bifurcations among churchmen were becoming apparent. The debate over various forms of Arminianism and Calvinism which had previously disturbed evangelical unity now seemed somewhat petty when compared to the nascent contests over the meaning of Christianity itself. Liberally inclined evangelical churchmen tried to wed orthodoxy to the "givens" of biblical criticism and evolution; others, impressed by the new findings and less concerned about orthodoxy, experienced an almost irresistible pull towards what became known as Protestant liberalism; still others moved in the direction of conservative evangelicalism which frequently accented a premillennial eschatology and a high view of Scripture (biblical inerrancy). In the more liberal groups were some churchmen committed to social change, although they increasingly confused it with the gospel. In the more conservative groups were many who severed the gospel from its social correlate as well as from the whole domain of learning. In Moody and later in Billy Sunday, the latter found the architects for a new coalition of faith, animated by the old zeal but now greatly limited in its social and intellectual concerns. The broad evangelical community, so influential in the second third of the nineteenth century, was now being ineluctably pulled apart.

The efforts of Princeton Seminary Professors Charles Hodge, B. B. Warfield, and of those writers who contributed to the series of pamphlets called *The Fundamentals: A Testimony to the Truth* (1910-1915) to reverse what

11

they considered to be a deteriorating situation encountered only limited success. Theological conservatives were definitely losing their capacity to exercise significant influence over American Protestantism, let alone over American culture in general.

In the years which followed, but especially in the 1920s and 1930s, their tendency to separate from theological error and evil within society was instrumental in bringing about massive denominational disruptions. Threatened by the intrusion of Modernism into the mainline denominations, many theological conservatives (often referred to as fundamentalists) withdrew to establish their own "purer" organizations which in turn sponsored "purer" educational institutions. The enemy—proponents of evolution, Marxists, theological liberals, Catholic immigrants—was fought on all sides, and nowhere was this better exemplified than in a courtroom in Tennessee.

The Scopes Trial of 1925, ostensibly about the issue of evolution, in fact posed a question of larger import: Could a representative of conservative Christianity repulse the challenge of "modern" science? As the town of Dayton awaited the answer, its streets were transformed into a festive hawker's haven with bustling crowds and reporters from the country's leading newspapers. During the proceedings, the large audience cheered, scoffed, and sat silent while the two giants did battle. William Jennings Bryan, the silver-tongued orator and three-time presidential candidate of the Democratic Party, now aging and clearly ill at ease in questions of a scientific nature, frequently was caught off balance by John Scopes' brilliant defender, Clarence Darrow. With the whole country looking on, conservative Christianity was not only repulsed, but seemingly crushed.

Conservative evangelicals were disheartened, not only by the Scopes Trial, but also by the ecclesiastical struggles in process. The departure of J. Gresham Machen from Princeton Theological Seminary in 1929 proved for many to be

12

the final straw. A kind of wilderness experience had begun for evangelicalism. Truncated by splits, understandably beset by a defensive mentality, suffering from a loss of confidence, it was but a shadow of its earlier strength.

The period from the 1930s to the 1960s, bracketed by the Depression on the one end and the Vietnam War on the other, was in many ways one of lonely consolidation. Wounds were licked, losses were counted, defenses were shored up. Thus when the liberal Federal Council of American Churches seemed to be acquiring undue power, a parallel movement, the National Association of Evangelicals, was formed in 1942 to represent those more conservatively minded. William Ward Ayer, who addressed an early meeting, argued that fragmentation had cost evangelicals a voice in the nation's affairs. Ayer's assessment of the consequences of two decades of withdrawal and division was undoubtedly correct, but his call to unity could only be partly heeded; Carl McIntire, whose concerns were more decidedly fundamentalistic, had already formed another organization, the American Council of Christian Churches (1941). Common to many evangelicals in this period was the belief that the gospel and the "American way of life" were not only correlates but almost synonyms. Coexisting with revivalistic faith was sometimes found idolatrous patriotism; the Flag was often draped over the Cross, and both were revered as belonging together.

In the 1950s the general "revival" in religious interest in the nation as a whole also benefited evangelicals. A more receptive climate was apparent. Conservative seminaries continued to enjoy growing support, and evangelical scholarship was given a boost by the founding of Fuller Theological Seminary (1947) in Pasadena, California, and its subsequent development. Billy Graham in his crusades was accorded a national hearing. Campus Crusade for Christ, founded by Bill Bright, began to recruit staff workers. Other organizations such as Youth for Christ and Word of Life effectively reached out to high schoolers.

For most Americans, however, this revival was as patriotic as it was religious. It often amounted to little more than the shining and polishing of the status quo; "revival" was virtually synonymous with the unmitigated complacency of traditionalism. Allegiance to an undefined "God," as Will Herberg has pointed out, obscured the multitude of divisions that had formerly set off Jews from Catholics and Catholics from Protestants. Thus the reception accorded to evangelical Christianity was neither more nor less than that accorded to other faiths.

By 1958, historians spoke of the revival as being in the past, and in one of those startling shifts of mood the Christian world found itself on the threshold of a revolutionary era. Toward the middle 1960s it became apparent that there was a sense of dislocation in the nation, of things being out of harmony, of institutions adrift, of antagonism—"us" and "them." A pervasive apprehension became apparent, its expression oscillating between anger and helpless docility.

Dramatic changes in accepted ways of thinking occurred. A search for new life-styles, for different modes of belief, and behavior, was initiated. This search blossomed into a vigorous and irreverent counter-culture. Across the land there was profound social turmoil, and in the minds of many of the young, a growing distrust of the whole American system. The peace movement, the sit-ins, the civil rights marches, and the agitations all grew out of a deeply felt outrage over the kind of values that our society had not only accepted but also institutionalized. In the midst of burning cities and bombed universities, it was hoped that human dignity could be recovered, the sanctity of human life could be reasserted, both in America and in Vietnam. Corrupt and decayed as society might have been, however, it resisted all those protesters who stormed it. It did not crumble; nor did it change very much.

Many of the young began to lose hope. Some became cynics. Others took refuge in the drugged sanctuary of their inner lives, still others began groping for new kinds of spirituality. Abandoning the world to its own destruction, they searched for that reality which, if unseen, would yet be more hospitable, and one whose continued existence would be more certain. In the process, some even turned away from the countercultural palliatives of drugs and promiscuous sex. By the end of the 1960s a new kind of rebel was emerging, one who was strangely quiescent, muted, preoccupied with other things, unresponsive to the manifest evils of society, passive in the face of its imminent demise.

It was during the 1960s that radical theologies blossomed and died. As a matter of fact, rank and file Christians caught in the agonies of a society trying to find itself amidst the onslaught of new and frightening problems found little help in the pronouncement that God was dead. To them, this was evidence, not of great originality, still less of truth, but merely of triviality. But it was in this period, too, that a resurgence of evangelical faith became more noticeable, providing a strange foil to the more pessimistic theologies that enjoyed their brief success.

The most flamboyant evidence of this, upon which the news media focused considerable attention, were the Jesus People. They were soon exploited commercially, with Jesus watches and sweatshirts being marketed nationally. Their attempt, however, to find primitive Christianity while surveying the fallen rubble of both secularism and the counter-culture, was soon passed off as a fad. Undeniably, there were encouragements to such an interpretation. Like many others before them, Jesus People often seemed to be looking down the long well of human history and seeing their own faces reflected at the bottom. Sometimes their Jesus was the drop-out carpenter who constantly wondered where things were at; at other times, he was the leader of the commune. Frequently, he was the critic of the

15

establishment, the one who had assailed the "military-industrial complex" of his time. Their faith was often not only simple but also simplistic; it was zealous but also anti-intellectual; it was fervent but also antisocial. Yet to many of these people, their faith had resulted in an escape from the horrors of the drug world, rescue from the free, but dehumanized love of the counterculture. It is not, therefore, to be despised.

As bizarre and newsworthy as the Jesus People were, they represented only a small part of a far wider, far more conventional resurgence of biblical Christianity evident throughout the land. It was the kind of expansion that alarmed Dean Kelley in his *Why Conservative Churches Are Growing* and which Donald Bloesch tabulated with some care in his *The Evangelical Renaissance.*

Whether it is proper to speak of this growth in evangelical commitment as a resurgence may be debated. It is certainly true that in national terms evangelical Christianity today enjoys only a fraction of the allegiance it had during its heyday in the nineteenth century. Its influence on national priorities, the cultural outlook, education, and social legislation remains small. It is "resurging," then, only in a limited sense. First of all, it is proper to use this expression when comparing the relative strengths of evangelical and nonevangelical Protestantism; the former is growing numerically and the latter is declining. Second, this term is appropriate to certain internal changes in evangelical faith, the most noticeable of which are the growth in scholarship, the renewal in social concern, and the more sophisticated political understanding which is developing.

That the emerging strength of evangelical Christianity has excited considerable interest, of both a favorable and unfavorable kind, is undeniable. This has occurred on the two hundredth anniversary of a nation founded on Enlightenment ideals and on the fiftieth anniversary of the disastrous Scopes trial and at a time when nonevangelical

Christianity is in eclipse. And yet no single volume has yet appeared which has sought comprehensively to define what evangelical belief is, from whence it has arisen, what is the numerical strength of its following, what is the sociological makeup of the community adhering to it and how it now relates to the intellectual concerns of the day, to culture, and to society. These are the questions that participants in the movement as well as observers of it would like to see addressed; these were the questions posed to the authors. Because of both the importance and the difficulty of such a study, we decided that it was necessary to invite the participation of both evangelical and nonevangelical scholars, for each group has a special contribution to make. The intimate knowledge of a participant is, in certain ways, preferable to the assessments of an outsider. On the other hand, the facility for criticism, as well as the ability to grasp the larger perspective and to assess the significance of a movement within the overall picture may elude that participant, and it may indeed be easier to come by for the outsider. Furthermore, it was obvious to us that a volume purporting to deal with American evangelicalism could not overlook, as some have done, the contribution of black Christians; for this reason, we also invited the participation of two black authors. Thus we have reached across both racial and ideological lines to find those authors who are best equipped to deal with the questions we wished answered. The majority, however, are evangelicals, but they write as academics not as churchmen, as analysts not as spokesmen. Their evaluations, therefore, are their own.

The essays are arranged in three sections. In the first are those essays which seek both to define the shared theological convictions of evangelicals and to give some account of their differences. The second category of essays aims at identifying those American Protestants who hold evangelical beliefs; their histories and sociological characteristics are particularly noted. The essays in the third section deal with the changing evangelical perspectives on science,

17

politics, and societal issues during the last fifty years. At the end of each section is an evaluation or critique in which the authors address themselves to the general issue highlighted in their section; they had no opportunity to read the other essays before they wrote their pieces.

Across the ages, Christian movements of all kinds have tried to recapture the teaching and spirit of primitive, biblical Christianity. This is not as hopeless a task as some have claimed. Primitive Christian faith had already reached a crystalline form by the close of the first century and its verities were being established in miniature creeds, some of which are embedded in the New Testament itself. There were "faithful sayings" (I Tim. 1:15, 3:1, 4:9; II Tim. 2:11; Titus 3:8), fixed formulae for baptism (Acts 8:16, 19:5; I Cor. 6:11), catechesis (Rom. 1:3, 8:34; II Tim. 2:8; I Tim. 3:16; I Cor. 8:6; I Tim. 2:5), apologetics (Rom. 10:9; cf. I Cor. 12:3), and worship (Eph. 5:14; Titus 3:4-7; Phil. 2:6-11; Col. 1:15-20; I Tim. 3:16). A general consensus as to what constituted the Christian message was early exemplified, for example, in the speeches in the Book of Acts. It was this message, validated by a council, established by the apostles, and endorsed in churches (Rom. 6:17; I Cor. 11:2, 23 and 15:3; II Thess. 2:15, 3:6) which was committed to faithful men and to posterity (II Tim. 2:2). To deviate from this message was to embrace a "different gospel" (Gal. 1:6-9) and to invite final anathema. Whatever were the nuances which accompanied it and the ramifications which followed it, primitive Christianity was beautiful in its simplicity. At its center was the infinite, personal, and triune God who, in the birth and death of the Son, exhibited his ultimate compassion for man whose spiritual faculties have been ruined by sin and whose innermost desires are agitated by an aversion for his Word, both living and written. It taught that unmerited forgiveness has been provided through the vicarious, representative death of Christ, that unexpected reconciliation with God

18

could be found by embracing the gospel's promise of pardon. Christianity undoubtedly always involved much more than this, but it was never less. Its genius lay in that unique and elusive blend of simplicity and profundity. It was so simple that the simplest Galilean peasant could understand it easily, but so profound that no one could understand it completely.

Evangelical Christianity seeks to reaffirm these truths and to do so in that paradoxical union of simplicity and profundity. There is no doubt that much of what passes as biblical piety today is blighted by an unbecoming superficiality, strong in its simplicity and weak in its profundity. But it is nevertheless apparent that the old power to transform lives, to give hope where only despair reigns, to give coherence where only fragmentation has existed, to provide forgiveness where only the gnawing pain of guilt has been felt is still contained within the gospel (Rom. 1:18-20). The old, old story told in the old, old way is, in at least these respects, doing for this time precisely what it did for the age of primitive Christianity.

D.F.W.
J.D.W.

Part I. What Evangelicals Believe

The Theological Boundaries of Evangelical Faith

John H. Gerstner

Everything that American Protestants once considered essential in Christian faith was conveyed by the word *evangelical;* for some time, to the general Protestant public, this has no longer been so. During the last century in particular Protestant theologians have debated the very essentials of Christianity, frequently with little agreement. To what extent the present situation is an outcome of these earlier debates has been variously discussed, but it is certain that during the 1960s the Christian faith was debated against the background of declining congregations, diminishing financial resources, collapsing seminaries, and widespread, unsightly capitulation of Christian faith to secular assumptions. Those who groped for answers often became gloomy and pessimistic about finding them. It was a period of low horizons and diminished expectations. But out of this situation unexpectedly emerged a robust evangelicalism that so many prophets had announced could never survive a thoroughgoing secular age. It became plain that by the early 1970s it was becoming a dominant religious option in the land. Not only had it survived but now it seemed to many, who formerly were not sympathetic to it, that it alone was equipped to help those who were

John H. Gerstner is Professor of Church History at Pittsburgh Theological Seminary.

caught in the deathly web of secularism and wanted to escape. But what is evangelicalism?

Any student of evangelicalism is first impressed by the extremely wide and varied usage of the root word evangelical. Many denominations, especially Lutheran, have taken this name. The Evangelical Lutheran Church of the United States, The Evangelical Lutheran Augustana Synod of North America, The Evangelical Lutheran Joint Synod of Wisconsin and other States, and The Finnish Evangelical Lutheran Church of America are but a few examples. But the Lutheran denominations have no monopoly on the name, for there has been an Evangelical and Reformed Church (now part of the United Church of Christ). There is an Evangelical Association, The Evangelical Congregational Church, The Evangelical Free Church, Evangelical Friends, the Evangelical United Brethren Church, and The Reformed Presbyterian Church, Evangelical Synod. There is The Evangelical Union in Scotland and the word *evangelisch* has been as prominent in Germany as its equivalent has been in the United States. Periodicals have been fond of this name: *Evangelical Inquirer, Evangelical Intelligencer, Evangelical Magazine, Evangelical Magazine and Gospel Advocate, Evangelical Magazine and Missionary Chronicle, Evangelical Missionary Quarterly, Evangelical Theological Quarterly, Evangelical Quarterly.* Many seminaries, too, designate themselves evangelical: one of the very largest is Trinity Evangelical Divinity School.

The word evangelicalism derives from the Greek *euangellismos.* The evangel is good news or gospel, and throughout the New Testament it designates the message of salvation. Paul was not ashamed of this gospel, for "it is the power of God for salvation to everyone who has faith, to the Jew first and also to the Greek" (Rom. 1:16). Because it was the message, the indispensable message of salvation, the Apostle pronounced the curse of God upon those who preached any other evangel whether himself or an angel from heaven (Gal. 1:8).

Despite the dominant usage of *euangellismos* in the New Testament, its derivative, evangelical, was not widely or controversially employed until the Reformation period. Then it came into prominence with Martin Luther precisely because he reasserted Paul's teaching on the *euangellismos* as the indispensable message of salvation. Its light, he argued, was hidden under a bushel of ecclesiastical authority, tradition, and liturgy. The essence of the saving message for Luther was justification by faith alone, the article by which not only the church stands or falls but each individual as well. Erasmus, Thomas More, and Johannes Eck denigrated those who accepted this view and refered to them as "evangelicals." [1] A modern Roman Catholic theologian, Algermissen, sees as the essence of evangelicalism the reformer's appeal to the sole authority of the Bible, but more perceptively another Roman scholar, R. K. Macmaster, writes: "In its widest sense, the term signifies the body of doctrine regarded as the essential message of the gospel. Although the precise meaning of Evangelicalism has varied with different historical contexts, it is generally applied to the doctrine of salvation by faith in Christ." [2]

Philip Schaff has argued that evangelical Protestantism was early distinguished by three factors which he designated as objective, subjective, and social. The first was the authority of the Bible as opposed to that of the Church in all matters of faith and conduct. The second was justification "by the free grace of God through a living faith in Christ, as the only and sufficient Saviour, in opposition to the Roman doctrine of (progressive) faith *and good works.*" The third, "the *universal* priesthood of *believers,* in opposition to the *exclusive* priesthood of the *clergy,*" affected the functioning and structure of the church. [3]

Although Luther himself disliked the name evangelical being applied to his followers precisely because he saw the evangel as absolutely essential to all Christianity, the term did become associated with Lutheranism. But in time

(1648, when the Peace of Westphalia recognized the Reformed as evangelicals; 1653, when the *Corpus Evangelicorum* appeared including Reformed as well as Lutheran creeds, and especially in 1817, when the union of Lutheran and Reformed churches in Germany was called evangelical), evangelicalism was freely applied to Protestants in general. In 1948, thirteen Lutheran, twelve United, and two Reformed ecclesiastical bodies united to form the *Evangelische Kirche Deutschlands*. Today in German usage, *evangelisch* is commonly a synonym for Protestantism in distinction from Roman Catholicism.

Wesley's work in England is often referred to as the evangelical revival; it is no coincidence that his German, pietistic forerunner, J. C. Spener, wrote a volume entitled *Evangelische Lebensbegriffe*.[4] While Wesley did not regard his Anglican communion as apostate he felt, as Luther had before the break with Rome, that the gospel was being covered over by liturgical formalism and that he needed clearly to declare it to perishing men. The nineteenth-century scholar Blunt protests the claims of evangelicals such as Wesley and his followers. Identifying them with the low churchmen of his communion, he wrote that the evangelical or gospeller movement was "deprecated for the arrogance of the assumption which it expresses, that they are the only faithful preachers of the Gospel in the Church of England." [5] An 1812 work by Bishop Richard Mant was of the same temper, being entitled *An appeal to the Gospel, or An inquiry into the justice of the charge alleged by Methodists and other objectors, that the gospel is not preached by the national clergy.*

Up to this point there was more tacit than expressed doctrinal content to evangelicalism. But as "Puseyism" and "Popery" became stronger, the evangelical movement began both to close ranks and to unfold its banner more conspicuously. The Evangelical Alliance [6] was actually formed in London in 1846 with almost eight hundred participants being present. Notable leaders such as the German F. Tholuck, the Swiss Merle D'Aubigné, and America's S. S. Schmucker as well as the English gathered for the occasion, but it was to Thomas Chalmers, the nonconformist Scot, that the movement looked for its inspiration. Significant was the spelling out of the doctrinal platform in nine affirmations: (1) the inspiration of the Bible, (2) the trinity, (3) the depravity of man, (4) the mediation of the divine Christ, (5) justification by faith, (6) conversion and sanctification by the Holy Spirit, (7) the return of Christ and judgment, (8) the ministry of the Word, and (9) the sacraments of baptism and the Lord's Supper.

These doctrines indicate that though the movement was single-minded it was not simplistic. Like Luther before them, these men showed their common consensus with the past in proclaiming the trinity and other catholic doctrines, while insisting on the indispensability of salvation by grace alone. Thus the evangelicals opposed otherwise orthodox Roman Catholicism and Anglo-Catholicism because these were thought to neglect the heart of all orthodoxy, the evangel. Although the Reformed bodies were most strongly represented in the Alliance it is highly significant that the doctrines enumerated are not distinctly reformed but merely broadly evangelical.

Early American theology had its principal roots in European and British pietism. William Ames was the dominant theologian of the founding New England fathers. While his theology was classically reformed, it had the activistic,[7] pietistic stress of his own mentor, often called the father of pietism, William Perkins. John Cotton, Thomas Shepard, Thomas Hooker, and virtually all the seventeenth-century theologians of the congregational establishment were covenant or evangelical teachers. Jonathan Edwards in the next century was greatly concerned precisely because he saw his age turning from the evangelical faith of the seventeenth-century fathers. He fought mightily against this trend as did Frelinghuysen, Jonathan Dickinson, the Tennents, and others in the Middle Colonies [8] and Samuel

Davies in the South. In fact, the New England evangelical awakening began in 1734 as a direct result of the sermon series on justification by faith in which Edwards stressed the gospel of pure grace not only against Romanism but against the advancing Arminian neonomianism among Protestants. Joseph Tracy has seen the secret, humanly speaking, of Edwards' success in his showing that "God has not appointed anything for men to do before coming to Christ by faith"; for Edwards, this faith itself was the gift of a sovereign God.[9] That is what evangelicalism meant.

We need not here enter into the controversy that is still raging as to whether Edwards was right in his appraisal of the historical situation. That may be a moot point, but it is hardly debatable that after the "orthodox sleep" of the latter half of the eighteenth century when the evangelicals finally awoke, liberalism was challenging the gospel.

It would have been serious enough if it had been only the liberalism that led to Channing, Emerson, Parker, and unitarianism. But in a sense, that was so obviously a defection from evangelicalism that evangelicals could recognize the danger of liberalism's teachings and the fact that unitarianism was an ultimate enemy of the evangel.

What was more serious than unitarianism was the wound which evangelicalism received at the hands of its friends. The New England theology was supposedly continued in the new divinity centered in the New Haven school, with its ablest exponent in Nathanael Taylor, a protégé of Edwards' grandson, Timothy Dwight. The Yale divine claimed to be orthodox, calvinistic, and evangelical; the Princeton school which had come to be recognized as the nineteenth-century standard-bearer of evangelical orthodoxy had a different estimate of him. According to Charles Hodge and others,[10] Taylorism was Pelagianism, the utter antithesis of evangelicalism. Meanwhile, the Lutherans were having their "Taylor" in the form of Schmucker. The Episcopalian and other denominations were also having similar struggles for the preservation of evangelical faith.

But a theologian still more ominous for evangelicalism than Taylor was to appear—Charles Grandison Finney. No one in the second quarter of last century had the ear of America in the spreading of what went by the name of evangelicalism as did Finney. B. B. Warfield, whom some believe to be the greatest scholar Princeton ever produced,[11] was to see in Finney the Pelagian that Hodge had recognized in his mentor, Taylor. Warfield was not alone in this view. William McLoughlin [12] and others have seen Finney as a religious expression of Jacksonian democratic principles, which in different language, carries the implications of Warfield's charge.

We cannot here follow the intricacies of the interesting story of Finney and evangelicalism. It is sufficient to note that through his influence evangelicalism underwent a major change in meaning. His Pelagianism subverted the Reformation's understanding of grace precisely because it denied the Reformation's view of man. If his gospel conveyed the evangel, it was in form different from what it had been earlier. To this extent Finney, the greatest of nineteenth-century evangelists, became the greatest of nineteenth-century foes of evangelicalism.

With the appearance of Moody, Sunday, and Graham, however, evangelicalism recovered from the distortion of Finney, but it has never since returned to its original, pristine character. Virtually all the earliest evangelicals such as Luther, Calvin, Zwingli, Knox, Cranmer, Ames, Cotton, to a lesser degree Spener and Wesley, and to the purest degree Edwards, Hodge, and Warfield believed that the biblical evangel was the message of salvation by grace alone through faith alone. The stress on the sovereign initiative of God in first providing salvation and then in disposing the sinner to receive it was never believed to undermine the place of human responsibility. For the theology of the Reformation is notable for the care with which

sovereignty and responsibility are mutually upheld, paradoxical as this may appear. Nor, indeed, was the stress
on God's initiative designed to circumvent or eliminate the
activity of evangelism. On the contrary, it was seen as the
sine qua non of all evangelism. Without God's gracious
interposition the preaching of the gospel will always be
fruitless. God's sovereignty undergirds evangelism; it does
not undermine it. But in the practice of evangelism since
Finney's day, the notion of human responsibility has been
greatly enlarged and changed. The price which has had
to be paid is a diminished doctrine of grace. Although
contemporary evangelists have recoiled from some of
Finney's distortions, the evangel is still presented as being
of divine origin but it is seen as needing human cooperation for its realization. The initiative of God in disposing
man to receive the gospel is not only seen as unnecessary
but some view it as pernicious since the freedom of man
is thereby violated. The dilemma of relating man's moral
inability to his ethical responsibility is not new to this
generation of evangelicals, nor are some of the solutions
that have emerged. But it is clear that the view common
to the Protestant Reformers, which was held with remarkable unanimity, has undergone serious modifications.

Another modification in the practice and meaning of
evangelicalism occurred with the formation of the Evangelical Alliance in 1846. Ironically, the Americans, who at
first could not enter fully into the Alliance because it took
a firm stance against slavery, began after the Civil War
to take a more energetic part in it, especially in the area
of social action. In fact, Josiah Strong became executive
secretary of the American branch in 1885, a capacity in
which he served until he resigned in 1898. Strong was also
famous as a noted forerunner of the social gospel and his
resignation was caused by the slow pace of the Alliance
in social reform. No doubt he would have been deeply
gratified to see the Evangelical Alliance lead to the formation of The Federal Council of Churches in 1908. The

Council stressed social involvement a great deal but in the process seemed to many evangelicals to be eliminating the gospel itself, though even Walter Rauschenbusch had argued strenuously that there could be no valuable social reform without the gospel.[13] For many years the Lutherans and others would not join the Council because of this presumed threat to the gospel.

It was about this time that fundamentalism became prominent. The turn of this century saw the emergence of this movement because the Evangelical Alliance and other ostensibly evangelical phenomena were seemingly becoming more liberal. The evangelical protest took the form of an insistence on the fundamentals of evangelical faith.

At its inception the movement which came to be called fundamentalism was a broadly-based, broadly evangelical, generally Protestant phenomenon. Writing for *The Fundamentals,* for example, were men like James Orr and B. B. Warfield, both of whom were staunch Calvinists. In fact the five fundamentals were formulated in 1910 by the General Assembly, Presbyterian Church in the United States of America when the denomination was still predominantly Calvinistic in witness. With the passage of the decades, the larger denominations, such as this Presbyterian body, have tended to reject fundamentalism without officially repudiating the fundamentals. The result is that conservative leaders in the larger Calvinistic denominations may still be fundamental without being dubbed fundamentalists. The various fundamentalist associations, such as the World Fundamentalist Fellowship, have of course worked outside such denominations.

Although the terms fundamental or essential have long been used in classical theology, the movement called fundamentalism is American and modern. Europeans today speak of *amerikanische Fundamentalismus* because around the turn of this century many concerned American conservatives believed that even the irreducible minimum of a supernatural Christianity was being abandoned or ques-

29

tioned by the liberal movement. To resist this trend, Bible conferences and schools came into existence. The actual "five fundamentals" (the miracles of Christ, the virgin birth of Christ, the satisfaction view of the atonement, verbal inspiration, the bodily resurrection of Christ) seem first to have been defined at the Presbyterian General Assembly in 1910, although other lists of essential doctrines had been drawn up by Evangelicals in the last half of the nineteenth century. Between 1910 and 1915, *The Fundamentals* was published at the expense of the Stewart brothers of California. This early phase embraced traditional reformed and Arminian theologians of the major Protestant denominations, together with dispensational conservatives usually found in the smaller, independent groups. They united to defend the fundamentals of the faith which they all shared in spite of many important differences about nonfundamentals.

During the last half-century there has been a slight shift in the use of the term *fundamentalism*. Conservatives in the major denominations are not so often called fundamentalists (partly because their denominations are not part of such bodies as the "National Association of Evangelicals," "American Council" and the like), which has come to be associated more commonly with the smaller, independent groups. J. Gresham Machen is possibly the last famous scholar in a major denomination commonly to be so designated though his position is still shared by many in his own and other major denominations. Because of the growing association of the term with separated bodies having inferior educational systems and a polemical outlook, the term has come in general parlance to represent not only the advocates of the traditional fundamentals but also those who are militant, schismatic, antischolarly, dispensational, and premillennarian. Indeed, Ernest Sandeen has argued that premillennialism was the background movement that came into expression as twentieth-century Fundamentalism.[14] There are, however, many who are not militant, schismatic, or antischolarly (or dispensational or premillennarian), but who are, nonetheless, proponents of the fundamentals. They call themselves evangelicals rather than fundamentalists, not because they repudiate the fundamentals but because they reject the image which fundamentalists have acquired.

The late Edward John Carnell was a case in point. His extremely able defense of fundamental Christianity being beyond dispute, he nonetheless became increasingly uneasy about the term and preferred to distinguish between classic and cultic fundamentalism, to the chagrin of many. In fact, the term neoevangelical or neofundamentalist has come into wide use by men to the right of conservative center such as Robert Lightner and to the left of it, like William Hordern, to locate the different shades of fundamentalism. Undoubtedly there are differences, but these are less of theology and more of mentality, culture, and outlook.

Consequently, it is possible to see the term evangelicalism acquiring both a broader and a narrower connotation in the twentieth century than it had had previously. On the one hand, it lost some important aspects of its Reformation heritage, especially as these relate to the doctrines of grace, the depth of human depravity, and the indispensable need of God's saving initiative not only in sending his Son, Jesus Christ, to accomplish salvation but also in inclining sinners to accept it. On the other hand, during the painful and protracted debate of the 1920s and 1930s, the latitude of thought which could be called evangelical was sharply limited and some of the concomitants of nineteenth century evangelicalism such as a deep social concern as generally expressed, for example, over the slavery question, disappeared. Controversy not only brought evangelicals together, but it also accentuated the issues which divided them from those of other persuasions. In turn, evangelicalism came to be defined in terms of these issues, some of which had not previously distinguished it. Thus a certain narrowing in connotation took place.

31

The history of evangelicalism during the nineteenth and twentieth centuries has once again highlighted an ambiguity that first surfaced in the Puritan period, namely, whether a distinction can be drawn between essentials of the faith and nonessentials. The issue is a complex and important one, for it goes to the heart of biblical authority. Evangelicals are agreed that Scripture is authoritative in all matters of faith and conduct. This means that nothing in faith or practice can be held against the teaching of Scripture. But does it follow that Scripture explicity informs the church on all matters of its conduct? Anglicans and Lutherans have argued that there are certain matters which are indifferent and upon which Scripture has not spoken; these would include matters relating to church government, forms of worship, and the use of liturgy. On these issues, Christian prudence is to be determinative. The nonconformist Puritans in England, however, contested this, arguing that the distinction between essentials and nonessentials, between matters relating to salvation and those which do not, is entirely arbitrary, for Christ's authority is at stake in both categories. This view was carried across the Atlantic by the early settlers and has come to characterize American evangelicalism. A practical distinction is made between essentials and nonessentials which enables evangelicals in different traditions and denominations to recognize one another, but denominational distinctives are nevertheless pursued because it is believed that Christ's authority is as much at stake in these matters as in the more weighty matters relating to salvation.

The presence of this theological unity that survives in spite of denominational distinctives has given rise to an ecclesiology in evangelicalism which some consider to be novel. What is stressed are the invisible aspects of the church rather than the visible, which partly explains why evangelicals are unenthusiastic about the ecumenical movement. To them, the most fundamental unity is not an organizational one but a spiritual one. Undoubtedly, this stress has sometimes allowed evangelicals to become irresponsible with respect to the visible, institutional church; and it certainly did nothing to discourage the denominational splintering of the evangelical witness which took place during the 1920s and 1930s. But it is important to note that this stress on the invisible church is not the invention of contemporary evangelicalism; it is also present in Augustine, Luther, Calvin, Hodge, Kuyper, and many others of earlier generations.

To the evangelical, theological precision at least on essential matters is vital. Others may imagine that anyone who shows religious earnestness, regardless of his views, or who engages in evangelism, regardless of the evangel which he preaches, can be called an evangelical. Those who have self-consciously assumed this title, however, insist that they have done so on account of their theology. The five points of fundamentalism remain central to evangelicalism, for all five relate to the person of Christ.[15] He alone, the historic, divine-human Son of God, is Christianity's essence; the thought of Christless Christianity, such as it is encountered in modern theology, is evidence neither of profundity nor of originality, but of sheer nonsense. And on these points, evangelicals deny that there is liberty for interpretation, distinctions between the facts and the theories about these facts, so that a person may profess his belief in them, while in reality holding as true something quite different.[16]

This is not to say that there are not different expressions given to this evangelical theology. In recent years, some of the cultural wrappings of fundamentalism have fallen away, and those who now maintain the old views often do so with considerable learning and sophistication. This has given rise to charges of capitulation from the fundamentalists; the new breed of evangelical is dismissed as "neoevangelical." But not all find this new development so disagreeable. William Hordern has described this development as the "new face of conservatism," saying:

33

The best description for this group is "new conservative."
A conservative is one who is marked by the desire to preserve the truth and values of the past, but his mind is not
closed to change if he can be persuaded that the change is
for the better. The use of the term "conservative" helps to
distinguish this group from a movement that can still be
called fundamentalist. This latter group is the "radical right"
of the theological world, and is often allied with the radical
right of the political world. The distinction between the
contemporary fundamentalist movement and the new conservatives is made evident by the fact that the fundamentalists
reserve some of their most bitter attacks for the new conservatives. . . . Riley Case locates the beginnings of the
new conservatism in three books beginning with Carl
Henry's *The Uneasy Conscience of Fundamentalism* in
1947 and continuing with the American Scientific affiliation's *Modern Science and the Christian Faith* and E. J.
Carnell's *An Introduction to Christian Apologetics* in 1948.[12]

In 1942 the National Association of Evangelicals was
formed with the purpose of representing "all evangelical
believers in all denominations and groups." There can be
no doubt it was the presumed departure of the Federal
Council of Churches from evangelical principles that led
to this development. In fact, it was a milder reaction than
the one that preceded it in 1941. The American Council
of Christian Churches required as a condition of membership that all denominations or individuals withdraw from
the Federal Council or from denominations affiliated with
it. This is sometimes called double separation—separation
from evil and separation from those not separated from
evil. It was because there were so many individual evangelicals in denominations affiliated with the Council that
the National Association of Evangelicals felt the need for
a fellowship of such persons even though involved reluctantly or critically with the Federal or National Council. In
1945 came the Evangelical and Foreign Missionary Association under the NAE. If one includes the missionaries
of this and other exclusively evangelical bodies such as the
International Fundamental Foreign Missionary Associa-

tion, not to mention evangelicals in the standard denominational agencies, well over fifty percent of the present-day foreign missionaries are evangelical.[18]

As used in the Bible, then, the term *euangellismos* refers to the way of salvation and was so understood subsequently. At the Reformation it came into prominent usage precisely because the Roman Church seemed to Protestants to have lost the gospel way of salvation. In the reformers' formulation and well into the nineteenth century, evangelicalism was God's way of salvation, not only in the offering of it to men but in the applying of it to their hearts as well. Last century, however, the evangel began to be seen more as the divine offer of grace and not so much as the divine application of grace. With the turn of this century even the offered gospel was challenged, and evangelicalism engaged in a mighty struggle to preserve the very fundamentals of evangelical faith. These fundamentals were, as the term suggests, the mere foundations of the gospel and not the full-orbed gospel itself.

The twentieth century has seen the emergence of "crisis theology" spearheaded by Karl Barth and going under the name of evangelical. Yet if the process of seeking definitions is valid, then it is plain that Barthians are not evangelical in an historical sense. If the term evangelical can include Karl Barth as well as Carl Henry, Emil Brunner as well as Jonathan Edwards, Oscar Cullmann as well as John Wesley, then we must give it a definition so broad as to be somewhat meaningless.

In an age that is characterized by a loss of meaning and an uncertainty about religious values, it is important for evangelicalism to offer a choice, not an echo. It is important for it to be clear where it has always been historically clear; it must become creative, able to stir the hearts of men again, powerful, and able to open to them the limitless depths of God's own being. To do this it will rely on its own strength only at its peril. For as the greatest of all American evangelicals, Jonathan Edwards, once remarked:

> We must come off from this [pride] to an absolute despair of helping ourselves, either in purchasing redemption for ourselves, or in applying the redemption already purchased. We must leave all hoping that we shall be able either to satisfy God's justice or to bring ourselves to an hearty acceptance of Christ's satisfaction. We must not imagine that we of our own ability shall either convert ourselves or uphold ourselves in a state of grace or do any good work of ourselves when we are converted.[19]

Notes

1. See Erasmus, *Epistola contra quosdam, qui se falso iactant Evangelicos,* published in 1529.

2. R. K. Macmaster, *New Catholic Encyclopedia* (New York: McGraw-Hill Book Co., 1967), 5, 688.

3. Philip Schaff, *Creeds of Christendom* (New York and London: Harper and Brothers, 1877), 3, 206-7.

4. See J. F. Spener, *Die Evangelische Lebens-Pflichten* published at Frankfort in 1707.

5. Blunt, *Dictionary of Sects, Heresies, Ecclesiastical Parties and Forms of Religious Thoughts* (London, Oxford, and Cambridge: Rivington, 1874).

6. See *Evangelical Alliance: A Concise View of its Principles, Objects and Constitution* published at Newcastle, England, in 1846.

7. It is characteristic of many Dutch Calvinistic writers to view Puritanism in this manner; cf., for example, Ralph Bronkema's *The Essence of Puritanism* (Goes, England: Ooaterbaan & Le Cointre, 1929).

8. See C. H. Maxon, *The Great Awakening in the Middle Colonies* (Chicago: The University of Chicago Press, 1920).

9. *The Great Awakening* (Boston: Tappan and Donnet; New York: J. Adams, 1843), p. 10.

10. See Charles Hodge's "Jonathan Edwards and the Successive Forms of New Divinity," *The Biblical Repertory and Princeton Review* (1858), pp. 585-620.

11. B. B. Warfield, *Studies in Perfectionism,* 2 vols. (New York: Oxford University Press, 1931).

12. See William McLoughlin, *The American Evangelicals, 1800-1900* (New York: Harper and Row, 1968), p. 13.

13. See Walter Rauschenbusch, *A Theology for the Social Gospel* (New York: The Macmillan Co., 1917).

14. Ernest Sandeen, *The Origins of Fundamentalism: Toward a Historical Interpretation* (Philadelphia: Fortress Press, 1968).

15. The virgin birth of Christ is not strictly essential to the doctrine of the deity of Christ, but it has often been so regarded by fundamentalists because many who explicitly deny the virgin birth are also implicitly opposed to the deity of Christ.

16. For example, evangelicals hold that it is not the resurrection but the *bodily* resurrection that is indispensable to orthodox belief. Likewise, it is not the "Lordship of Christ" but the "eternal deity of Christ" that is the evangelical fundamental. A large number of ministers in the Presbyterian Church in the U.S.A. have made the distinction between facts and theories in their "Auburn Affirmation" (1923).

17. William Hordern, *New Directions in Theology Today* (Philadelphia: The Westminster Press, 1966), I, 77-78.

18. See J. H. Kane, *A Global View of Christian Missions from Pentecost to the Present* (Grand Rapids, Mich.: Baker Book House, 1971).

19. This is from an unpublished manuscript of a sermon on Luke 9:23, preached during the fall of 1726, quoted with the permission of the Beinecke Library and Rare Book Room, Yale University, New Haven, Conn.

Unity and Diversity in Evangelical Faith

Kenneth S. Kantzer

On October 31, 1517, a brilliant young monk in Wittenberg set in motion a train of events of which contemporary evangelicalism is both an integral part and an important outcome. For while Martin Luther's protest, delivered in the ninety-five theses, was aimed primarily at ecclesiastical abuse, undergirding it were two fundamental principles which are still central to the present day heirs of his protest.[1] The first sees justification occurring at the beginning of one's Christian life rather than the end. God's loving favor is entered into through faith in Jesus Christ; it is not a reward for moral earnestness or ecclesiastical obedience.[2] The second principle asserts that Scripture, as illumined by the Holy Spirit, is the only trustworthy guide in moral and spiritual matters. The weight of tradition no less than the continuing teaching of the church must alike be subject to this higher authority.[3]

The phenomenon of unity in the midst of diversity which characterized Christian faith in the sixteenth and seventeenth centuries also characterizes it in the twentieth. Evangelical Christianity stands in a line of direct descent from Luther, Melanchthon, Calvin, Zwingli, Knox, Cranmer, Hooker, Chemnitz, Arminius, Menno Simons, and all but

Kenneth S. Kantzer is Professor of Systematic Theology and Dean at Trinity Evangelical Divinity School.

the most radical Anabaptists. Their basic faith has been perpetuated and binds Christians together in a remarkable unanimity that has defied the shifting of cultural patterns and the passing of the centuries. At the same time, the perplexing and even frustrating individuality evident then is evident now.[4] At the center is a commonalty of faith, but the edges have become frayed through misunderstanding and internecine warfare, for evangelicals have consistently shown a remarkable willingness to fight and die for inconsequential nuances.[5] Yet in their better moments, each one gives thanks to God that there are men and women living in the midst of a blasé and skeptical world who are willing to believe anything passionately and commit themselves to what they hold to be good and true.[6]

I. The Formal Principle

The formal principle of biblical authority is the watershed between most other movements within the broad stream of contemporary Protestantism and the movement (or movements) of twentieth-century Protestantism known as fundamentalism, which is a term often poorly used for the purpose it is intended to serve, or evangelicalism or conservative Protestantism.

Luther's articulation of the formal principle, the enduring authority of Scripture in matters of faith and conduct, was as controversial and divisive in his day as it is in ours. And it is certainly plain that in recent years it has often suffered from unwarranted caricature. Evangelicals who follow Luther in this regard are accused of holding that Scripture must be "literally" interpreted regardless of its variegated literary forms and its rich profusion of word pictures, metaphors, and similes, that its authors were stenographers to whom the Holy Spirit dictated, that the Bible is either a book of rules or a book of science, and that acceptance of these and other beliefs is necessary for salvation. It is safe to say that no educated evangelical

39

and few who wish to describe themselves as fundamentalists would acquiesce to any of these views.[7]

It is, of course, true that in providing theological safeguards for the idea that the Bible is to be heard and heeded in all the circumstances of our lives and in seeking to explain how the Bible is divinely authoritative, evangelicals have traditionally described its inspiration as plenary and verbal, the results of which are that it is infallible and inerrant. Yet none of these words, if properly understood, lends any encouragement to the continuing caricature to which they are exposed in some circles. God in his providence so guided the authors in the choice of their words and the use of their sources, without in any way negating their individuality, that their words are also and really his (verbal inspiration). And this guidance extends to the whole of Scripture not merely to its more "elevated" or more "religious" parts (plenary). The result of this is that Scripture is incapable of stating error (infallible) or of wandering from the truth (inerrant).[8] None of these words relates to the method of inspiration—how God providentially guided the authors—but only to the results.[9] Scripture is complete; it is trustworthy. Those who build their lives upon its truths will not be disappointed or mislead. On the contrary, this is the means by which God both guides and addresses man. Yet it remains a means rather than an end, for faith never terminates in the Bible itself, even if it is structured and informed by it, but in the God who speaks through his biblical Word. The Lausanne Conference of July, 1974, which assembled the most representative gathering of evangelicals in this century, affirmed these same truths:

> We affirm the divine inspiration, truthfulness and authority of both Old and New Testament Scriptures in their entirety as the only written word of God, without error in all that it affirms, and the only infallible rule of faith and practice. We also affirm the power of God's word to accomplish his purpose of salvation. The message of the Bible is addressed

40

to all mankind. For God's revelation in Christ and in Scripture is unchangeable. Through it the Holy Spirit still speaks today. He illumines the minds of God's people in every culture to perceive its truth freshly through their own eyes and thus discloses to the whole church ever more of the many-coloured wisdom of God.[10]

Undoubtedly, the manifold discussions that have taken place about original autographs, inspiration, illumination, inerrancy, and infallibility have appeared to some almost like a heavy layer of dust that has settled on this subject. The situation, however, is not dissimilar from that which arose earlier in the church's life over the doctrines of the trinity and of Christ's person. The simple confession that Christ should be honored as God may be preferable to the affirmation that was developed in highly technical and complicated language known as the Chalcedonian Definition, but in an age where the truth of Christ's person was imperiled, the simple confession was also imperiled. Without technical and complicated underpinnings, it could have been undermined. It is certainly the case that evangelicals should see, and usually do see, their discussions over Scripture in this light. God has given his Word to the church, not to provide a topic for discussion, still less for controversy, but primarily that people may become acquainted with his means of forgiving sin (justification) and learn how to live in the daily power of Christ's conquest over sin (regeneration and sanctification). Thus evangelicals, in sharing their faith with others, do not see themselves as superior philosophers, nor yet as those having a more enlightened view of reality, but simply as people who have received God's cure for the haunting and indelible guilt of sin and that corrosive emptiness of the heart for which Christ is alone the enduring solution. For this reason they have a message to share. And in the midst of the complexities of contemporary life, God day by day meets his people in Scripture which serves as an instrument for comfort, rebuke, and cleansing; this is why

41

evangelicals place great importance on the daily reading of and meditation upon Scripture.[11]

In the first third of the twentieth century the future of evangelicalism looked exceedingly bleak. The flood gates were washed away, and it seemed evident that it was only a matter of time before the doctrine of biblical infallibility would join the dodo and the dinosaur, although some conceded it might linger on in isolated rural areas of the Middle West and Deep South.[12]

In recent decades, particularly in the fifties and sixties, evangelicalism has experienced a general resurgence accompanied by renewed affirmation of its formal principle. At the same time traditional liberalism has declined, and its dominant role on the American scene has been taken over by a chastened liberalism and a conservative neo-orthodoxy, both of which have a far greater appreciation for the Protestant heritage than had the older liberalism. This radical change in the American church has brought conservative evangelicals back once again into dialogue with those of other persuasions.[13]

If evangelicals are in general agreement regarding the divine inspiration and authority of the Bible and its function as an adequate guide for the life of the church, the same cannot be said for the way in which they seek to prove or defend their doctrine of Scripture. Broadly speaking, contemporary evangelical apologetics falls into two categories: traditional and presuppositional. The traditional apologists maintain that: (1) There is an objective case to serve as an adequate ground for confidence in the truth of Christianity. (2) The human mind, even sinful man's fallen mind, permits a common ground, epistemologically speaking, on the basis of which a Christian apologist may appeal for a rational judgment. (3) The source of this possibility lies in a relic of the image of God and in prevenient or regenerative grace. (4) The Christian witness ought to present to the unbeliever evidences to persuade him to believe Christ is worthy of trust as well as values to motivate him to choose Christ. (5) Evidences are also appropriate to confirm the faith (in so far as it involves knowledge) of a believer already committed to Christianity. (6) The act of faith, in so far as it is an intellectual act, is buttressed by evidence. (7) Only by the grace of God does the divine Spirit create truly saving faith with full certainty or certitude of the truth of Christianity. (Following Calvin, evangelicals frequently refer to this as the "witness of the Holy Spirit.") [14]

Although betraying an obvious debt to Augustinian wisdom, the structure of these traditional apologetics varies widely. At one end of the spectrum is a Protestant variety of Thomism exemplified by Stuart Hackett and Norman Geisler. They insist upon the adequacy of the familiar theistic arguments to prove to a certainty the existence of God and of historical evidence to show that Jesus is the God-man, the supernatural Savior of men, and that the prophets of the Old Testament and the apostles were divinely commissioned and inspired to provide an infallible revelation of the mind of God.[15]

At the other end of the spectrum are "Christian mystics" who, like E. Y. Mullins, argue that the Christian experience provides data which can only be adequately accounted for on the basis of the existence of God and the living Christ who by His Holy Spirit works regeneration and sanctification. This type of argument from experience is usually supplemented with historical arguments for the deity of Christ.[16]

Between near-Thomism and Christian mysticism falls the vast body of historical apologists. Ablest representatives of this viewpoint from the past generation would be T. C. Hammond,[17] William Henry Green,[18] George Park Fisher,[19] B. B. Warfield,[20] and the greatest of them all, James Orr.[21] More recently this position has been defended by Floyd Hamilton,[22] J. Oliver Buswell,[23] John Stott,[24] and Bernard Ramm in his earlier works.[25] According to these thinkers, natural revelation is valid to establish the existence of a supreme being to whom man is responsible, but the God known from natural revelation is inadequate to satisfy the human heart. The noetic effects of sin render this limited natural revelation still more ineffective so that by it alone man can never fulfill his ultimate need. Special revelation is thus necessary and is based upon historical evidences, to which some would also add experiential evidences. Through these historical evidences we can establish the deity of Christ, and also the historical validity of a divine revelation vouchsafed to the prophets of the Old Testament and the apostles of the New Testament. The argument then usually takes two mutually supporting turns —one based on the testimony of the divine Christ and the second based on the claims of the prophets and apostles.

The case for biblical infallibilty based on the authority of the divine Christ is simpler to follow and in the twentieth century has proved a powerful apologetic weapon. The very evidence from history that serves to support the divine Lordship of Jesus Christ is equally clear and convincing that he taught the infallibility of the Old Testament Scriptures and gave a similar authority to his selected apostles for the New Testament. Whoever accepts the Jesus Christ of the New Testament as Lord, therefore, cannot stop short of acknowledging also the infallible authority of the Scriptures.[26]

The same doctrine, moreover, is taught by the biblical authors themselves. Whatever confidence one has that the Old Testament prophets received a true revelation from God and, similarly, that the New Testament apostles were commissioned by Christ with authority, represents precisely the degree of confidence one may have that their works are an infallible revelation from God, for this doctrine is just one of those which they very clearly maintain they received from him.[27]

The evangelical insists, therefore, that his confidence in biblical infallibility is not a blind faith. It is accepted on the basis of authority, but not an authority unauthenticated. The authority of Christ and the religious authority of the apostles are accepted on grounds of adequate evidence. Neither is the argument circular because the evidences for the deity of Christ and for the commission of the prophets and the apostles do not include the presupposition of any particular view of biblical inspiration. The fact that many who do not believe at all in the infallibility of the Bible still acknowledge that there is adequate evidence for believing in the deity of Christ illustrates how the doctrine of Christ's deity is not logically dependent upon a traditional view of inspiration. Nonetheless, anyone who accepts the Lordship of Christ has no logical alternative but to acknowledge the complete trustworthiness and divine authority of Scripture, for that is what he taught.[28]

A variation of this common type of traditional apologetics is presented on the contemporary scene by a number of evangelical apologists best represented perhaps by John W. Montgomery and Richard Longenecker. Claiming to be a christocentric apologist, Montgomery, without denying a natural revelation, still does not find it apologetically useful but appeals exclusively to the historical arguments for Christ without seeking to place them in a framework of apologetic theism. Longenecker, who also stresses the christocentric nature of his apologetics, insists upon some value for natural revelation but keeps the focus upon the historical evidences for the deity of Christ and for Christ's teaching about the authority of Scripture.[29]

A significant variation in the traditional methodology of supporting biblical inspiration is the inductivist approach. According to these writers the divine nature of Scripture may be ascertained by examining its characteristics, the so-called *indicia*. The Bible, for example, has been confirmed by innumerable archaeological findings; it has survived in spite of the most assiduous efforts to destroy it; it is the greatest influence for moral good in the world; it is the most widely translated and published book in human history (less used since Soviet mass production of *Das Kapital);* although produced by over forty authors from many cultures spread over nearly two millenia, the books we call the Bible reflect the unity of a single mind. The point is that only a book divinely authored and guarded would have these characteristics. Usually, of course, these arguments are climaxed by the claims of the biblical authors to divine authority and the confirmation of the teaching of the divine Christ. In its simplest form this inductive type of apologetics is probably more frequently relied upon by the laity in evangelical churches than is any other. It is probably least trusted by instructed evangelicals, particularly since the scathing analysis of Søren Kierkegaard has become well known in the American church.[30]

In spite of radically different ways of presenting the evidence and even quite contradictory ideas as to what constitutes the appropriate evidence, there is solid agreement as to the conclusion. This is what constitutes these divergent thinkers as evangelicals. They will agree that to be convinced of the truth of Christian faith necessitates a work of divine grace by which God prepares the resisting human heart. When the Holy Spirit rejuvenates the sinful mind of the unbeliever, however, appropriate evidence may take effect. To what degree the act of saving faith then turns on the evidence will vary considerably. For some it is wholly dependent on evidence, for others only partly so and for still others not dependent at all. Also there is a difference of opinion as to the degree of certainty or probability to which man may be led by the evidence. Except for the Thomists, all argue for a probability and certitude of such a degree that one must believe if he chooses to act in an intellectually responsible way.[31]

Although all of the traditional apologists believe there is a valid case for the truth of the gospel and for the divine authority of the Bible, they not only vary greatly as to the type of argumentation used, but also more fundamentally as to specific metaphysical positions to which they have committed themselves. Few would care to identify themselves with any contemporary philosophical movements. Many, however, will admit special indebtedness to a particular viewpoint or thinker. For example, in the earlier part of the century the philosophy of personalistic idealism was reflected in the works of many Protestant apologists.[32] In later years there is a traceable influence of the linguistic analysis philosophy. Arthur Holmes and Jerry Gill both acknowledge a direct indebtedness to Ian Ramsey.[33] John W. Montgomery shows strong influence from the early Wittgenstein.[34] And, of course, all have been immeasurably influenced by the great Christian thinkers of the past from Augustine to Paley as well as from the cultural heritage of the Scottish "common sense" realism, which so profoundly penetrated the philosophic and apologetic thinking of religious America during the nineteenth and early twentieth centuries.[35]

The second major group of evangelical apologists is the presuppositionalists. Some rational presuppositionalists, like A. H. Strong, will admit that there is no proof for theism. The traditional arguments for theism are all fallacious. They are all, to say the least, short at both ends. There is no starting point from which man may base confidence in the validity of the human mind so he can present a valid case; and the evidences themselves, even if we were to grant the trustworthiness of the human mind, do not adequately establish the existence of God. The finite cannot get at the infinite.

This does not mean that Christianity must be accepted irrationally as an arbitrary act of will. Theistic arguments may be effective with the unbeliever, first negatively, showing him how incoherent is his own unbelieving position and second positively, illustrating how reasonable and intellectually satisfying it is to make the presupposition of full theism, which once made brings all else into an appropriate, coherent, and rational whole. The historical arguments for supernatural Christianity, moreover, are

47

valid if one employs them within the rational framework of theistic presuppositions. Faith in Christ and apostolic authority are evidenced in much the same way as is held by the various types of the traditional apologists. Intellectual faith in the truth of Christianity is supported at least in part by the evidences.[36]

A much larger group of presuppositional apologists have been distinguished as Dutch apologists or presuppositionalists because the chief impetus for their position came through the Dutch theologians of the last century, Kuyper[37] and Bavinck,[38] and in this century through Valentine Hepp,[39] the theologian Berkouwer,[40] and the philosopher of law, Herman Dooyeveerd.[41] The most vigorous proponents of presuppositional apologetics in the United States have been Cornelius Van Til [42] and Gordon Clark.[43]

Presuppositionalism is the dominant apologetic within contemporary American evangelicalism and now numbers among its advocates Carl Henry, best known and most widely read of evangelical theologians;[44] Bernard Ramm;[45] James Packer (English);[46] Francis Schaeffer;[47] and the late Edward Carnell.[48]

According to the theistic presuppositionalists of the type represented by Cornelius Van Til, there is a natural revelation; but in endeavoring to establish this position we cannot start from any neutral point of view. The traditional arguments for theism, as with all presuppositionalists, are reckoned to be fallacious. It is impossible, moreover, to appeal to the unbeliever on the basis of common ground. Epistemologically speaking, the unbeliever has no ground on which to stand. No appeal can be made to logic or to the laws of human thought, for apart from theism, neither human logic nor its processes of thought have any meaning or validity. No appeal can be made to facts supporting theism, for apart from theism there are no "brute facts." All so-called facts involve interpretation and thus presuppose a viewpoint and the meaningfulness of human thought.

Only by positing Christian theism—the truth of the self-revealing God of Holy Scripture—can facts be recognized as facts, and the laws of human thought be acknowledged as laws. Only then will natural revelation discover its validity. The man who chooses to be autonomous in his thinking has really no right to know anything.

On a very different level, of course, there is common ground between the believer and the unbeliever. It lies in the sense of deity imprinted indelibly on the soul of unfallen man which natural, unredeemed man seeks to suppress but never quite manages to eradicate from his mind. This knowledge of God is the seed of a truly valid knowledge, but it never blossoms into a right knowledge unless man is regenerated by an act of God's special grace and thus brought into submission to the God of the Bible and his supernatural revelation.

It is possible, nonetheless, for the believer to place himself in the thought of the unbeliever for the sake of argument in order to show him the bankruptcy of his own non-Christian presuppositions. Likewise he can ask the unbeliever to share the believer's Christian presuppositions for the sake of argument. Never, however, does he give up the only rational ground of all thought in order to argue with an unbeliever on nontheistic presuppositions.

The true word of the self-revealing God is self-authenticating. It both presupposes and is presupposed by the sovereign triune God. The Bible's content and the fact that it is the word of God unite as the object of a single act of faith not depending on anything above or beyond the Scripture but coming through the work of the Holy Spirit, sealing the truth of the Bible and its saving word on the mind of man.

Exactly the same can be said regarding the historical arguments adduced in support of supernatural Christianity. Only on the basis of the presupposition of the triune God of the Bible can the facts of historical revelation be known as facts and such arguments find validity.

On the other hand, if we presuppose the triune creator God of the Bible, then all the data of special revelation will fit into a coherent whole. Christianity, thus, is reasonable only to the regenerate mind which has already accepted the truth of the God of the Bible. The presupposition of Christian theism as presented in Scripture is the only possible ground for belief in a rational world where facts can be known as facts and where history can have any meaning. The only absolutely certain proof of the truth of Christianity is that, unless its truth is presupposed, there is no proof of anything.

Faith, thus, never builds on evidences for theism, either for the divinity of Christ or for the authority of Scripture. Rather by an act of will man must choose to accept the triune God of the Bible. This can only be done by regeneration of the soul and the creation of faith by the Holy Spirit. Faith once created by God may be confirmed by evidences which are logically valid and fully supportive of the truth of supernatural Christianity. Such evidence, however, is valid only so far as it is firmly grounded on the presupposition of the triune God of the Bible.

Van Til, therefore, does not consider himself a mere fideist or antirational. On the contrary, biblical Christianity is the only rational interpretation of the universe; and theistic presuppositionalism alone is acting in a truly rational way, for it alone safeguards the very principle of rationality. The presuppositional case for biblical theism enables man to know God as he really is (*i.e.,* analogically, within the limits of a creature made in the divine image) and to know him with certainty.[49]

In similar fashion Gordon Clark argues for a theistic presuppositionalism, but unlike Van Til he will not allow for any validity of natural evidences for theism (though he will acknowledge a limited natural revelation) and further rejects historical or experiential arguments as invalid either to lead to faith in supernatural Christianity or to confirm the faith of the regenerate. Clark employs many of the traditional arguments of both ancient and modern skeptics to show that all arguments for theism or for supernatural historical revelation are simply invalid when considered either as apodictic or heuristic. Without some sort of presupposition, in fact, no knowledge at all is possible, and certainly no philosophical construction. Everyone, of course, has an *apriori* presupposition of which he may or may not be conscious. Only the biblical and Christian *apriori* is acceptable, however, for other presuppositions fail to pass the test of consistency. Like Van Til, Clark insists that fallen man suppresses a genuine but mutilated innate knowledge of God by creation in the image of God. Natural revelation, as Clark understands the term, refers exclusively to this "sense of deity" and "sense of oughtness" to which nature calls man's attention. Without special revelation, however, this extremely meager inborn knowledge serves only to render sinful man without excuse for his ignorance of God.

Saving faith is created in man by divine grace so as to enable man to choose to believe in the God of the Bible, but faith does not terminate on the evidence either wholly or partly. It makes sense only as one presupposes the supernatural revelation set forth in the Bible—a presupposition not grounded on or confirmed logically by evidence, yet a presupposition that is the very opposite of irrational, for it alone enables anything to have meaning. However, the regenerate believer can show a higher degree of internal consistency or coherence of the data on the basis of his Christian theistic supposition than is possible with all alternatives which are necessarily inconsistent at their foundation. In this way Clark presents the unbeliever with a challenge either to speak rationally and in a Christian-like manner or to be silent in irrational unbelief. Once the truth of Scripture is accepted as the basic axiom of thought, then all truth necessary for man may be derived inductively by an analysis of its teaching. Man thus can trust his mind, within limits, as the product of God, safely employ the law of contradiction as willed and revealed by the God of truth, understand meaningfully the world which God created to be known even as he created man's mind to know, discover right and wrong as the sovereign God reveals his will, and hope for the future based on the promises of the omnipotent and omniscient sovereign of the universe.[50]

In spite of their significant disagreement as to the method by which they defend the divine authority of Scripture, therefore, twentieth-century evangelicals preserve historical continuity with the formal principle of Reformation theology and with evangelicals of the past. The Bible is both the record of the sovereign acts of God and the divine preinterpretation of what those acts mean. It is the inspired book of instruction (Torah-instruction) for the guidance of God's people. It comes to man as God's gift of grace— to guide man so he need not continue on his lost way, but may find the path to life. It is the instrument employed by the Holy Spirit to speak God's word today to the mind and heart of the faithful believer. It is the only infallible rule by which man can test his thinking and his action so as to bring them into conformity to the will of his heavenly Father. Theology, therefore, must not be drawn from reason (though for the most part the evangelical acknowledges his dependence on consistent reason and logical processes), not from experience (though he recognizes that without experience by which it is personally appropriated, good theology is not only unattainable but is utterly worthless), and not from tradition (though he treasures it with gratitude and freely acknowledges that without tradition his spiritual understanding would be impoverished and he might never come to faith). The evangelical, rather, seeks to construct his theology on the teaching of the Bible, the whole Bible, and nothing but the Bible; and this formative principle represents a basic unifying factor throughout the whole of contemporary evangelicalism.[51]

The Material Principle

Following Martin Luther, traditional Protestantism, of course, has held not only to the formal principle of biblical authority but also to the material principle of the gospel of Christ. This material or content principle of Reformation Christianity has been worded in various ways but essentially refers to the good news of how man can be rightly related to God and represents the second great unifying factor of modern evangelicalism.

The so-called fundamentals, so prominent in theological disputes of the last half-century, served to unify fundamentalism in its battle against liberal theology and continue to unite the evangelical movement of the last quarter of the twentieth century.[52] These fundamentals invariably include the formative principle of the infallible authority of Scripture together with certain teachings regarding the person and work of Christ highly mooted by nonevangelicals of the last century. Following a certain logical arrangement rather than any order of importance, the fundamentals are: (1) the eternal preexistence of the Son as the second person of the one God; (2) the incarnation of God the Son in man as the divine—human person—two natures in one person; (3) the virgin birth, the means by which God the Son entered into the human race and, without ceasing to be fully God, became also fully man; (4) the sinless life of Christ while sharing the life and experiences of alien men apart from sin; (5) the supernatural miracles of Christ as acts of his compassion and signs of his divine nature; (6) Christ's authoritative teaching as Lord of the church; (7) the substitutionary atonement in which God did all that was needed to redeem man from sin and its consequences; (8) the bodily resurrection of Christ as the consummation of his redemptive work and the sign and seal of its validity; (9) the ascension and heavenly mission of the living Lord; (10) the bodily second coming of Christ at the end of the age; (11) the final righteous judgment

53

of all mankind and the eternal kingdom of God; (12) the eternal punishment of the impenitent and disbelieving wicked of this world.[53]

This entire list is seldom cited but rather, by a sort of synecdoche, part is left to stand for the whole. Lists are by no means uniform, but those doctrines most frequently set forth in short creedal statements are the virgin birth, substitutionary atonement, bodily resurrection, and the second coming. For completeness' sake, however, all the above aspects of the person and work of Christ must be included. No true evangelical would admit for a moment that anyone who clearly denied any one of the above is evangelical in the full sense of the word.

For the instructed evangelical, however, the essential elements or fundamental doctrines of evangelicals do not really constitute the fundamental basis of evangelicalism. They represent, rather, clear teachings of Scripture essential to a consistent, healthy faith and obedience to the Lord of the church. They have come to the forefront of debate in part because, in one way or another, they have become highly controversial issues in the battle between fundamentalism and modernism in the latter part of the nineteenth and earlier twentieth centuries and also because they are essential to the *bene esse* (well being) of a believer's faith even though not to its *esse* (existence).

In the mind of the evangelical, therefore, not all of these doctrines stand on exactly the same level in relationship to the fundamental structure of evangelical faith. Certainly few would suggest that one must believe in evangelicalism (*i.e.* in all the doctrines essential for recognizable evangelicalism) in order to be saved or rightly related to God. The true fundamental of biblical Christianity is the divine grace available to sinners in Christ by faith. The gospel is the good news for all who believe in Christ, not specifically for those who believe in the virgin birth or substitutionary atonement, or bodily second coming of Christ.[54]

This list of fundamentals, moreover, either in its long

or short form does not by any means represent a complete spectrum of basic Christian doctrine. It was hammered out in the throes of a life-and-death battle between orthodoxy and its foes and betrays all too clearly its original historical context. Many of the most trusted evangelical leaders repudiated such "shortcut creeds" even in the heyday of fundamentalism.[55] All would admit, for example, that the doctrine of the trinity is essential to historical Christianity and certainly also to evangelicalism. The divine attributes of omniscience, omnipotence, omnipresence, eternality, holiness, love, and truth are clearly fundamentals of any biblical Christian faith. No complete listing of evangelical faith could omit the doctrine of creation and divine providence; of man created in the image of God; of the fall, in which this image was thoroughly defaced but not completely eradicated; and of sin as inherited corruption and guilt. For the most part evangelicals insist that the human race became sinners as a result of the fall of the first man Adam. Even those who are willing to grant the possibility of human evolution often insist that there must be a first man from whom all the human race is descended and whose fall brought the human race to sin, divine wrath, and condemnation.[56]

Beneath the protective layers of doctrine, then, there is an intellectual and ethical commitment that welds evangelicals together into a self-conscious community with generally clear boundaries. But if evangelical faith is to be defined at its center as an adherence to the Reformation's formal and material principles, it should not be simplisticly reduced to these commitments. Within evangelical Christianity there is an amazing diversity that is vigorously—indeed, sometimes too vigorously—pursued. This variety of belief and practice arises from two main overlapping sources: denominational distinctives and doctrinal differences.[57]

The major denominations which trace their origin to the Reformation still preserve the differences that divided

55

their forefathers: conservative Lutherans above all stress the cross and the sacraments; conservative Presbyterians and those in the reformed churches underscore the sovereignty of God and are characterized by a vigorous Puritan ethic; evangelical Anglicans take the lead in ecumenical ventures; and in America, the most diverse of the groups, the Anabaptists, continue to stress the difference between the "gathered" church—those adults who have made a conscious commitment to Christ and are baptised accordingly—and the "folk" church whose membership is indiscriminate. To these age-old traditions has been added Pentecostalism whose arrival shortly after 1900 has signaled a new emphasis on the supernatural gifts of the Spirit as normative for the church today and as indicative of a higher level of Christian experience.[58] All of these groups are to be distinguished from, rather than confused with, those cults such as Christian Science and Mormonism which have departed from the two fundamental principles of the Reformation. If there is a third force in Christendom, it cannot be artificially made up of groups which have little or nothing in common.

Furthermore, there are, within an overarching evangelical commitment, strong doctrinal differences which sometimes follow, but more often than not, cut across the lines established by denominational preferences. Ecclesiastical separation, for example, still is a matter of lively concern, although the force which it generated in the 1920s and 1930s has generally subsided. On the one side are those committed to working in the older denominations on the ground that the drift toward liberalism or even outright disbelief will be more pronounced if an evangelical witness is withdrawn; on the other side are the separatists who argue that any evangelical witness within these denominations serves only to obscure rather than to sharpen the difference between true and false Christian faith.[59] Dispensationalism as a method of understanding and relating the different parts of Scripture to one another is likewise a matter of considerable discussion. Indeed, Carnell even defined fundamentalism as the perversion of orthodoxy into a cultic aberration by its emphasis on separation and dispensationalism,[60] whereas Sandeen, by confusing fundamentalism and conservative evangelicalism, claims to have discovered the origins of evangelicalism in J. N. Darby's dispensationalism and the verbal inerrancy doctrine of the Princeton school.[61] The fact of the matter is that there is a whole spectrum of belief on this issue, ranging from those who insist that the Old Testament law must be obeyed, even to the point of observing Saturday as the sabbath,[62] to those who regard only Paul's prison letters as normative for today.[63] What is at issue is not what parts of Scripture are inspired and what are not, but which parts are applicable to the Gentile church today and which are not; and a growing tendency towards unity at the center is discernable in evangelicalism. Thus George Ladd, typical of many anti-dispensational thinkers, argues that Israel as a body is distinct from the New Testament church so the promises made to the former will be realised, not in a spiritualised form in the latter, but actually and nationally during the millennium.[64] Similarly, Charles Ryrie, a stout defender of dispensationalism, argues that despite the differences in the way God deals with men under his different dispensations, grace and faith remain the conditions of right relationship with God that are common to them all.[65]

Closely related to the hermeneutical differences that surface in the debate over dispensationalism are issues of eschatology. While evangelicals are united in their agreement over the literal, physical return of Christ, the bodily resurrection of both the just and the unjust, the former to receive a final evaluation of their lives after being received into heaven and the latter a final condemnation for their sustained rejection of Christ resulting in an eternal separation from God, not all are agreed over the details of God's program for the future of mankind. Dispensationalists are invariably premillenarian, holding that after his return Christ will set up a thousand-year kingdom on earth characterized by peace and perfect righteousness.[66] Non-dispensationalists are divided into premillenarian, post-millenarian, and amillenarian, the prefixes "pre," "post," and "a" locating the coming of Christ with reference to the millennium. Premillenarians argue that the world will never come to peace and righteousness until Christ personally returns and rules over it; [67] postmillenarians argue that this peace will come and will be the condition for Christ's return; [68] amillenarians argue that no such earthly kingdom is to be expected. Promises made to national Israel are realized spiritually in the New Testament church or refer to the final state of all the redeemed in eternity.[69]

In a different area, it is clear that even if evangelicals are agreed that a witness to Christ's power to save is obligatory upon the church, they are divided over how best this might be done. Differences of style—whether or not to use gimmicks, sports personalities, emotional appeals, or compelling music—are not as important as differences in understanding what the Great Commission means. Christ's command to go into the whole world and preach the gospel is understood by some to mean preaching the good news of Christian faith as a whole. Evangelism is, therefore, largely identical with the educational task of the church. Others define the gospel narrowly as the good news of salvation from sin requiring active faith in Christ marked by a decision for him.[70]

Although divisive issues within the evangelical community display no signs of disappearing, a growing assimilation of the divergent groups within the movement is clearly evident. With a few notable exceptions, sharp corners of difference have been rounded off. Most dispensationalists, for example, recognize that there is one way of salvation for all of God's people. "Pretribulationism" [71] is not quite so crucial as it was once thought to be, though it is still included in the doctrinal statement of many schools of theology and hence will continue for the foreseeable future to be a source of division among evangelicals. Premillennialism, generally in the past merely tolerated in the church, has managed to disassociate itself from bizarre features of a former chiliasm and is the characteristic stance of the majority of American evangelicals. At the same time, it has ceased its rapid gains of the early middle part of the century and has probably come to a sort of stalemate with amillennialism, both being accepted as legitimate within the framework of consistent evangelicalism, while the postmillennial view for all practical purposes has dropped out of sight.

Conclusion

Renewal and growth best describe contemporary evangelicalism. Proof of this is evident on every hand, ranging from percentages of increase set by Sunday schools, local congregations, conservative denominations, youth groups, and renewal movements to publishing records, retreat houses, missionary societies, conservative ecumenical structures, evangelical seminaries, preaching campaigns, popular magazines, new translations of the Bible, devotional literature, and hymnody. Why, it is often asked, after nearly a century of liberal domination, during which time liberalism in its various forms has taken over leadership in almost all the older mainline denominations, did this ever come about? How could such an outmoded viewpoint, lingering on like a spiritual appendix, suddenly begin to function with renewed vitality on the religious scene at the end of our twentieth century? All sorts of sociological explanations have been put forth both by evangelicals and nonevangelicals. The sociological factors cannot be ignored. Wieman, however, gets at a more fundamental explanation for the apparent anomaly of resurgent evangelicalism. He ascribes it to the way in which it fosters a sense of life on a higher plane of human existence than is provided by other alternatives together with its more coherent, fully elaborated world and life view by contrast with any presented by its contemporary rivals.[72] Essentially the same analysis is set forth by Dean Kelley in his volume *Why Conservative Churches Are Growing*. The root reason for the evangelical renaissance, he asserts, is to be found in the meaning it provides for human life and existence.[73] Liberalism had its day; and in spite of the fact that much in it was scintilating and brilliant, its ultimate religious bankruptcy eventually became apparent. Disillusioned liberals, like Niebuhr in this country and Bultmann or John Robinson abroad, have not proved able to meet the void in the human heart. Likewise the complicated intricacies and irrational overtones of a Barth or Brunner could seldom be understood and almost never proved attractive to the man or woman in the pew. Decade by decade, as the twentieth century slipped away, modern man found the newer panaceas less and less fruitful. The traditional optimism of Americans lost the ring of genuineness. Ultimate meaninglessness seemed to close in upon man and hope faded for this life or the future.[74]

In the last decade evangelicals have become increasingly aware of the devastating way in which their stance has been warped by their battles against liberalism during the preceding century. It is not that liberalism is no longer recognized as an enemy of faith; from an evangelical perspective, liberalism has simply taken on a new face, as chastened liberalism or as neo-orthodoxy, both of which are woefully inadequate perversions of Christianity. In spite of this, however, evangelical Christianity has come gradually to see its need to be itself, to rest upon the base of the historical and supernatural Christ as he is set forth for man in the Bible, interpreted for today's world by the power of the Holy Spirit, and not in opposition to any other religious option.

To a lost and confused generation evangelical Christianity holds out hope and meaning by giving voice to the good news of the gospel. In obedience to the instruction of the Lord of the church, Jesus Christ, and his written Word of Holy Scripture, evangelicals once again, more boldly than ever, are addressing the lost, confused, and desperately needy world of the twentieth century with the gospel of God's redeeming love and the sure biblical chart for sailing on life's uncharted seas. And the cry of hope echoed back from the ancient sage of another and earlier day is heard again: Man's heart can find no rest until it finds its rest in Thee, O God. This is where evangelicalism finds its power.

Notes

1. See *The American Evangelicals 1800-1900,* ed. by William McLoughlin (New York: Harper & Row, 1968) for a defense of the continuity (not identity) of evangelicalism with orthodox Protestantism. In the nineteenth century and earlier the two terms were practically synonymous.

2. Steven E. Ozment in his chapter "Homo Viator," from his edited volume, *Reformation in Medieval Perspective* (New York: Franklin Walls, Inc., 1971), establishes conclusively in my judgment that Luther and his Roman Catholic antagonists were facing the same problem and had come up with different and mutually exclusive answers. In the interests of ecumenical harmony this is sometimes glossed over.

3. For a summary of traditional Lutheran views of biblical authority, see Robert Preus, *The Theology of Post-Reformation Lutheranism* (St. Louis: Concordia Publishing House, 1970). For a traditional reformed view, see Norval Geldenhuys, *Supreme Authority, The Authority of the Lord, His Apostles, and the New Testament* (Grand Rapids: Eerdmans Publishing Co., 1953). James I. Packer defends the position of an Anglican Evangelical in *God Speaks to Man: Revelation and the Bible* (Philadelphia: The Westminster Press, 1965).

4. In 1844, Robert Baird, for example, lists the evangelical denominations (in America) as Episcopalians, the Congregationalists, the Baptists, the Presbyterians, and the Methodists (with all their various subdivisions) and adds: "In doctrine we have but two great divisions—the Calvinistic and the Arminian . . . but when viewed in relation to the great doctrines which are universally conceded by Protestants to be fundamental and necessary to salvation, then they all form but one body, recognizing Christ

61

as their Common Head." (quoted in McLoughlin, *The American Evangelicals,* pp. 31-32).

5. Martin Luther rejected Zwingli's alien spirit and advised Schwenkfeld (which he deliberately misspelled as Stinkfield) that he would do better spreading manure than spreading the gospel. So today, some strict Baptists return the favor by denying that they are rightly termed Protestants.

6. So wrote Auguste Dorner on the plaque celebrating the Marburg colloquium in Marburg castle, Germany.

7. The reformers were not above employing the word *dictate* to describe the divine productivity of Scripture, but in doing so they made very clear the distinction in methodology between ordinary dictation and biblical "dictation." See John F. Walvoord, ed., *Inspiration and Interpretation* (Grand Rapids: Eerdmans Publishing Co., 1957) pp. 102-103. Few modern evangelicals employ the word dictation to describe biblical inspiration. No evangelical scholar of this century has argued for a dictation method of most of the Bible, and almost all have expressly repudiated the term.

8. The doctrinal basis for the Evangelical Theological Society reads: "The Bible in its entirety is the Word of God, written, and therefore inerrant in the autographs."

9. Evangelical views of biblical authority, of course, are based on the validity of so-called propositional or "meaning" revelation rather than upon an exclusive wordless revelation only through God's acts left uninterpreted such as is promulgated by almost all nonevangelicals writing on this subject. An analysis of the Greek word *apocalupto* as it is used in the New Testament sustains the evangelical position (Walter Bauer, *A Greek-English Lexicon of the New Testament and Other Early Christian Literature,* . . . (Chicago: University of Chicago Press, 1957).

10. *The Lausanne Covenant* (Minneapolis: World Wide Publications, 1974).

11. Note, for example, Os Guinness, *The Dust of Death: A Critique of the Establishment and the Counterculture—and a Proposal for a Third Way* (Downers Grove, Ill.: Inter-Varsity Press, 1973). See also Francis Schaeffer, *Escape from Reason* (Downers Grove, Ill.: Inter-Varsity Press, 1968).

12. See Emil Brunner, *The Mediator* (New York: The Macmillan Co., 1942), p. 185; Karl Barth, *Das Christliche Verständnis der Offenbarung* (München: Chr. Kaiser, 1948), p. 29; Millar Burrows, *Outlines of Biblical Theology* (Philadelphia: The Westminster Press, 1946), pp. 9, 44. Modern thought and especially modern science, so the inference is drawn, render the evangelical view of the Bible intellectually disreputable if not outright dishonest. When they get down to a bill of particulars, however, nonevangelicals invariably either refer generally and often vaguely to viewpoints by which no evangelical recognizes himself or revert to internal verbal contraditions within Scripture or what appear to be historical discrepancies known at least as well to Jerome and

Augustine in the ancient world or to Luther and Calvin and their immediate successors in the Protestant churches. Not new scientific data but new ways of looking at ancient data have made the difference.
13. Donald G. Bloesch, *The Evangelical Renaissance* (Grand Rapids: Eerdmans Publishing Co., 1973), pp. 13-18. Studies of contemporary American evangelism include Richard Quebedeaux, *The Young Evangelicals Revolution in Orthodoxy* (New York: Harper & Row, 1974); Bruce Shelley, *Evangelicalism in America* (Grand Rapids: Eerdman's Publishing Co., 1967); Ronald Nash, *The New Evangelicalism* (Grand Rapids: Zondervan Publishing House, 1963); R. R. Lightner, *Neo-Evangelicalism* (Findley, Ohio: Dunham, 1961).
14. In traditional Protestant terminology saving faith includes *notitia* (knowledge), *assensus* (consent of the mind to truth), and *fiducia* (trust).
15. Stuart Cornelius Hackett, *The Resurrection of Theism* (Chicago: Moody Press, 1957); and Norman Geisler, *Philosophy of Religion* (Grand Rapids: Zondervan Publishing House, 1974).
16. Edgar Young Mullins, *Why is Christianity True?* (Chicago: Christian Culture Press, 1905), pp. 241-303, 359-77. See also Lewis French Stearns, *Evidence of Christian Experience* (London: J. Nisbet, 1890).
17. T. C. Hammond, *Reasoning Faith* (London: Inter-Varsity Fellowship Press, 1943); and *Age Long Questions* (London: Marshall, Morgan, and Scott, n.d.).
18. William Henry Green, *A General Introduction to the Old Testament: The Canon* (New York: Charles Scribner's Sons, 1898); *Higher Criticism of the Pentateuch* (New York: Charles Scribner's Sons, 1902); and *Unity of the Book of Genesis* (New York: Charles Scribner's Sons, 1910).
19. George Park Fisher, *Grounds of Theistic and Christian Belief* (New York: Charles Scribner's Sons, 1915).
20. Benjamin Breckenridge Warfield, *Studies in Apologetics* (New York: Oxford University Press, 1932).
21. James Orr, *The Christian View of God and the World* (Grand Rapids: Eerdmans Publishing Co., 1947).
22. Floyd E. Hamilton, *The Basis of Christian Faith: A Modern Defense of the Christian Religion* (3rd rev. ed., New York: Harper and Brothers, 1946). Between the earlier evangelical apologists who flourished at the turn of the century and this more recent group of apologists towered the lonely figure of J. Gresham Machen who stood head and shoulders above his colleagues as an apologist for evangelical Christianity.
23. James Oliver Buswell, Jr., *A Systematic Theology of the Christian Religion* (Grand Rapids: Zondervan Publishing House, 1963), I, 72-101, 183-213; II, 32-39. See also his strictly apologetic works, *Behold Him* (Grand Rapids: Zondervan Publishing House,

63

1938); and *A Christian View of Being and Knowing* (Grand Rapids: Zondervan Publishing House, 1960).

24. John R. W. Stott, *Basic Christianity* (Grand Rapids: Eerdmans Publishing Co., 1958).

25. Bernard L. Ramm, *Protestant Christian Evidences* (Chicago: Moody Press, 1953). In more recent years Ramm has shifted to a thoroughgoing VanTilian system of apologetics.

26. See Hugh M'Intosh, *Is Christ Infallible and the Bible True?* (Edinburgh: T. and T. Clark, 1902).

27. John H. Gerstner, *A Bible Inerrancy Primer* (Grand Rapids: Baker Book House, 1965); and *Reasons for Faith* (New York: Harper and Brothers, 1960).

28. The issue thus becomes not one of biblical authority but of Christology. See H. Dermot McDonald, *Ideas of Revelation* (London: Macmillan & Co., 1959) and *Theories of Revelation: An Historical Study, 1860-1960* (London: Allen & Unwin, 1963).

29. John Warwick Montgomery, *How Do We Know There is a God? and Other Questions Inappropriate in Polite Society* (Minneapolis: Bethany Press, 1973) and *Where is History Going?* (Grand Rapids: Zondervan Publishing House, 1969).

30. Henry Clarence Thiessen, *Introductory Lectures in Systematic Theology* (Grand Rapids: Eerdmans Publishing Co., 1949), pp. 51-63 and especially pp. 108-11. See also his *Introduction to the New Testament* (Grand Rapids: Eerdmans Publishing Co., 1944), pp. 81-91.

31. For Calvin's defense of the validity of a probable argument for the existence of God from nature and for the truth of supernatural Christianity and biblical authority from the evidence of history, see *Institutes of the Christian Religion*, trans. by Henry Beveridge (Grand Rapids: Eerdmans Publishing Co., 1957), vol. I, chapters V and VIII. For a similar view in Luther, see *Lectures on Romans*, in *Luther's Works*, trans. by Walter G. Tillmans and Jacob A. O. Preus (St. Louis: Concordia Publishing House, 1972), pp. 25, 156-58.

32. Edgar Young Mullins, *The Christian Religion in its Doctrinal Expression* (Philadelphia: Roger Williams Press, 1917); Floyd Hamilton, *Basis of Christian Faith*, pp. 40-43.

33. Arthur Holmes, *Christianity and Philosophy* (Chicago: InterVarsity Press, 1960), pp. 166-67; Jerry H. Gill, *The Possibility of Religious Language* (Grand Rapids: Eerdmans Publishing Co., 1971), p. 8.

34. Note his *Tractatus Logico-Theologicus*, unpublished printed text for classroom use, 1971.

35. See the influential writings of the Princeton philosopher James McCosh, *The Intuitions of the Mind Inductively Investigated* (3rd rev. ed.; New York: Robert Carter, 1877) and *Christianity and Positivism* (New York: Robert Carter, 1871).

36. A. H. Strong, *Systematic Theology* (Valley Forge, Pa.: Judson Press, 1907), I, 53-62.

37. Abraham Kuyper, *Encyclopedia of Sacred Theology* (New York: Charles Scribner's Sons, 1898).

38. Herman Bavinck, as can be noted from his *The Doctrine of God* (Grand Rapids: Eerdmans Publishing Co., 1951) is a presuppositionalist only with considerable qualification (pp. 41-80).

39. Valentine Hepp, *Calvinism and the Philosophy of Nature* (Grand Rapids: Eerdmans Publishing Co., 1930).

40. Gerrit Berkouwer, *General Revelation* (Grand Rapids: Eerdmans Publishing Co., 1955).

41. Herman Dooyeweerd, *A New Critique of Theoretical Thought* (Philadelphia: Presbyterian and Reformed Publishing Co., 1953).

42. Cornelius Van Til, *Defense of the Faith* (Philadelphia: Presbyterian and Reformed Publishing Co., 1955), pp. 179-259.

43. Gordon H. Clark, *Religion, Reason, and Revelation* (Philadelphia: Presbyterian and Reformed Publishing Co., 1961); and *Christian View of Man and Things* (Grand Rapids: Eerdmans Publishing Co., 1952).

44. Carl F. H. Henry, *Notes on the Doctrine of God* (Boston: W. A. Wilde Co., 1948), pp. 42-74; and *The God Who Shows Himself* (Waco, Texas: Word Books, 1966).

45. Ramm's shift towards a presuppositional apologetic is evident in *Types of Apologetics* (Wheaton, Ill.: Van Kampan Press, 1953).

46. James I. Packer, *"Fundamentalism" and the Word of God* (Grand Rapids: Eerdmans Publishing Co., 1959), pp. 115-29.

47. Francis A. Schaeffer, *The God Who is There* (Downers Grove, Ill.: Inter-Varsity Press, 1968)), especially pp. 87 ff.

48. Edward John Carnell, *An Introduction to Christian Apologetics* (Grand Rapids: Eerdmans Publishing Co., 1948). See also his *Christian Commitment: An Apologetic* (New York: Macmillan, 1957).

49. Van Til, *Defense of the Faith*, pp. 179-259; *A Christian Theory of Knowledge* (privately printed notes, 1957); *An Introduction to Systematic Theology* (privately printed notes, 1955).

50. For an excellent review of Clark's apologetic stance see Ronald H. Nash, ed., *The Philosophy of Gordon H. Clark: A Festschrift* (Philadelphia: Presbyterian and Reformed Publishing Co., 1968).

51. So Carnell's definition of Protestant orthodoxy is "that branch of Christendom which limits the ground of religious authority to the Bible." As a definition, this is defective in that it fails to note the all important material principle of orthodoxy. See *The Case for Orthodox Theology* (Philadelphia: The Westminister Press, 1959), p. 13.

52. Evangelicals like Carnell who repudiated fundamentalism took extraordinary pains to show that they did not reject the so-called fundamental doctrines of fundamentalism.

53. The General Assembly of the Presbyterian Church U.S.A. in 1923 affirmed five "essential" doctrines.

65

54. This is illustrated by the extraordinarily high regard in which conservative evangelicals hold such writers as C. S. Lewis.

55. Machen was strongly opposed to the short creeds characteristic of fundamentalism.

56. James Orr, *Christian View*, p. 180.

57. Many attempts have been made to separate the schools of thought within evangelicalism into simple yet meaningful groups. Terms used most frequently are fundamentalists, evangelicals, and neoevangelicals.

58. Pentecostalists are frequently distinguished from neo-Pentecostals. The latter are often defined either as those outside the older Pentecostal bodies who claim a present gift of speaking in unlearned tongues or those who practice the gift but do not see in it a sign of a higher level of spiritual progress such as the baptism or filling of the Holy Spirit.

59. The dividing line today is more frequently drawn not between Puritans and Separatists but between "first-degree" Separatists, who will not join traditionally protestant denominations if liberalism and other forms of unbelief are openly tolerated within the leadership, and "second-degree" Separationists, who consider it wrong to affiliate with other evangelicals who are not Separatists in practice.

60. Carnell, *The Case for Orthodox Theology*, pp. 113, 114, 117-19.

61. Ernest R. Sandeen, *The Origins of Fundamentalism: Toward a Historical Interpretation* (Philadelphia: Fortress Press, 1968), pp. 2-24.

62. *Seventh-day Adventists Answer Questions in Doctrine . . . ,* prepared by a representative group of Seventh-day Adventist leaders, Bible teachers, and editors (Washington D.C.: Review and Herald Publishing Association, 1957).

63. Cornelius R. Stam, *The Fundamentals of Dispensationalism* (Milwaukee: Berean Search Light, 1951), pp. 233-43.

64. George E. Ladd, *A Theology of the New Testament* (Grand Rapids: Eerdmans Publishing Co., 1974), p. 538.

65. Charles C. Ryrie, *The Grace of God* (Chicago: Moody Press, 1963), pp. 43-55.

66. See J. Dwight Pentecost, *Things to Come: A Study in Biblical Eschatology* (Grand Rapids: Zondervan Publishing House, 1958); A. J. McClain, *The Greatness of the Kingdom* (Grand Rapids: Zondervan Publishing House, 1959).

67. Allan A. MacRae, *The Millennial Kingdom of Christ* (privately published sermon, n.d.); and Buswell, *A Systematic Theology*, II, 389 ff.

68. Lorraine Boettner, *The Millennium* (Philadelphia: Presbyterian and Reformed Publishing Co., 1938), pp. 3-105.

69. Louis Berkhof, *Systematic Theology* (Grand Rapids. Eerdmans Publishing Co., 1946), pp. 695-719.

70. See James I. Packer, *Evangelism and the Sovereignty of God* (London: Inter-Varsity Press, 1961).

71. See John F. Walvoord, *The Rapture Question* (Grand Rapids: Zondervan Publishing House, 1957).

72. Henry Nelson Wieman and Bernard Eugene Meland, *American Philosophies of Religion* (Chicago: Willett, Clark and Co., 1936), pp. 67, 68.

73. Dean Kelley, *Why Conservative Churches are Growing* (New York: Harper & Row, 1972), pp. 36-55.

74. For the way in which this theme is often incorporated into an evangelical apologetic, see Francis Schaeffer, *Escape from Reason,* and especially Os Guinness, *The Dust of Death.*

Contemporary Evangelical Faith: An Assessment and Critique

Paul L. Holmer

Epistemological Considerations and Evangelicalism

This essay is written with an acknowledgement of a standing debt to the evangelicals. That debt is not only for childhood nurture which made Christianity vastly momentous and more than a hobby, but also for that stream of reminders that the evangelicals provide which keeps alive the radical breach that the gospel is from the *nous* of this world.

In a peculiar but hearty way, most American evangelicals, amid their cantankerousness and splitting up over doctrine and practices, have also not quite succeeded in being respectable. They look marginal if you are very churchly; they appear intolerant if you are ecumenical; they seem antiintellectual just when everything looks systematic and about to be settled. But my point is that they have kept the mood of conventicles, the mood of Christianity being a minority movement, alive amid their erstwhile success. The oddness of God is almost shown you in the difficulties the evangelicals have in being true to him. The more smoothly run ecclesiastical outfits by comparison tend also to tame God, almost to the degree that they get culture, doctrine, and buildings in agreeable conjunction. God begins to seem a silent partner, terribly acquiescent

Paul L. Holmer is Professor of Theology at Yale Divinity School.

and tolerant, to the operations of a genial religiosity. But not amid the evangelicals.

Thus, the very roughness and somewhat abrasive demeanor of the evangelicals, who are usually trying so volubly to stay straight on the God of the Bible, gives me, at least, the impression that God is not the invention of the churches. He does not show a placid hand. He is not a genial benevolence nor a surrogate for moral value. He looms up in evangelical practice and talk pretty much as you would expect if you had been fed on Job, Abraham, and Isaac, the last judgment, the creation story, the flood, the accounts of miracles, and the taking notion that becoming and being a Christian was and is a shattering experience, neither a churchly performance nor an alternative code of life.

So what I have been rather slowly and painstakingly getting clear for myself by fighting my way through philosophical and theological thickets turns out to be not altogether different from what my parents, with their evangelical ardor for my very soul, told me when I was too young to accept or to desist. And long since, suffering the angularity of trying to be evangelical and an intellectual, I was pleasantly surprised to find that the evangelicals had never completely forgotten how hard it is to integrate God with what we want to make of ourselves. The God of the Bible will have us his way, or not at all. However deeply that runs against the grain, that is a note never quite obliterated in the so-called "third" component in American and world Christianity.

To this extent, then, a debt is acknowledged. But there are some rough edges not made by God. It is these I want to discuss around the formal notion of epistemological considerations and evangelical faith. Put more briefly, it is: what about the claims to knowing God? My concern here is with what theology has become within the evangelical tradition and its popular preaching front stance. It is not as if I am here juxtaposing a liberal temper and disposition

69

against the conservatives; neither am I urging more fulsome antiintellectualisms and experience upon the intellectual and doctrinal side of evangelical Christianity; and surely, I am not speaking for this-worldliness versus other-worldliness, for philosophy versus theology, for modernity versus tradition, for reason versus revelation, not even for the demise of fundamentalism. I am not even indulging that easy shrug of dismissal and disdain which might have characterized the Eastern establishment's attitude toward the rugged religiosity of the frontier, the missionary enterprise, and of plainer people. On the contrary, it is because those rough edges appear in a swatch of discourse that ties the reader all the more closely to the New Testament that they are so troublesome. If one were toying with an episode or even an aside, matters would not be serious at all. But evangelical Christianity, by keeping miracles, God, the Bible, and consciousness of every believer in the flux of worship and preaching also manages to link itself with themes that are deeply ecumenical. Those themes have to do with the Bible and Jesus, on the one side, and the essential spiritual need of human life, on the other. Here the evangelical's thrust finds its allies in Augustine, in Luther, in Calvin, in Wesley. Seen from the outside, even these authors, along with the evangelicals, seem to be testifying to an extraordinary and tough unanimity of biblical faith. Here a kind of consensus also grows, out of which the evangelicals, with the biblical authors and the theologians noted, are talking about pretty much the same thing.

This kind of ecumenicity, a sameness over the ages, a converging likeness within differing periods, groups, countries, styles, and cultures make these rough edges all the more cutting. I want to take note of several factors *seriatim* that seem to me extrinsic to that evangel and that could be corrected without loss. They are: first, the peculiar epistemological issues hovering around the evangelicals and their putative doctrines of the Scripture; second, the notion of theology in relation to the Bible; third, something about belief and its logic; then fourthly, some remarks in a more logical vein about the philosophical theism with which the evangelicals became entangled. All of these, again, are so important because they keep the development of the individual's Christian life, his pathos, and devotion almost at bay when evangelical preaching is directed precisely at it.

II

First, then, something about the Bible and its use within the evangelical contexts. I am not here complaining about the unabashed espousal of miracles and the virgin birth, nor even the notion that God reveals himself in exceedingly unlikely ways. Far be it from me to invoke modern naturalisms or a so-called scientific mentality as if these were, because they are new, therefore necessary. For, with the early Wittgenstein, it seems easier by far to be skeptical and jaundiced about these so-called modern conceptions of the world than to use them as criteria for judging every other conception. For they are, indeed, founded on the strange and faulty illusion that "the so-called laws of nature are the explanation of natural phenomena," as if these laws are inviolable and really discovered, not in fact conceptual nets, designed for a given purpose.[1] So what I here say is not said in any general criticism of the Bible itself or on behalf of a notion that it ought to be read scientifically because we all are that way today.

On the contrary, I repeat that being ordered by the Scripture seems to me to be right for all Christians; for at the very least this is the way to stay in touch with those who knew God. This is not to make a remark on the apostles' immediate acquaintanceship with Jesus; but it is to say that God was shown to them in his life and teachings and to us, there also, but also in the apostles and the entirety of the Scripture too. There is something elemental and right about the evangelicals staying with the Scripture. But the rough edges begin to show up.

For one thing, there is far too much said about the Bible, almost as if the Bible cannot speak for itself and show one the Savior without sundry helps. Of course, we ought to know that no words ever say anything by themselves just as no words have, strictly speaking, a meaning of their own. Therefore, the words of the Bible are like words anywhere: they are only meaningful and say something when they are conceived to belong to speakers, to situations, to occasions. Words do not mean; they do not say; people mean and say something or other with them. It is not taking anything away from the Bible to say that this maxim holds true there too. On the other hand, I am not here arguing that everything said in the Scripture must, therefore, be studied with an eye to the *sitz-im-leben* and that the historical setting is definitive. By no means. Historical-critical methods might be useful in this place or that—this is not the issue with which I am here concerned.

Rather, it seems to me that with all the Bible-centered talk that the evangelicals get pushed by their epistemic stand on the Scripture into a position that is comparable to that that they are eschewing in contemporary historical-critical studies. For admittedly, once the scholarly machinery of the present day gets into gear, the historical scholars seem prone to talk about everything but what the scriptural authors themselves say. We soon learn that a lot that is said is essential, but it begins to veer us in the direction of linguistic, stylistic, and historical issues. And whether the Bible is the word of God gets lost in the naturalized and conventional devices of technical study. It is almost with a wrench of mood and temper that one can even begin to think it is also something so worth saying and believing that men might die for it, be persecuted for what it avers, or live radically new lives on its account. This desacrilized mode of study is not of itself irreligious or anti-Christian, but it is a long way from reading the book in fear and trembling of its God whose expensive and costly way of redeeming the race makes for its chief point.

The insistence of the evangelicals is that the Bible is the word of God. But the 'how' of that insistence is what makes for a kind of learned talk, maybe quasilearned, that also diverts the listener. For instead of learning who God is and how to live in his accord, one learns a lot of things also about the book. If it is the word of God, then one should learn with it, for it is a lamp to our feet, a light in the darkened world, by which to find one's way. But strangely enough, theories about dispensations, inspiration, authorship, and a lot else, begin to intervene. It almost looks as if a chief piece of theology, a kind of knowledge of God, has to be made up by evangelicals to get the business moving. And soon the fireworks are not in the gospels and the epistles but in the evangelical spokesmen's scheme about the book.

I suppose it not strange, therefore, to have "redlines" from Genesis to Revelation; elaborate notions of how each part of the Bible supports other parts; pictures of conceptual identity being drawn about salvation, promise, inspiration, and a host of other things. I am not here ruling on the truth or falsity of these issues; but I am asserting that by looking so intently at the Scripture, trying to say impressive things about it, trying to defend it with constant polemics, that evangelicals also divert attention from God and from oneself. One becomes too conscious here of uniting themes and too little conscious of oneself and the Almighty.

While I can sympathize with the evangelical's notion, fairly well represented in several centuries, that the whole Bible ought to be used for Christian nurture and preaching, it does not seem to me that evangelical practice and theology really permits it anymore than pericopes do. Admittedly, the pericope texts tend to edit the Bible a bit; and they seem to fit the scriptural themes to a scheme like the church's year and to a round of very impressive services and ecclesiastical extravaganzas. Surely the pericopes are old and tried, and they probably do not utterly fail the purpose of our faith. But, they also omit a lot, and they tend to make the Bible fit the church practises and the rather demure way that most worshipers have of being domesticated to churchly life.

Clearly there was something robust and zestful about the evangelicals, in this setting and that, insisting that only the whole Bible must be exploited in order to do justice to its dramatic God. But, instead of exploring that book in the interest of the blinding light that God will bring, it is as if the whole book must be praised, massaged by some phrases, and its message summarized and encapsulated for a more ready consumption. It is not clear whether pericopes fail all that much when one considers what these meta-claims often do. Obviously it is a serious diversion for many to be defending the Bible, when the point of the Bible itself is that every life is being conformed to worldliness and about to be vanquished by evil itself. The Bible is the means to the light; by it, one can see everything anew.

The consequence of all this is a host of things. One of the most serious is that instead of getting to know God, one tends to get to know the Bible. By itself this is not bad. The point is that evangelical talking about the Bible, loosely a kind of theological position taking, never quite distinguishes the two. Surely, the Bible is the means; knowing God with certainty, love and constancy is the end in view. The Bible, not Cicero, Plato, and general human history, is the context in which he is shown to us. For even what the authors say in the Bible is not in consequence of their observational knowledge of God. For no man has seen him at any time. But they did get to know him. The strangeness of a nonobservational and practical knowledge of God is another story, but it is important that he was shown, was revealed, to them as he also is to us. Only with the knowledge of God can we be said to be redeemed, and we must start with that Scripture. After all the controversy, it looks as though the evangelicals have put something between God and man that does not have to be there.

Rail as we might at church life, at sacramentalism, at continuing sacrifices, the evangelicals have the appearance of being brave enough to give up a lot of tradition in the name of a single mediator, Jesus Christ. But inerrant Scripture gets to be an epistemic crutch, a pseudo-certainty, which while it purports to push doubt away, also inserts a humanly devised conceptual scheme by which to get the Scriptures to disclose the Almighty.

Fortunately, a lot of people disregard these dangerous notions; and this is probably also due to the vitality of the evangelical preaching which feeds mostly on the biblical content anyway. But that rough edge often catches one unawares. Perhaps more subtle in all of this, though, is another matter: the nature of theology itself that seems to ensue.

III

If one wishes to know why the Apostle Paul concluded for the Corinthians that the gospel of the Lord Jesus Christ looked foolish to the Greeks and a stumbling block to the Jews, then one could turn to Jesus' ministry and compare that with the public lives of Greek and Jewish teachers. Or the seven words of Jesus from the cross might mark out the oddity and strangeness that helps generate Paul's judgment. Our point is that Paul's remarks (I Cor. 1) do mark out a feature by which one learns more exactly what Christianity is. And thereby one proposes some knowledge of God, in short, theology. This theology is the kind of remark that is not quite a piece of new information, at least it is not the same as a novel fact. But Paul says something that is true and that is startling; however, it is more like a reflective comment, a reminder made about the very morphology and logic of the gospel itself. One gets the essence of the matter laid out in an imaginative and arresting way.

Paul certainly was explaining what he knew and what in a sense was already present, the life and ministry of Jesus. He was not inventing and proposing unheard of novelties. He was working over materials, remembered and knowable, that were in the public domain. Furthermore, what he does seems to me a biblical example of how to do theology, one which would therefore be binding upon all who make the Bible their norm. At this juncture, though, the theology of biblically-oriented evangelicals seems to me to become strangely alien to the biblical content. Along with many theologians since the earliest days, the strange notion has developed that the form and style of discourse is an option or simply an accident of choice or of the age. The correlative is that one can, supposedly, say the same gospel in any one of a number of ways.

If this is true, then one can have juridical manner, logical grids, question-and-answer methods, scientific methodologies, all or any of them by which to state the same Christian content. But already the issues get confused. The evangelicals, whatever their religious affiliations and historical settings—Lutheran, Baptist, Calvinistic, free-churchly, high or low—seem pushed by an enthusiasm for the Bible and a zeal to convert everybody, to make the knowledge of God eminently accessible. However laudable the motives, the results are frequently lamentable.

Two results are manifest. The casual and almost fortuitous character of the Bible, its multitude of *ad hoc* pieces, in metaphorical colloquial speech, is refashioned by the theological reformulations. A kind of literalism is, thus, everywhere asserted. And in case the hearer and reader cannot get the literal truth in the texts, the theology and the preaching tend to state it for him. For it is almost as if the richly metaphorical speech, so much like our daily talk about ourselves, about psychological matters, about thoughts, about emotions, is really distrusted, and another set of language ploys, the theology, as it were, states the meaning. This, then, is the first consequent.

The second is a little more complex, but it involves an issue earlier noted, namely, of letting one part of Scripture interpret another. As a polemical point, this contention can surely be joined; for it is in certain circumstances an apt way to protest a diffuse way of using Christian Scripture as a summary of earthly wisdom when its thrust is something quite different. Our point here is the misuse of this pedagogical and homiletical admonition in the direction of treating the Scripture as if it were a literary and metaphysical and casual gloss on a literal and systematic structure that it otherwise hides. The everlasting search among evangelicals for that structure, that is literally true and that is interconnected, makes Scripture often look like an introduction into a better theological scheme that lurks within it.

So the literalism issue and the systematic tendency, both perpetuated for worthy aims, always are projected as a fruit of study and a way to state the meaning. In this way, again, the Scripture, though it is mightily praised, gets treated as a point of departure, not for the business of becoming a Christian (which the Scripture aims at), but for the business of stating God's truth. And there is, consequently, a very high stake in that systematic and literal skein of thought, the correct theology, that is the meaning of the Scripture.

One must remark here that in this very respect the evangelicals are very much of the same mind-set as most of the liberals. For Hegel, Bultmann, Kant, and Bishop Robinson are not all that different in this regard. They, too, conjugate the Scriptures to get at the hidden meaning, and it is no wonder that evangelicals find the battles so numerous. They continue to stay in the same league intellectually. For many so-called liberals, along with the evangelicals, are convinced, too, that the Bible is the point of departure; and the assertion of literal truth is not enough to keep evangelicals from reading past the actual texts and placing them as they are, into another more organized scheme that looks more precise, legible, and easier by far to understand.

Theology becomes ascertaining of the Bible. Once that game is played, I'm afraid there is no stopping the discovery of meanings. For when one cannot discover them, one makes them up; and the point of demarcation is hard to fix. And theology, besides, becomes exceedingly important, not because the knowledge of God alone is important—which it surely is—but rather, because the system, which is logically tighter, conceptually better defined, looks like the literal rendition of what one otherwise has in parables, epistles, and the miscellany of admonitions, indicatives, and moodful literature of the Bible. Systematic theology of the evangelical sort gets to be a kind of tenseless, moodless tissue of erstwhile truths, ineluctable, shiny, and necessary. Besides, it becomes teachable, tangible, and orthodox.

But the point being made is that hereby a dubious intellectual posture, however widespread, is being proposed as though it were required by the Bible itself. I do not think that it is, but it is urged by the evangelical theologians very often indeed. This is what has led the evangelicals, who want the whole Bible's message, who have a case against dead orthodoxy and much of dead theology, to sire one of their own again. And besides that, they begin to look longingly at philosophies of various kinds to help in the task. Is it surprising to find how often the evangelical Christianity that is full of primitive homiletical surges seems to require a commitment to some kind of philosophical scheme when its intellectuals try to defend it against liberalism and other attacks? For James Orr and Edgar Sheffield Brightman, Scottish realism and various kinds of rationalism do have something in common when they can elicit the evangelicals' advocacy.

It is hard to say exactly what that is. But this yen for a systematic net of truths and mutually supporting concepts, looks like a must for evangelical Christians who long to get after that meaning of Scripture. Again, the discontent with the natural metaphysics and ordinariness of Scripture probably bespeaks the notion that it is ambiguous as it is; and that the ambiguity will be removed and divisions will be healed when the literal plain truth is harvested. But there is more. Evangelicals, like other Christians, have their fair share, too, of those who want to prove, to argue, and to polemicize on behalf of the Christian message. And this sought-after philosophical scheme promises to give one the logical tools as well as the ontological commitments to get proofs working at all.

But often times, this need for philosophical groundings, in order to make the theology seem warrantable, involves a kind of dogmatism that again makes for a very rough and cutting edge. It is almost as if an area of immense confusion and of massive self-assertiveness, the erstwhile pure epistemic side of philosophy, is invoked as though it had to be the necessary and nonnegotiable foundation for New Testament thought and significance. Though this side of philosophy is considerably less interest-saturated than morals and the search for wisdom, it is still a very "iffy" business at best. Besides, I think it a mistake to ask Christians who are intellectuals to make a commitment that is ontological and epistemological in philosophical terms when it is precisely these areas in philosophy that are the least settled and also where the canons of sense and nonsense in these matters are in debate.

Furthermore, we do make ontological commitments anyway if we are Christians, if for no other reason than we come to believe that there is a God to talk about. But the notion that every ontological commitment made by a Bible believer is an instance of a commitment to a philosophical scheme implicit in the Scripture (or a theological scheme with philosophical roots) is both a logical mistake and a slander upon the Scripture's viability to stand by itself.

I am not here suggesting that scriptural believing is a shallow matter or involves only an assent to its words. On the contrary, we can learn about God and not only about more Scripture. So there is sense to the notion that we come to know God and to become theists, if that notion is understood thus far in biblical terms. God is a person who loves and cares. But evangelicals tend to identify via their theology and their philosophy the God of the Bible with the God of philosophical theism. In the interest of defending Scripture and erecting apologetic structures to support and amplify it, the evangelicals—like certain strands of orthodoxy before them—tend to the notion that the biblical narrative is like a series of incomplete symbols, needing another scheme of concepts within which its meaning will become manifest.

Obviously, the scriptural narratives and panoply do need something else to become meaningful. But that something else is the life-history of the reader. When it becomes qualified by shame, fear, guilt, and sin-consciousness, those words of Scripture turn out to be not only the words of Paul and the apostles, manifesting God, but also find others' mouths in which and for which they are full of vitality. But this is to swing over into another difficult arena for discussion which was previously promised attention. Belief in God again becomes somewhat distorted by this malformation in evangelicalism.

IV

Let me reaffirm what was said earlier: the evangelicals do seem to keep the biblical evangel vibrant and exposed. But they do this through a rich and folkish hymnody, devotional preaching, and *ad hoc* worshipful use of the Bible. Perhaps these features of evangelicalism could be improved in detail; but the overwhelming impression that strikes me is that by staying open to all kinds of possibilities, there is also room for the God of the Bible. Again, though, I have a misgiving about what happens to the concept of being faithful within all of this, especially as soon as the minister gets a little more education and starts to do doctrine with a vengeance. For the pattern into which the evangelicals work themselves seems to me to put a strain upon the variety of ways that one can follow, obey, assimilate Scripture, and be a Christian. Far be it from the author to suggest anything like an implicit faith or a tacit kind of belief. The point is, rather, that the kind of biblicism we have noted makes believing a theology about the Bible almost more important, if not foundational, for believing its content; this same biblicism tends to force belief into a pattern of first assenting to a kind of theism read from between the lines before one can go on to use the lines themselves.

This is to remark upon a distortion of belief, the very concept and its related practices, which takes place. We might typify it in this way. If one's adaptation to or use of the Scripture, one's very educability by the Word of God, is the issue for evangelicals, then it is important to get the notion of what believing actually supposes. Is it a process? An activity? An occurrence? One would think from Scripture itself that a variety of ways of believing or truly believing (in contrast to nodding one's head) might be noted. For one thing, there is the simple following of Jesus and assuming his ways; there is going back to one's daily tasks and sinning no more. For some, the point of departure is leaving everything else; for others, like John, not being offended in his name. If one asked, "When does one believe?" the answers are terrifying multiplex but also tellingly simple. It seems that one cannot be believing if one does not love; and believing in God is not evinced if one has not done his commandments. On the contrary, believing in a treacherous and superficial way is castigated by the thought that the evil one can also believe—but without any of the above noted features.

The logic of belief is obscure to most of us, as it is in

81

most intellectual contexts. One can safely say that the reason for the ramified character of the concept in the Scripture is probably that believing in God itself is not a single-track enterprise. Probably an analogy would help. If one found someone who said that he believed that the earth was round but then expressed fear in taking an ocean voyage because he might fall off the horizon's edge, then that fear would be a symptom of non-belief. All the asseverations to the contrary, the fact of believing would be immediately dubious. In some like fashion, believing in God rules out certain kinds of anxiety, despair, and intellectual sloth; and the Bible never isolates belief as if it were a act separate from hope, love, and a zestful and joyous life.

This impacted character of Scripture on belief, or more properly, on faith in God, is not, I suspect, due to intellectual confusion and refusal to think. But right here the issue is that what looks like a many-sided and many-tracked set of endeavors in the Bible is made simpler and more definable in the evangelical's theologizing. For faith itself is therein refined in the direction of an act of belief. It is as though the evangelicals, with all kinds of theological antecedents on their side (including Augustine), want to make believing an activity, something that one does, a kind of intellectual process that one undertakes. Then it becomes a matter of assenting to a state of affairs, that being adumbrated in the theological account. For the theology is far easier to believe—if assenting is the mark of believing—than is the Scripture.

It is almost as though evangelicals, too, want to tidy up the picture a bit. Becoming and remaining a Christian looks like a strange business if the formless and nontheological New Testament is all that we have. Of course, for those who were chastened by the theological abuses and church practices and wanted the simplicities of the Bible instead, there must have been a temporary contentment with the unfettered texts. But the next generation, and now seemingly most of the evangelicals who want to justify themselves and their positions, now needs devices by which to prove and to argue. Then a notion is born anew—though it turns out to be an old idea at that—the pieces of Scripture are really part of a vast hidden structure of thought. Believing begins to look as if it has an armory of reasons in reserve; so one believes, then, not because of the attractiveness of Jesus or out of dire need or because of a chastened consciousness seeking forgiveness; instead the theology is like a system of warrants, a passel of guarantees, that shows you that the verses are true, and therefore believable.

Once again, then, we can see what a stress upon theology does, when the knowledge of God is thought to demand a special form and structure. The theological structure, hid within the New and Old Testament pieces, does tend to define itself, also, as a kind of philosophical theism. And, then, believing in the Bible turns out to involve also the subtle requirement of understanding that Bible's meaning; but the meaning is stateable only in another tissue of prose, one which is more formal, less metaphorical, more precise, and supposedly, less ambiguous. When that is achieved we get the doctrine; and now the question is—What do we do with it? The answer seems, again, that we believe it.

So, several matters are at stake. The multitudinous and rich ways of being faithful in the New Testament get more precision in the theological schematisation that states its essence. In the latter scheme, it is as if belief (an activity, something that one does rather patently) looms up as the organizing and necessary action constituting faithfulness. This emphasis is correlative to the theistic tissue, usually philosophically articulated, that is said to be implicit in the whole of Scripture. I think that this makes evangelicals put more emphasis upon an act of belief than New Testament faith actually requires. The morphologies of the Christian ways of living and acting get an artificial formalism that New Testament characters do not illustrate otherwise. Again, this act of belief becomes too rich and too important when it is remembered that the Bible itself is treated as though it were an interlocking, self-referential set of writings, whose substantial meanings can be arraigned in a conceptual system of doctrines. Then the act of belief has as its object nothing piecemeal, the way New Testament content seems to depict, but the whole Bible and/or the whole scheme of doctrine at once. I find this picture of belief too much indeed.

But what is wrong is that believing in a Christian sense is only seldom quite so clearly a matter of this kind of activity. And that only when confrontations with stated opposites demand a choice. Otherwise, belief is not a starting point; instead, it is like a capacity rather slowly achieved by a Christian living in daily prayer, sacrificial obedience, devoted conformity to a variety of other scriptural teachings. Even more particularly, the core of the scriptural teaching is that becoming a Christian is more like a blood transfusion, a kind of invasion by God into this paltry flesh, so that Christ will live within each person who yields to him. This kind of resuscitation by God is the consequence of the impartation of new motives, of new goals, of an entirely new and inconceivable teleology for this life. It is like a new birth. The whole of the world takes on a more incidental and temporary mien, almost as if that God of love, mercy, and wrath will not allow anything but mortals to put on immortality. The shift in outlook, habit, pattern of response, disposition, and judgment is to follow suit. One comes to that in a lifetime of devotional Christian nurture.

For all that, however, the act of belief is altogether too slender a base—the very language and word *belief* is too narrow for all that a Christian faith must include. Believing indeed will go on, but sometimes before, sometimes with, sometimes after these other things. Human beings are much too variegated psychologically ever to make an act of

belief that decisive; and Christian faith is much too rich
a mode of life to have an activity like assenting play such
a role. The confusion is created, certainly, by the fact that
we cannot even begin to decide whether to take Christianity
with seriousness until we know what it is. We need to
know something before we can begin. There is a sense
in which a theological summary like the Apostles' Creed,
or John 3:16, or Phillippians 2 gives one something to
think about. But the beginning is not always an assent to
these things as much as it is that in some manner or
another there is a lingering sense that here is something
to think about. Those pieces of Scripture may condemn,
console, incite, inform; but it pushes too hard to say that
some kind of binary statement is always supposed therein
to which one must assent. Sometimes yes and sometimes no.

Putting all this in another key, it is as if the evangelicals'
interest in having a converted, sin-forgiven new life in
Christ, with all its biblical vividness, is seriously diverted
by too much emphasis upon one subjective power at the
expense of all the other powers and capacities. For this
gives a dubious account of human subjectivity itself. Evangelicals must have a concern with assurance, certitude, fear
of the Lord, hope, love, and a host of other subjective (*i.e.,*
occurring in subjects) manifestations of Godliness. These,
too, are requisite. Surely it is an oversimplified psychological account which would allow us to think that believing
would produce loving and hoping. Why not loving produc-
ing in some cases the believing? Think of the subtleties
here and absurdity of a standard view of the relationships.
They go in a rich variety of ways.

These, then, are the reasons for saying that too much
stress is placed on belief; and belief itself is probably
misdescribed as an activity, whereas it usually is in Christian contexts more like a God-given capacity. So a standard
formalization here is—however regal looking and intellectually impressive—a snare and delusion. It is a poor way,
another ineptitude of thought, that has been given to

great a status in evangelical religiosity. The net effect, again, is to vitiate the religious vivacity that is being sought by recourse to the radical New Testament faith. So many evangelicals become, it is sad to say, defensive and self-protective, and it seems to me victims of bad logic rather than victors in Christ Jesus. Certainly spending so much effort in defending a doctrine about Scripture, that is not quite in Scripture, is bad enough. But to be asking that on every point in Scripture one knows, if not prove, before one tries much of anything, seems to me to take the heart out of a great scriptural theme—namely that by doing and following, by seeking with all one's heart, by being pure in heart, one will surely find God. By refashioning those conditions or otherwise subsuming them, evangelical intellectualisms do a disservice, albeit promising so much!

All through these remarks I have noticed a fairly consistent pattern among evangelicals to develop a dependence upon a scheme that is fairly called philosophical theism. The point is that most evangelicals become rather uncomfortable with the radical proposal of Pascal that the God of the philosophers is not the God of Abraham, Isaac, and Jacob. Of course, there are the obvious difficulties with Spinoza's, perhaps Hegel's and the Aristotelian kinds of God-concepts. But the thrust is still strongly in the direction of a God who is absolute, infinite, necessary, timeless, etc. It is the claim among evangelicals, as with many orthodox Protestants and Catholics, that a certain kind of philosophical theism explicates fairly and acutely the God of the Bible. The upshot, then, is a more formal predication about who God is and what he does than is immediately apparent in the Scripture.

Part of the force of theology is that there is, indeed, knowledge of God. And that means that one must make some predications about God's person. At this juncture, my argument gets abstract, but I hope neither unilluminating nor needlessly obtuse. For the question we must ask here trades rather heavily upon the logical issues involved in certain kinds of predication.

If there is to be a kind of nonbiblical and independent knowledge of God such as philosophical theism supposes, then the question is how one gets it. The answer is not an easy one. I choose only a few examples to illustrate a very rich and complex mode of argument. One might call this kind of argumentation dialectical and mean that philosophical theism proposes some knowledge about God to be drawn from purely conceptual considerations. This is quite different from settling issues by research into the facts and resultant new information.

So, consider for a moment, our facility at making some large disjunctive, categorical remarks. We can say that everything is either finite or infinite, thereby proposing that these two categories are exhaustive, that there is no third possibility somewhere in between. Much of what passes for "understanding" comes by placing a thing in a category. We seem rather confident that to put something in the right category is to understand it, at least a little. Again, if everything that is is either finite and limited or infinite and unlimited, it looks as if deciding what is which is an increment to knowledge.

A disjunctive pair of categories like this, finite or infinite, will only be useful if we can treat that pair as if they are also actual predicates of what is. To say they are predicates means that finite and infinite are not just words and not just categories. They have to be qualities of what philosophers might call being, which is all that is. The long-standing logical scheme in which a certain kind of philosophical theism really works is the one that says that when we enunciate paired opposites like existent and nonexistent, absolute and relative, necessary and contingent, actual and potential, unlimited and limited, etc., that these polar terms are universal in scope and that they are descriptive of the way everything must be. For this reason, the category-schemes of the Western philosophical tradi-

87

tion have looked like the minimal kind of logical grid upon which anything could be known. Of course, this is a kind of slender but, nonetheless, a very impressive kind of knowing. We seem to place everything within a single and necessary scheme.

Needless to say, this is also the heart of metaphysics. For this kind of metaphysical remark is purely dialectical, again meaning that it is conceptual and is achieved not by empirical description as much as it is by analytic and definitional exactness. Besides, a category schematisation has the power and authority to give a sense to the notion that everything is rationally commensurate, at least to the extent that anything that is can also be put into the frame of concepts that includes everything else. The category outlook has the plainest features of rationality about it, which features most of us want if the world is going to make sense.

Remembering, then, the outlook of Christian evangelicals, that God has spoken through the prophets, Jesus Christ, and the Bible, it is exceedingly tempting to think that Jesus, the Bible, and God himself must be minimally describable in this same kind of scheme. This does not appear to be asking too much, nor does it seem to require a denial of Christian fundamentals. On the contrary, with the plausible notion that God surely is not irrational and a sheer whimsy, it also looks likely that God is rationally knowable, but only by way of saying that he is infinite, absolute, timeless, necessary, and pure actuality. If it is rational to think disjunctively because everything must be either this or that, then God must also be one or the other. He is someone about whom one can predicate something. He exists; he is necessarily, not because he was caused; he is absolute and is never changed by the world as all the rest of things are. This kind of dialectical evocation has a rich sonorousness about it that makes it ring out so that we say: "Surely this is what the God of the Bible also is."

By exploiting a disjunctive categorical scheme, which functions as a kind of logical grid, many thinkers (including theists) find themselves involved in something quite exhilarating. I suppose the remark of J. Lukasiewicz, a Polish logician, might give us a little of a clue as to how this logistic scheme looms up. He says:

> I have the impression that I am confronted with a mighty construction, of indescribable complexity, and immeasurable rigidity. This construction has the effect upon us of a concrete tangible object, fashioned from the hardest of materials, a hundred times stronger than concrete and steel. I cannot change anything in it; by intense labour I merely find in it ever new details, and attain unshakable and eternal truths. Where and what is this ideal construction? A Catholic philosopher would say: it is in God, it is God's thought.[2]

There is something much like this in those evangelicals who begin to do a kind of rationalistic and idealistic kind of philosophy. For idealism is very much in this dialectical stream that exploits conceptual matters to the extreme. And it is not for naught that so many evangelicals feel drawn into a kind of subtle form of idealism, in which knowledge of God is not drawn so much by inferences from nature (in the natural theology mode) as in the dialectical and conceptual fashion we have noted.

Once again, let us think a bit about the disjunctive kinds of categories. The difficulty with categories is a logical one. If the category scheme is as Lukasiewicz suggests, a construction, then the categories are probably not quite discovered as much as they are made. Instead of being the most general traits of all that is, predicates of being, they might be the way that men have learned to categorize for this purpose and that. Then the necessity becomes internal and only within the application of the categories; and one cannot use the categories to establish God's existence and nature except by the additional and noncategorical, ever daring proposal that hereby we will also define God. But this changes things. And we don't get to the God of the Bible that way. If the categorical scheme is now understood not as a kind of general tracing of what is, but more like a projective device or series of tools, with a variety of purposes, then categories are in fact laid down. We can argue within them; but the arguments for them and from them are what is so difficult. Much of contemporary philosophical inquiry is about such foundational matters in logic and mathematics. These areas are difficult and unsettled. Resolutions here will come only by the most concentrated and detailed work. We do not know if logical schemata came before or after existence, and the issue is too confounding to resolve. It does not make much sense to suggest that God also was a rationalist or is subject to such a scheme, when the devices and rules by which we establish rationality seem to have been conventional. But our point here is not to decide these difficult and technical matters. It is rather to suggest that the evangelicals, along with other philosophical theists, are not entitled to the sureties that these dialectical exploitations serve up. The root questions are really where all the fun is in modern philosophy; and it is a dubious business to pin too much of eternal salvation's lore, let alone the Bible itself, upon so abstruse and difficult a range of matters.

It is almost as if evangelicals feel impelled to throw the burden of believing, the difficulty of being faithful, the need to be certain upon another range of erstwhile indubitables. If there were a realm of fixed indubitables, a necessary categorical scheme, which would be blatantly foolish, to reject then it would be very nice, indeed, to get the things of God so integrated. Then they could force somewhat a stubborn intelligence. Such forcing is possible if one said that only a fool would refuse a two-value (true and false) logic. But this only ties one down to a logical matter and that is relatively trivial. The dialectical theism that evangelicals threaten one with, promises that logical allegiance entails a knowledge of God. But that only means

90

anything at all if the categories are predicates of all that is; however, as we have already said, that is where the difficulties lie and the exciting intellectual questions are being raised.

But we have to pause a bit. I am making these philosophical matters sound as if they are resolvable if and when more work is put upon them. That is not quite right. Instead, these vast issues, about which so many philosophical theists are asserting things and where other logicians and philosophers are querulous, are also matters upon which people speak a lot of nonsense. Here we get metaphysical in such a way that we have to say that there are no criteria at all, and no sense is being made one way or the other. It seems a dubious practice to me, therefore, to put a great premium on these matters. Besides, there is an arrogance about philosophical sureties anyway; and the picture of such philosophers and theologians ministering to the broken-hearted and the contrite gets more than ludicrous too.

We have been alluding to the difficulty of metaphysics as an independent philosophical discipline. Metaphysics tries to tell us about "what is" in universal and necessary terms, with only dialectical and conceptual analysis as its court of appeal. Because evangelicals have wanted to assert that God is real, that he really did make the world and sent his only begotten Son, it has also seemed that they were already involved in making metaphysical claims. The Bible itself is, when read in this way, making all kinds of "metaphysical" assertions, for it is telling one what is, especially, God and his created world. This is the familiar way to reason here.

But, if what we have been saying makes any sense at all, there is a simpler way to understand the Scripture here. Clearly, the Bible is replete with instances of people who have made ontological commitments. But then all that is meant by that is that people do in fact, in the Old Testament and the New, learn to talk about God. The

91

word, "God," is used with confidence. But there is no philosophy that is invoked to teach people how to do that. When people do not believe, it might be that they think there is nothing to write about or know about with respect to God. The Bible makes no sense to them. The issue then seems to me to be very deeply religious and not, in any sense I can quite imagine, theological or philosophical. Intrusion of the latter factors could only make matters worse, especially if one began to do so as so many evangelicals want to do when they begin to look for backing and warrants for the Bible.

It seems to me obvious enough that there is something very wrong, if not truly nonsensical, in thinking that the religion of the New Testament could have a foundation at all in anything like a philosophical scheme or a metaphysical reality. The whole notion is a terrible confusion; and it does violence to the New Testament as well as make people bay for a philosophical moon! Oddly enough, it supposes that a theologian or a philosophical theist is a kind of religious expert, one who deals in foundations and proves things and deals in knowledge of God. Again, there is no reason in this for quarreling with anyone who tries to see what follows from what has been said, who gets ideas straight, who sees to it that there are no nonsequiturs and major inconsistencies. We are not contending with a real teacher who gets rid of confusion, but there is little in that kind of tough logical work (theological also, if you will) that will make anyone an expert and a master on God.

Besides, it is an illusion that the kind of dialectical work on concepts, even religious ones that evangelicals like, such as justification by faith and a salvation scheme, as well as those metaphysical disjunctions, that could ever lead anybody to a belief in God. The Bible asks for something so different. It demands a kind of trust in God and a kind of fear of him. Arguments do not do that. The notion of God as an infinite "X," an absolute, a *causa sui* all strike me as being almost completely irrelevant to the Old and New Testaments.

It is exceedingly difficult to see how the glory of God, the wonder that is due him, can be related at all to the kind of distinction one makes when we say God is absolute, whereas the rest of the world is relative, etc. That whole way of getting the God-idea thrust into our lives is so tame and so irreligious, so dull and trite. As if God were different in a way that we can really measure and comprehend. But that is the effect of the epistemological trappings that even the evangelicals always threaten to pin so much on. They are looking for a common measure in a rational system of some sort. The fact is that the New Testament is not a system at all; but it is a kind of nest of notions that belong together. They fit with one another. But their import, taken together, seems to me to teach the Bible reader that the disparity between God and man is so great that only God's grace can bridge it. Any other way to put God and man in a happy relation, even by reason (whatever that is), looks to me like more than a logical blooper—it borders on blasphemy!

Is it not true also that the other issue we have noted, that of believing in God, can be seen in a different light as well? Evangelicals, I have said, are tempted to think that they can analyze that notion by trying to sketch a new understanding for us, both of God and of believing. All too easily we drift into the notion that the Bible might be too indirect or metaphysical and that the theology can show us that God stands for an objective reality in some literal sense. Then believing, in some obscure but supposedly true sense, gets to be a matter of assenting to that objective reality. Now it is important both religiously and logically to be very careful here. For the notion of God's being objective by analogy with other objects and in contrast to being subjective is to trade again on an absurd disjunctive pair of categories. God is real; but he is not an object. He is not like anything else except persons, but when do we say persons are objective?

So, too, with belief. For when I talk about belief in Einsteinian in contrast to Newtonian physics, I mean something different than when I say I do not believe in ghosts. But both are different than believing in God. For here a kind of trustfulness that pervades one's whole life is called for. To believe in God does not mean holding views about him nor is it really a matter of getting to know him the way one gets to know physics or archaeology. God is not knowable or believable like that. If I believe in God, then I say: "Thou art the Lord," I give up a lot of fretting and vain trying, and I rejoice in him.

But this is only to say that the New Testament teaches one to seek God and to find him in ways that are not via hidden and implicit reasons. If I read Job, Paul, Isaiah, and King David, I think this other kind of belief is awakened in me. One moves from spiritual and moral death to spiritual and moral life.

Thus I end where I began. The evangelicals, despite everything that has been said, have made it very clear that God is not to be taken lightly or as one chooses. In fact, God himself is found in the Bible, which is the language of Christian faith. But he is not really described there; he shows through! To want to turn that language of faith into a language that is about God almost as if one were to describe a matter of fact—this is the epistemic mistake of evangelicals. It is that which makes them want to make Scripture a testimony on one or more theological themes or to make it a piece of talk limning a deeper theism. That is the crucial confusion.

That Bible, that language of the Christian is all tied up with the Christian life. To get to understand it seems to me to require that one become childlike, full of wonder even like a Christian; and in becoming a Christian one also acquires that language of faith. The notion that there is another way, another religious gnosticism, seems at best gratuitous and illogical; at worst, unbiblical. What could be more dilemmic for evangelicals?

Notes

1. See Ludwig Wittgenstein, *Tractatus Logico—Philosophicus,* trans. by D. F. Pears and B. F. McGuinness (London: Routledge and Paul, 1961), pp. 137-43. Note especially entries numbered 6.342 and 6.37 ff.

2. J. Lukasiewicz, "W obronie Logistyki," *Z zagadnień logiki i filozofii* as quoted in Christopher Coope, Peter Geach, Timothy Potts, Roger White, *A Wittgenstein Workbook* (Oxford: B. H. Blackwell, 1971), p. 22.

Part II. Who Evangelicals Are

The Religious Heritage of Blacks

William Pannell

That the religious beliefs of blacks were powerfully influenced by the great revivals of the eighteenth and nineteenth centuries is undeniable. Some black scholars have tended to regard this influence negatively. Joseph Washington complains that the Africans had foisted on them the whites' "compromising beliefs, moralities, attitudes, values and behavior," [1] and Gayraud Wilmore claims that blacks "recoiled" from this.[2] Yet it seems clear that in the nineteenth century at least, it was the revivals themselves that generated the main impulse behind the antislavery crusade. The climax of this struggle came in the Civil War, at the center of which was ostensibly the question of slavery. The nation passed through this trauma, but in the process something happened to its psyche.

Those evangelicals who had formerly championed the cause of abolition also emerged from the struggle bruised and somewhat spent. The aftermath of the War brought freedom to many blacks but little change to the overall attitudes of whites towards them. Blacks still smarted from the indignities which they had suffered, and not even the best efforts of the Radical Republicans during the Reconstruction Era (1865-1877) won them real acceptance in

William Pannell is Assistant Professor of Evangelism at Fuller Theological Seminary.

the northern or southern states. Moreover reforming white evangelicals of a conservative bent generally turned their minds to other matters than that of the blacks' cause. After Reconstruction, black Christians who had received so much of their religious instruction from white evangelicals found themselves even more alienated not only from Southern evangelicals but from Northern and Western ones as well.

The black religious experience did not, of course, begin in America. John Mbiti has rightly noted that Christianity was planted in Africa long before the great Islamic expansion in the seventh century, and by this time it had already produced great scholars like Tertullian, Origen, Clement of Alexandria, and Augustine. "Christianity in Africa," he concludes, "is so old that it can rightly be described as an indigenous, traditional and African religion." [3] By the time slavers were crossing oceans in search of cargo, Christianity in its various forms had spread from the north of Africa down both the east and west coasts, even reaching into the heart of the continent.[4] How much this faith was embraced is difficult to discern; what Christian convictions the slaves might have brought with them to America is hard to judge.[5]

Once the ships docked, however, the slaves who survived the "Middle Passage" were given a fresh exposure to "Christian" ideas, for it needs to be recalled that slavery was conceived almost in missionary terms, as the deliverance of victims caught in the vice of heathenism. These Africans were being emancipated to enjoy the light of Western civilization which was casually equated with Christianity. Yet the major defect of heathenism was not so much its lack of true religion as its lack of true civilization. "Being a Christian," Jordan has said of this age, "was not merely a matter of subscribing to certain doctrines; it was a quality inherent in one's self and in one's society." [6] Where Western civilization ended and Christian faith began was altogether obscured.

97

White Americans also inherited from their old culture a subliminal distrust of blacks that expressed itself in crude racism. In the English language, blackness, by a long tradition of usage, had come to symbolize evil, malignancy, and death. Consequently, the color of the African slaves was a matter of no small fascination to the colonists. Almost instinctively, the Africans were treated as inherently base and, even in their pathetic confinement, as strangely menacing.

American colonists with evangelistic tendencies who sought to convert the slaves not merely to a transposed European culture but also to a saving faith thus found themselves in a perplexing situation. Were converted slaves really Christian brothers? Christianity from the start had been a faith with universal pretensions, but so, too, was Western culture. The distinction between religion and irreligion therefore melted into that of race and race. And at this point, evangelical Christianity was unsure of how to absorb the slaves on the level of faith without absorbing them into the culture.[7]

If this form of racism was not "the congenital weakness" with which the society was afflicted, it was present in the view these colonists had of themselves and their destiny. This latent nationalism had its roots in Old Testament thought centered in the experience of Israel in the wilderness. The imagery, expressed in the sermons and literature of colonists and Europeans from the beginning, saw the land as the New Eden and these strangers as forerunners of a new order on the earth. This long standing tradition "helped to shape the American's image of himself as the new Adam of the West, a being unemcumbered by the fears and superstition of a mouldering civilization, a wise innocent dwelling in a terrestrial paradise."[8] It was this tradition, along with the futurist doctrine of the later revivalists, that gave America its "federal theology." Perry Miller asserts that the American situation, "as the preachers saw it, was not what Paine presented in *Common Sense*—

a community of hardworking, rational creatures being put upon by an irrational tyrant, but more like the recurrent predicament of the chosen people in the Bible." [9]

But this image of the New Eden did not include a black Adam. For that matter, the destiny of the country did not provide for the survival even of the Indian. This was to be a white man's country, and while such a notion has been fiercely contested at times by a few, a strong protest to the contrary has never been effectively mounted. Although the evangelical movement was dedicated from the start to the conversion of lost persons, it also began to serve the political consensus in the young country.

Nonetheless, the origins of the black Christian experience in America were evangelical in nature. Some elements of evangelicalism could be found in the early attempts of the Church of England to convert and baptize the blacks. Unfortunately, the Anglicans placed so much emphasis on the ability to recite the Creed and the repetition of liturgical prayer in the expression of Christian worship that their movement made little headway among those whose knowledge of English was limited. Through its Society for the Propagation of the Gospel in Foreign Parts the Church sent to the colonies numerous missionaries, teachers, and instructors in catechism to further the work of conversion among the blacks. Similar attempts were soon registered by the main Protestant denominations in the country, with the Methodists, Baptists, and Presbyterians having the most success among the slaves. [10]

Richard Allen's conversion and subsequent ministry within the Methodist Church serves as somewhat of a paradigm of African experience within America prior to the Civil War. Allen, born a slave in 1760, was later converted and joined the Methodist Society. His master, Mr. Benjamin Chew, was also converted and came to the conviction that slaveholding was inconsistent with his Christian profession. He offered Allen and his brothers a chance to buy their freedom, and they did. Taking his new freedom to Wilmington, Delaware, Allen began a preaching ministry that was to catapult him to eventual leadership as Bishop of the African Methodist Episcopal Church, and we find him working in Baltimore, Philadelphia, and Southern regions—"slave countries, the Carolinas." At one point, refusing an itinerant ministry with the famed Bishop Asbury because of the segregated conditions under which such a ministry would be sustained, Allen was drawn to his African brethren and was led to associate with St. George's Church in Philadelphia. There, alongside such growing stalwarts as Absalom Jones, William White, Darius Jennings, and others, he developed a significant and widely accepted ministry in the Methodist and other churches throughout eastern Pennsylvania.

Allen seemed to embody the prevailing character of the early black leaders in the emerging independent churches. He was passionately spiritual after the style of the revivalists. He was committed to the religion of the heart and engaged tirelessly in evangelism aimed chiefly at his African brothers. Mays, in his early book entitled *The Negro's God,* correctly understands Allen as a man committed to "traditional views of God," which were current in his day. "Many of his traditional ideas of God were developed along social and racial lines. He accepted the orthodox view of God relative to sin and salvation. He believed that sinners would be lost and that conversion was a miraculous act of God. God forgives and saves the repentant sinner." [11] This form of orthodoxy characterized the black church from the beginning and was based squarely on the Scriptures.

True to this biblical perspective, Allen led the church in its missionary outreach. The black church, after the spirit and example of Allen, Jones, and Daniel Coker, became a missionary church early in its history. Coker was elected as a bishop of the African Methodist Episcopal Church, although he declined the position. It may be that his heart and mind were elsewhere, for a few years later he sailed with ninety other blacks for Liberia as part of the colonization and missionary ambitions of the American Colonization Society.[12] He is generally regarded as the first "martyr" of the A.M.E. Church "to the cause of missions." [13]

This missionary zeal extended to the Baptists as well. The appeal of the Baptists was due to several factors directly related to the Great Awakening. Like their Methodist brethren, Baptists preached and practiced "heart religion" and considered emotional expression a vital credential of genuine Christian experience. The role emotion played proved most attractive to many blacks. Baptists, however, differed from the Methodists in their willingness to recognize spiritual gifts among the people and to encourage their use in the ministry. Thus it was possible for a black man to become a preacher or exhorter in less time than it took to dry off from the waters of baptism. He was not required to pass a theological exam or display knowledge attained in the schools. For blacks, not yet exposed to formal education, this proved most attractive. A further advantage enjoyed by the Baptists derived from their more flexible structure of worship and service. This flexibility, coupled with a long history of antiestablishment sentiment, gave the Baptists a decided advantage among the poor, both black and white. "Impatience with institutional forms, creeds, theologies, and liturgies," says Herberg, "constituted another aspect of this attitude, for these were all held to invade the rights of the sovereign individual and to inhibit the free flow of the spirit." [14] The triumph of the Baptists was the triumph of "frontier religion."

Blacks were part of white Baptist congregations in the late 1700s, and the first all black church may well have been that on Mr. George Galphin's plantation at Silver Bluff, South Carolina, in 1773 and 1774.[15] Similar experiences were a part of the initial slave exposure to white ministries and their congregations. Blacks worshiped with whites, and whites established separate "situations" for black meetings. These were not attempts at either integration or autonomy, but the experience of blacks was anything but congenial to the full expression of the Christian life. The period from 1773 to 1820 probably marks the period of the most intense efforts to evangelize the black community. These efforts produced many outstanding black leaders, some of whom achieved widespread fame. Others responded to the call of missions and served admirably abroad. Chief among the latter group was David George, who in 1792 led a mission to Sierra Leone. Prior to this, the Georgian preached among Baptist congregations in Nova Scotia. Rev. George Liele, another Georgian, began his preaching ministry in the area around Savannah. Later, fearing for his life and unwilling to risk reenslavement, he fled to Jamaica where, in 1782, he founded the First Baptist Church in Kingston.[16] In 1815 Lott Carey became the first black missionary sent forth by an interracial congregation. Carey, a former slave, was a member of the Baptist Church of Richmond, Virginia.[17]

This brief outline may serve to demonstrate that black Christians, whether meeting with whites or conducting their own congregational life, did not differ from whites in their overall understanding and practice of the Christian faith. They were evangelicals, deriving their faith from the tradition of evangelicalism in white Christianity, especially as found in the Baptist and Methodist movements.[18] Indeed, it has long been an axiom in the black community that if one was not Baptist or Methodist someone had tampered with his religion. These churches, now hoary with age, trace their roots to pre-Revolutionary times and to a theological heritage saturated with evangelical content. It was a heritage alive with social concern, too, and the failure to implement in society what were seen to be moral necessities, goes a long way in explaining the subsequent development of black Christianity.

The decline of religious fervor, and hence social reform,

after the Great Awakening was recaptured in the Second Awakening. The impulse for social reform that declined with the demise of the Second Awakening has never been recaptured. What had happened in the interim between the Revolution and the Civil War was that white America, including its religious institutions, had to redefine itself in terms of its national destiny. Threatened by dissolution from within as a result of an expanding West and social and economic upheavals between North and South, increasing attention had to be given to holding the country together. The enemy was now within, and the old weapons by which a successful war was waged against England were no longer adequate. The emergency called for new measures that would unite the country. This the revival did. Miller's sweeping assertion sheds much light on the connection between the Protestantism of the Revolution and that which obtained prior to the Civil War:

> Between the Revolution and the Civil War an alteration was worked in the mind of American Protestantism which is in fact a more comprehensive revolution than either of the military irruptions. With the political order separated from the ecclesiastical, yet not set against it, the problem had become not how to enlist the community into a particular political crusade for any social doctrine, but how to preserve a spiritual unity throughout a multitude of sects amid the increasing violence of political dissension. On the one hand, the revival movement and the extension of the voluntary system could not prevent the Civil War, as conceivably the theology of the covenant might have; but what these forces could do was to formulate a religious nationalism which even the war could not destroy. Whatever blood was shed and scars remained, the battles were fought upon the assumption of a cultural similarity of the contestants, one with another, which could surmount the particular issues in dispute and thus become, after 1865, a powerful instrument of reunification.[19]

This assumption of a cultural similarity did not include black people. It was a logical extension of the assumption

103

that Englishmen brought with them to these shores. It was an expression of what would come to be known later as "the rightness of whiteness," that would later dissolve into "romantic racialism," and then harden into the vicious forms of Jim Crowism in both society and the churches. For the churches, who had in all their history in America insisted upon liberty for themselves as a corollary to the Christian faith, failed to insist upon the same standards for blacks. When white survival and comfort are at stake, black men have been forgotten. The trick has been to pass legislation which serves to uphold the basic tenet of the national faith, and then in times of stress to forget it in the pursuit of majority ambitions.

It was in recognition of these early failures that black Christians took their future into their own hands. They revolted in the same manner and with the same rationale as had their white counterparts. They had been made pawns in the struggle between conservatives arguing for repatriation (colonization) and Southern slaveowners whose fear of economic loss overcame any commitment to the ideals of the Revolution.

The churches, preoccupied with their own internal problems, had little energy for social reform. Furthermore, the churches on the eve of the Civil War had begun to move upward on the social ladder. The American dream had begun to pay off. The old "frontier religion" evolved into middle-class faith. "As the frontier grew in stability and prosperity, and as the frontiersmen became the solid middle class of the American commonwealth," said Reinhold Niebuhr, "the 'first fine careless rapture' of Evangelical Christianity was lost." [20]

The gradual withdrawal of evangelicals from the arena of social reform did not go unnoticed by blacks, especially the free blacks of the North. They had never enjoyed real freedom and equality with their white brethren, for integration in white churches usually took some form of second class status for the Africans. The Africans had never accepted this arrangement with equanimity. Like their white mentors, they had begun to use Scripture to secure equal status and responsibility in the body of Christ. This action was usually carried on in good spirit and with the hope of continued fraternal relations. But the die had been cast, and when Richard Allen led the African contingent out of St. George's Church to found the Free African Society in 1786, later to become the African Methodist Episcopal Church, he signaled to all black communicants North and South that the romance with white evangelicals was dying.

This action formed fears and fired the prejudices of whites. Recalling the earlier revolts of Gabriel Prosser (1800), Denmark Vesey (1822), and Nat Turner (1831), the country, especially Southerners, moved to prevent any further uprisings. But uprisings there were, as indeed there had always been. In order to downplay these revolts a vast propaganda scheme was conceived which pictured the African as docile and childlike and altogether too dull to engage in anything like an insurrection.[21] Yet these pronouncements about the happy slave were made with a wary eye cast toward the slave house.

One recollection must have been especially painful to the evangelicals in the churches. Vesey, Prosser, and Turner had accepted their role as liberators by reading the Bible. They were Christians, and members of emerging black Methodist churches had supported them.[22] These men may not have understood the psychological, political, and sociological jargon in use today to explain their actions, for theirs was a simple concern—to flesh out in liberation terms the plain teachings of the Scriptures. They, and other stalwarts such as Henry Highland Garnet, Frederick Douglass, and Henry McNeal Turner may force a new definition of what it means to be evangelical.

The white evangelical church moved on up into the solid middle class and abandoned its heritage to those whose message was social reform without the gospel. After the Civil War white evangelicals failed for the most part to meet the spiritual and material needs of the waves of immigrants that arrived in the country. Moreover, their general failure to work for the cause of blacks (coupled with the outright racist attitudes of some) meant the end of white evangelical influence on the blacks who had begun the great push northward to settle in the burgeoning cities. In brief, white evangelicals and black Christians continued more than ever to go their separate ways at the same time that they shared so many religious beliefs in common. The divorce between them was becoming very evident.

Black Christians who had been freed at last by the Civil War set about to consolidate their new liberties. They did not last long in the political and economic areas, but the black church survived as one of the chief and viable expressions of black power in the community. It exists today, often without its earlier evangelical content, as the cradle of black protest in America.

Notes

1. Joseph Washington Jr., *Black Sects and Cults: The Power Axis in an Ethnic Ethic* (Garden City, N.Y.: Anchor Books, 1973), p. 83.

2. Gayraud S. Wilmore, *Black Religion and Black Radicalism: An Examination of the Black Experience in Religion* (Garden City, N.Y.: Anchor Books, 1973), p. xii.

3. John S. Mbiti, *African Religions and Philosophy* (Garden City, N.Y.: Anchor Book, 1970), p. 300.

4. *Ibid.*, p. 302.

5. Cf. Richard Jobson, *The Golden Trade* (New York: Da Capo Press, 1968). It is probably so that as Jobson wrote, the African reflected "many . . . things our sacred history makes mention of, but it is likely that these expressions of similarity are traceable to their Muslim origin rather than Judeo-Christian."

6. Winthrop D. Jordan, *White Over Black: American Attitudes Toward The Negro, 1550-1812* (Chapel Hill, N.C.: University of North Carolina Press, 1968), p. 24.

7. *Ibid.*, p. 21.

8. George M. Fredrickson, *The Black Image in the White Mind: The Debate on Afro-American Character and Destiny 1817-1914* (New York: Cornell University Press, 1971), p. 7.

9. Perry Miller, *From the Covenant to the Revival*. Reprint Series in History (Indianapolis, n.d.), p. 342.

10. Washington, pp. 49, 50.

11. Benjamin E. Mays, *The Negro's God* (New York: Atheneum, 1968), p. 30.

12. Wilmore, pp. 143-45. There is evidence that Coker's refusal of the office of bishop was due to his color. Leonard L. Haynes, Jr., *The Negro Community Within American Protestantism* (Boston: Christopher Publishing Company, 1953), pp. 133, 134.

13. Charles Wesley, *Richard Allen, Apostle of Freedom* (Washington, D.C.: Associated Publishers, 1935), p. 170.

14. Will Herberg, *Protestant, Catholic, Jew* (Garden City, N.Y.: Anchor Books, 1960), p. 106.

15. W. H. Brooks, "Priority of the Silver Bluff Church," *Journal of Negro History,* VII, 174.

16. Wilmore, pp. 146, 147.

17. F. S. Monroe, "Lott Carey, The Colonizing Missionary," *Journal of Negro History,* VII, 328-426.

18. Washington, p. 49.

19. Gilbert H. Barnes, *The Anti-Slavery Impulse, 1830-1844* (New York: Harcourt, Brace and World, Inc., 1933), p. 361.

20. Reinhold Niebuhr, "The Impact of Protestantism Today," *The Atlantic Monthly* (Feb. 1948).

21. Fredrickson, p. 52.

22. Wilmore, pp. 74-136.

Bible Believers in the Black Community

William H. Bentley

The black community is the natural home of the black evangelical, even though with increasing frequency he is coming to be found in white dominated suburbia. Sensitive to the negative connotations conjured up by the term "ghetto" blacks prefer that the area where they live be called by the name community. It was the social scientist, not the neighborhood resident, who first informed blacks that they lived in a ghetto. Prior to that, blacks knew about slums, for many of us lived in them. Large numbers of us, however, lived in areas which could not accurately be so described. Imagine the great surprise and chagrin in discovering that the entire black community had come to be defined as the ghetto.

Ghettos were originally European and designated the quarters to which Jews were segregated. Following the mass migration of Jews to the United States in the early part of this century, the term became Americanized and enlarged. It still referred to the place where Jews resided, but it took on the additional sense of self-segregation. As soon as the Jews as a group became prosperous enough, virtually all of them moved up and out. In America there are virtually no Jewish ghettos at the present time unless one refers to some of the most affluent parts of suburbia. These are not ghettos in the traditional sense of the word.

Thus while the Jew, and other white ethnic minorities might have preceded blacks in the ghetto, they were not

William H. Bentley is President of The National Black Evangelical Association.

perpetually forced to remain there. Despite the fact that a very small trickling of middle-class, and an even smaller number of upper-class blacks are allowed to make the transition to the promised land of suburbia, the vast majority of their fellows are most effectively kept, willingly or not, in the areas rigidly designated for black occupancy.[1]

That blacks as a group have had little or no control over where they choose to live can easily be traced to the existence of a vast and complex network of structures designed historically to perpetuate the racial status quo. Virtually all white institutions, including the white church, either directly or indirectly profit from and in some degree enjoy an unearned increment from the racial status quo. That is why it is so extremely difficult to make meaningful changes in it.

Added to this lack of power to determine their own place of residence, blacks must bear the onus of the attribution of "sickness" to their community. All their institutions are said to partake of this sickness. The affliction is described as moral, spiritual, ecological, social, economic, political, and cultural.[2] The ghetto is therefore a bad place to live, and its relation to the larger society may be understood as a zone of quarantine.

The black evangelical is an integral part of the black community. As such, he is shaped, affected, and interpreted by the collective experience which all blacks historically share. Try as he may, and many do, he cannot escape from his identity as an indissoluble part of Afro-American humanity. His relationship to the larger white world of evangelicalism, therefore, cannot be divorced from this social reality.

The Term "Evangelical"
as Applied to the Black Christian

The word "evangelical" itself is ambiguous, notwithstanding etymological attempts to fix its precise meaning.

109

Theologians of such widely divergent views as E. J. Carnell, Carl Henry, Paul Jewett, Clark Pinnock, Karl Barth, and Emil Brunner all use the term, but with widely divergent meanings. To blacks, at least the mainstream ones within the major black denominations, the word has little historical relevance. Instead, "Bible believing" is the more widely used descriptive term.

Because blacks until recent times seldom consciously used the word "evangelical" to differentiate themselves from others who identified themselves as Christians, it has often been erroneously assumed, both by blacks who consciously call themselves evangelical and whites of the same persuasion, that there is very little true evangelicalism to be found within black Christianity. Blacks who were trained in white seminaries and Bible schools were confronted by this defective analysis of the black church. For example, it was often argued that theological orthodoxy was incompatible with the free expression of emotion characteristic of the less status-oriented churches of the black masses. Why this was so, if indeed it was, was never explained to us. Very few of us dared challenge this dogma, and thus we returned to our communities seeing the black church through white eyes. Thus the black evangelical movement began to be somewhat emasculated. There was little historical continuity with traditional black Christianity. It is therefore to this larger group, which represents what most blacks themselves call the black church, that we must look for the largest reservoir of spirituality within our own community.[3]

As indicated above, when we did return to our own communities, it was with a feeling of deep shame, and few of us willingly chose to identify with our people. It also drove many of us to attempt to impose white standards upon a people who had in part been historical victims of those values and standards. We seemed to be totally unaware of the fact that the survival of our people in America

110

was largely through the medium of the black church, and that church had survived because it had developed its own standards in the crucible of the Afro-American experience. It was this complex of negative attitudes, more than anything else, that explains why as a distinct religious approach black evangelicalism has been considerably less than successful in reaching the black masses. To this moment, it remains for the most part, outside the mainstream of black Christianity. With the possible exception of black Pentecostals, black evangelicalism is distinctly a middle-class religious phenomenon and has much more in common with its white counterpart than with the black. Consequently, one of the most pressing needs of black evangelicalism is to begin to see its own church through black eyes and in total relationship to its own community first. Only as it becomes aware of and accepts its heritage can it speak prophetically, not merely critically, to it. Only as black evangelicals pay their dues in identification with mainstream black Christianity can they emerge as America's most viable bridge between the separated communities.[4]

Use of the term "Bible believer" may be deceptive. The tendency is to regard it as unsophisticated. Yet there is probably no better name to be used in describing a complex of belief-systems which spans the gamut from simple credulity to real profundity.[5] Bible believers are to be found in all the major black denominations and in virtually all the smaller ones. Most of the smaller groups are relative "Johnny-come-latelies," being able to trace their origin only to the late nineteenth and early twentieth centuries. And while the National Baptist Convention-U.S.A., Incorporated, the National Baptist Convention of America, and the Progressive National Baptist Convention represent a more recent institutional adaptation, nevertheless Baptists and several Methodist groups preserve the continuity of the historical black protest and quest for identity.[6] Their crucial contribution, as noted above, has been to keep alive the time-tested traditions that enabled the Afro-American to survive the harsh crucible of white America.

Theological awareness or sophistication within mainstream black denominations, even among those who qualify as Bible-believers, may be found in varying levels and degrees. The black church has always been gifted with outstanding leaders, some of whom possessed training. But on the whole, development of explicit theological systems has thus far not been the contribution made by those leaders. Such theology as has been developed has been largely existential and pragmatic. In this context James Cone has rendered a great service to the church by pointing out the fact that the Negro spirituals in their totality reflect a theological awareness that is much more than merely rudimentary.[7] Nevertheless, it is an implicit rather than formalized approach to theology. It is not the theology of the Academy, it is the theology of the involved participant-actor on the stage of life. In this restricted sense it may be more American than the theology of most academies which are to a great extent based on a European model and reflect implicitly a European social experience.

Other strains of black Christianity also contain Bible-believers or evangelicals. We refer specifically to blacks within the major or mainstream white denominations such as Presbyterians, Congregationalists, Episcopalians, Lutherans, and to a lesser extent, though growing in numerical significance, members of the traditional Reformed groups. In addition black communicants are coming to be found among Mennonites, Evangelical Friends, and other largely white ethnically based Christian groups. Pentecostals and Holiness groups constitute, as briefly mentioned above, a major source of black evangelicalism. With the exception of this latter mentioned group, identifying who is evangelical is subject to the identical vagaries and difficulties which confronts the white investigator of the white church.

Membership in the major white denominations is an important factor in assessing black Christianity for at least two reasons. First, it shows that not even the major black groups could attract all the believers. Secondly, it points up the factor of class identification and stratification among Afro-Americans. It shows that all of us tend to seek membership in organizations with which we identify socially, economically, and culturally. There is no other way to explain why the blacks within these denominations persisted throughout the several centuries in maintaining membership in communions where all too often they were not wanted. The literature on the relationship of class stratification to religious identification is too voluminous to cite. But among black scholars who have written on the subject, E. Franklin Frazier and Nathan Hare stand out.[8] Both point out that as blacks climb the ladder of affluence they generally seek membership in churches which they regard as reflecting and possessing the values they have so newly acquired. It is also clear that much of the success of the Roman Catholic Church in post-World War II black America has to do with this same complex of self-perceptions. To be sure, this is not intended to deny the presence of religious orthodoxy in upper status blacks. Nevertheless, it is wise to pay some attention to the fact that acceptance of higher status church membership is often accompanied by rejection of religious orthodoxy as being a relic of a less enlightened mentality to be sloughed off in the process of putting on a new Christian skin. Evangelicalism as a term of identity is heard less often here.

With respect to the Holiness and Pentecostal groups, we are on a much firmer identity ground. These are entirely evangelical. And yet among blacks who are of this persuasion the term as such is not in widespread use. Once again we are faced with the fact that, in the black church tradition, the sharp distinction between those who are known for strict adherence to Bible-based doctrinal systems and those who are not is not consistently drawn. Exactly how this came to be is obscure. It may, however, have to do with the fact that doctrinal controversy of the

113

magnitude which seems endemic within traditional white Christianity has never assumed such importance in the black experience. This need not mean that doctrinal issues are absent nor their debate or discussion irrelevant. Black people in America have never had enough leisure time on their hands for disputes of this type.

Black Evangelicals: Who Are They and Where Are They?

1. *Black mainline denominations.* These are: The National Baptist Convention U.S.A., Incorporated; the National Baptist Convention of America; the Progressive National Baptist Convention, Incorporated; the African Methodist Episcopal Church; the African Methodist Episcopal Zion Church; and the Christian Methodist Episcopal Church. According to the standard reference works[9] these groups contain over eleven million members with well over eight million of them being Baptists. Since there is no statistical breakdown into those of the Bible-believing persuasion and those who are of other persuasions, we cannot with any degree of certainty state the number of evangelicals to be found here. Almost all studies, however hostile or laundatory, that have been made attribute a very large amount of evangelical sentiment as being prevalent within these groups.[10]

2. *Black Christians within white church structures.* Alex Poinsett[11] estimates that there are about 1.6 million such members, less than one percent of the 123.3 million total U.S. church membership. Harry Richardson[12] estimates the number of blacks to be found within such white denominations as the United Methodists, Protestant Episcopal Church, the Congregational Church, Seventh-Day Adventists, Presbyterians, American Baptists, and Church of God to be around 800,000. Blacks are also coming to be found in increasing numbers within the smaller white Protestant groups, as noted above. If we estimate the total

number of black members within the above named structures to be around one million, we would still not know what proportion could be classed as evangelical. Available statistics by denomination simply do not classify membership by orthodoxy of belief.

3. *Black Christians—independent.* These are members of organizations for the most part rather loosely structured and aligned with neither black denominations nor white ones. They are also assertedly orthodox theologically and would respond favorably to the epithet "fundamentalist." Thus they are clearly evangelical. Among them are the Brethren Assemblies, offshoots of the Plymouth Brethren, Independent or Fundamentalist Baptists (a name used to distinguish them from the larger Baptist groups which are regarded as somewhat apostate), and a few unaligned Methodist assemblies such as the Israelite Methodist Church in Chicago. Statistics are not available for these groups which seldom list their membership within the standard reference works.

4. *Black Holiness and Pentecostals.* Although there are significant numbers of black Christians within white Pentecostal and Holiness churches, it cannot be gainsaid that the overwhelming number is to be found within organizations founded by men and women of their own race. The reason for this separation is the same one which separated all other Christian groups. Pentecostals, despite their claims, have suffered from the same hang-ups in the area of race as others; a survey of the role played by blacks in the founding of the movement readily shows this.[13] Of these black groups, the Church of God in Christ is the largest. Statistics on this body have changed little since this writer first became a Christian within its communion over thirty years ago. In my judgment, the figures given in the reference works are low. Their membership is usually placed at between four and five hundred thousand. My estimate, based on rather careful observation of the growth of this church, would place the number at around seven

115

hundred and fifty thousand. Other smaller Pentecostal groups such as the United Holy Church of America, the Fire Baptized Holiness Church, the United Pentecostal Council, the Mount Calvary Pentecostal Movement, the Arturo Skinner and other Deliverance Movements, plus the Apostolic Faith movement, and many others too numerous to mention, would easily bring the number of black Pentecostals to well over one million. The Holiness tradition among Afro-Americans is much less significant statistically than is the Pentecostal. Among blacks, as was equally true among whites, the tongues phenomenon marked the doctrinal parting of the ways. Probably the outstanding representative of the Holiness movement among blacks would be C. P. Jones' Church of Christ-Holiness. Its membership fluctuates around the twenty thousand mark. The Holiness movement within the black community has never approximated the strength of Pentecostalism.

5. *Fellowship Associations.* They are so designated because they are not, strictly speaking, connected with any denomination and are variants of the independent approach to Christian service. Of these we list two as representative: The Michigan Association of Negro Evangelicals and the National Black Evangelical Association. The former is headed by Warren Lawrence. The latter has had a succession of Presidents from Marvin Prentis through Evangelist Howard Jones, George Perry, and the present writer.

The Michigan group is locally oriented; the National Black Evangelical Association is national in scope. It was founded in 1963 in Los Angeles, California, for the purpose of promoting fellowship and ministry with a major focus on Afro-America. Although its membership includes whites the Association has for the most part honestly sought to cultivate in-depth relationships with the black community. It seeks to be a voice of credibility and authenticity to that community. It also seeks to be a bridge between the two divided communities—the white and the black. NBEA is an organization of organizations and includes within its scope other groups such as the Tom Skinner Associates, John Perkin's Voice of Calvary, Reuben Connor's Black Evangelistic Association, Carver Foreign Missions, Teen Challenge, Fellowship Bible School of San Francisco, Mel Banks' Urban Ministries, and the African Christian Teachers Association, headed by Etta Ladson of New York.

Of the evangelistic associations undoubtedly the best known one is Tom Skinner and Associates. Its major thrust is evangelism but other vital ministries also flow from the organization. Associates include Carl Ellis of Campus Ministries and Henry Greenidge, who heads the Creative Arts ministry. Other evangelistic associations include Robert (Bobby) Harrison Ministries, Sam Dalton's ministries, and black members of the Billy Graham Evangelistic Association—Ralph Bell and Howard Jones. Other well known evangelistic ministries are those of Charles Williams, William Pannell (presently on the staff of Fuller Theological Seminary), and men of high caliber such as John Lawrence of New Jersey, and Donald and Richard Henton of Chicago.

Finally, there is the growing list of those blacks who serve God through the profession of teaching. We list only a few: Ozzie Edwards of the University of Michigan, Professor of Sociology and head of the department of Afro-American Studies; Wesley Roberts, member of the Department of Theology and Professor of Apologetics at Gordon Divinity School; Abraham Davis of Messiah College and Houghton College; Ruth Lewis Bentley, Head of Minorities Affairs and member of the counseling staff at the University of Illinois Medical School.

In the absence of careful pioneering work on black evangelicalism which will delineate its precise sociological makeup, establish its exact numerical strength, and clarify its theological solidity, present observers have had to work more from speculation than from clear data. Nevertheless it

117

seems fair to say that evangelicalism is probably far more prevalent among blacks than is usually realized. Those who seek for truth in this matter must not limit themselves to the often prejudiced value judgments of some blacks who openly accept the name evangelical but who hold themselves outside mainstream black Christianity and regard it as virtually apostate. No one black person or group can speak for all the others; the facts come from a variety of sources.

A final word is in order. Blacks who are evangelical have come to terms with themselves and with others of like theological persuasion in matters of orthodoxy of doctrine. Now they, both individually and as a group, must likewise come to terms with the awareness of their ethnic identity, something that white evangelicals are also having to do. The creative possibilities of this are both troubling and tremendous. By virtue of their unique experience in both secular and sacred America, black Christians of evangelical persuasion, by accepting freely and positively the ties that bind them to their community of their origin and nurture, may be used of God to help bring healing to a community sorely in need of it. In accepting this role, they must do so without negating blackness as the price of racial harmony within the Christian context. This, in essence, is but the religious aspect of a problem that is really much larger: How can one be genuinely black in white America?

Notes

1. The following works discuss the formation, institutionalization, and perpetuation of the black ghetto. Ulf Hannerz, *Soulside: Inquiries into Ghetto Culture and Community,* (New York: Columbia University Press, 1969), p. 11 ff. Max Geltman, "Is a Slum a Ghetto?" *The Confrontation: Black Power, Anti-Semitism, and the Myth of Integration* (Englewood Cliffs, N. J.: Prentice-Hall, 1970), contains an excellent though brief discussion of the origin and usage of the term "ghetto" as largely derived from *The Uni-*

versal Jewish Encyclopedia. Hannerz applies the term more specifically to the Negro commmunity, particularly that portion of it which he selected for his research. Allen Spear in *Black Chicago: The Making of a Ghetto* (Chicago: University of Chicago Press, 1967) shows how the black ghetto of Chicago was formed and perpetuated. Karl and Alma Taeuber in an article, "The Negro Population In the United States," in John P. Davis, ed., *The American Negro Reference Book* (Englewood Cliffs, N.J.: Prentice-Hall, 1967), present statistical data on the composition of the black community across the country. Other works such as Myrdal's *American Dilemma,* St. Clair Drake and Horace Cayton's *Black Metropolis,* and Lewis Knowles and Kenneth Prewitt's *Institutional Racism,* shed additional light on the complex political, social, economic, and educational features of the ghetto. William K. Tabb, *The Political Economy Of The Black Ghetto,* the *Kerner Report* (*Report of the National Advisory Committee On Civil Disorders*), and the entire issue of the February, 1972, *The Black Scholar,* entitled "The Black Colony, U. S. A.," all focus on the ghetto as the product of the larger society, its zone of "quarantine."

2. The so-called "Moynihan Report" is a most apt illustration of this particular orientation. It reflects the tendency of white social science to study black institutions as deviations from the white norms. This shallow piece of research was based almost entirely on secondary sources which did a more comprehensive job of analysis. It was a propagandistic piece of material, hastily concocted as a rationale for building "War on Poverty" strategy. That "war turned out to be no more than a skirmish." Moynihan has been so effectively and comprehensively critiqued that we will present no exhaustive list of authorities who have pointed out his inadequacies. The entire discussion may be found in the book edited by Rainwater and Yancey, *The Moynihan Report and the Politics of Controversy.* (Cambridge: M.I.T. Press, 1967.) For a convincing argument that implicit bias found in the "consensus model" of "functionalism oriented" social science often leads its investigators into glaring inaccuracies in their analysis of nonwhite institutions, see the articles by Ronald W. Walters, "Toward a Definition of Black Social Science," and Dennis Forsythe, "Radical Sociology and Blacks," in Joyce A. Ladner, ed., *The Death of White Sociology* (New York: Vintage Books, 1973). More constructive approaches to the study of black institutions in which they are seen as viable subjects for research in their own right can be found in the many writings of W.E.B. DuBois, particularly his study of the "Black Church" in the famed *Atlanta Series* and *The Philadelphia Negro.* Other names to be added to the list would include Joseph Washington, *The Politics of God;* Carter G. Woodson, *The History of the Negro Church;* Mays and Nicholson, *The Negro's Church;* the December, 1969, issue of Nathan Hare's *The Black Scholar;*

Gayraud Wilmore's *Black Religion and Black Radicalism;* and Robert Staples, ed., *The Black Family: Essays and Studies.*

3. Dependable statistical studies of the composition of the black church in terms of the precise identity of the evangelicals within it are almost non-existent. Virtually all students of the black church recognize a fairly high percentage of what could be called "evangelical sentiments" within it, but little or no serious attempt is made to statistically isolate them. This is partly due to the fact that "evangelical" has never been a term in wide use within mainstream black Christianity. That the doctrinal sentiment without conscious use of the name (as is true in the case of white Christianity) has from the first been a part of the black Christian belief system, is seen in the fact that Richard Allen and the early founders of the black church subscribed to the evangelical beliefs of the Wesleys and those that followed them. The authorities cited above also indicate that in the subsequent development of the black church there has always been a significant element of what whites call "evangelicalism." There has never, however, been a fundamentalist-liberal controversy within black Christianity in America.

4. See William Bentley, *The National Black Evangelical Association; Reflections On The Evolution Of A Concept Of Ministry* (privately published, 1974).

5. See footnote 2. In addition, Lerone Bennett's *The Negro Mood* (Chicago: Johnson, 1964) contains a profound discussion of the inner dynamics of the faith of black Christians as providing the main bulwark against the inhumane and dehumanizing corrosions of the American racism of which they were the victims. He shows how faith was made doubly hard because, though there were significant exceptions, those who forced slavery, segregation, and discrimination on them, called themselves Christians and used the authority of the Bible and theology to justify it. See also Benjamin Mays, *The Negro's God* (New York: Atheneum, 1969).

6. Joseph Washington's *Black Religion,* and E. Franklin Frazier's *The Negro Church in America;* W. E. B. DuBois's *The Philadelphia Negro;* James Cone's *A Black Theology of Liberation;* and perhaps best of all, Wilmore's *Black Religion and Black Radicalism* show the protest element as being a major motivating force within black Christianity. See also John Hope Franklin, *From Slavery to Freedom* and the entire issue of the December, 1969, *The Black Scholar.* The protest motif provides a unique element that is not found within white American Christianity.

7. Joseph Washington's *Black Religion* (Boston: Beacon Press, 1964) indicted the black Church for existing outside the mainstream of Western theology. He pointed out that blacks have never produced outstanding theologians and therefore are ethically rather than theologically based. The "genius of the Negro folk religion is the drive for freedom." Washington reverses himself in his later writings, but it is to James Cone that we must turn, especially his

The Spirituals and the Blues (New York: The Seabury Press, 1972), to learn that although explicit and formal theology was not a feature of traditional black Christianity, nevertheless the slaves, and later the freemen, had definite and substantive ideas of God, man, and the universe. Cone probably is best known for his writings on black theology. Other major contributors in this area are J. Deotis Roberts, Major Jones, Vincent Harding, and the provocative and probing William R. Jones in his *Is God a White Racist?* These and other works point to an increasing dissatisfaction with the cavalier manner in which the black experience has been dealt with in the traditional expositions of white Christian theologians.

8. E. Franklin Frazier, *The Negro In The United States* (New York: The Macmillan Co., 1957) and *Black Bourgeoisie* (New York: The Free Press, 1957). *Black Bourgeoisie,* together with Nathan Hare's *Black Anglo-Saxons* (New York: P. F. Collier, 1970), deliver a withering attack on the social pretensions of the newly affluent post-World War II blacks. A milder discussion may be found in St. Clair Drake and Horace Cayton's *Black Metropolis* (New York: Harcourt, Brace and World, 1962), II.

9. Constant H. Jacquet, Jr., ed., *Yearbook of American Churches,* (Nashville: Abingdon Press, 1974). Also John P. Davis, ed., *The American Negro Reference Book* (Englewood Cliffs, N.J.: Prentice-Hall, 1966).

10. Carter G. Woodson, *The History of the Negro Church* (Washington, D.C.; The Associated Publishers, 1972); Benjamin Mays and Joseph Nicholson, *The Negro's Church* (New York: Negro Universities Press, 1969); William Banks, *The Black Church in the U.S.* (Chicago: Moody Press, 1972). In addition, an excellent anthology of writings on the black church is to be found in Hart Nelse, Raytha Yokley, and Anne Nelsen, eds., *The Black Church in America.* (New York: Basic Books, 1971); C. Shelby Rooks, "Toward the Promised Land: an Analysis of the Religious Experience of Black Americans," in *The Black Church* (Boston: The Ecumenical Commission of Massachusetts, 1972), vol. II, no. 1.

11. Alex Poinsett, "Negroes and the Christian Church," *Negro Handbook* (Chicago: Johnson Publishing Co., 1966). The latest edition of 1974 is expanded and rewritten, but the statistics have not changed from those of the earlier edition. In part this reflects poor denominational census practices.

12. Harry Richardson, "The Negro in American Religious Life," in Davis, *The American Negro Reference Book.*

13. Leonard Lovett, "Perspectives on the Black Origins of the Contemporary Pentecostal Movement," *The Journal of the Interdenominational Theological Center* (Fall, 1973).

From Fundamentalism to Evangelicalism: A Historical Analysis

George M. Marsden

"In what sense can this country be called a *Christian* country," asked the retired President of Yale, the Reverend Theodore Woolsey, in an address to the Evangelical Alliance in 1873. "In this sense certainly," he answered, "that the vast majority of the people believe in Christ and the Gospel, that Christian influences are universal, that our civilization and intellectual culture are built on that foundation, and that the institutions are so adjusted as, in the opinion of almost all Christians, to furnish the best hope for spreading and carrying down to posterity our faith and our morality." William F. Warren, the President of Boston University, addressing the same audience, concurred entirely. "There never was a time," he announced, "when the leavening progress of Christ's kingdom among men was so rapid and irreversible as the present." America, President Warren admitted, had had a few infidels—Thomas Jefferson, Thomas Cooper, and Thomas Paine (the "three doubting Thomases") and more recently Transcendentalists, Owenist socialists, spiritualists, and phrenologists—yet at the present "on all the ranks of American unbelievers the Christian apologist of learning and ability can nowhere find a foeman worthy of his steel." [1]

George M. Marsden is Associate Professor of History at Calvin College.

Fifty years later in 1924, H. L. Mencken remarked that "Christendom may be defined briefly as that part of the world in which, if any man stands up in public and solemnly swears that he is a Christian, all his auditors will laugh." [2] The status of evangelicalism had plummeted so drastically from the days of extravagant confidence of the 1870s to the debacle of the fundamentalism of the 1920s that Mencken's characterization seemed plausible. William Jennings Bryan debating Clarence Darrow at Dayton, Tennessee, in the summer of 1925 came to epitomize the popular image of the defense of the traditional faith, and the derision of foes of learning and ability appeared irrespressible. "For the first time in history," Maynard Shipley wrote in his popular *The War on Modern Science,* "organized knowledge has come into open conflict with organized ignorance." [3]

The stark contrast of the images of American evangelicalism at these two points—a century ago and half a century ago—accentuates one of the principal paradoxes of the movement in relation to American culture today. Viewed in the shorter perspective of its fundamentalist past, evangelicalism today appears to be the somewhat moderate outgrowth of an essentially eccentric and separatist religious subculture. On the other hand, viewed in the perspective of a century ago, contemporary evangelicalism can be seen as embodying some of the most deeply rooted traditions and characteristic attitudes in American culture. At times it appears as a beleaguered sect; at other times it still poses as the religious establishment.

This dual heritage leaves today's evangelicalism with a variety of unresolved ambiguities as well as some strengths. This essay—which is primarily a set of interpretive suggestions, rather than an attempt at a closely-documented survey—will seek to suggest implications of these two aspects of evangelical history in America. Prior to that more formal interpretation, however, the scene will be set by an overview of the series of developments that have

123

shaped and reshaped the movement during the past century.

A Century of Changes:
Four Stages of Evangelicalism

The first of four major stages that can be distinguished is the period from the 1870s until the end of World War I when, on the surface at least, the evangelical version of Christendom still appeared to be intact in America. By the end of the period, however, the ancient ideal of a Christian society had become little more than an illusionary superstructure only partly masking revolutionary changes in the basic intellectual assumptions, values, and social patterns of the culture—changes that had eroded or removed almost every support except moralism and sentiment.

Despite some sense of crisis within the Protestant community during this period, the predominant feature of the religious life of the era was more innovation than alarm. The most prominent creative response to the new situation was the emergence within evangelicalism itself of a strong liberal element which increasingly adopted the "modernist" principle of assimilation of modern assumptions and values into the Christian tradition. The theological liberals accordingly emphasized (in varying degrees) God's immanent work through evolutionary, natural, and historical forces, the development of Scripture out of natural processes, and the continuing revelation of God especially in the growing application of Christian principles to society.[5]

While the theological liberals remained within the major denominations, an important element of evangelicals who retained the essentials of the revivalist tradition moved during this early period in an innovative and separatist direction. These were the Holiness and the Pentecostal movements that developed out of the Methodist-pietist tradition. Their new emphases were essentially the opposite

124

of the modernist principle, giving heightened expression to the revivalist teachings of the supernatural transformation of individuals by the power of the Holy Spirit, separating converts decisively from the world through lives of holiness and "baptisms" with other spiritual gifts. Such separatist teachings fostered a proliferation of groups whose histories were largely isolated from other Protestant developments in the next era. The Holiness and Pentecostal movements, however, closely resembled and paralleled fundamentalism, so that the heirs and emphases of these somewhat distinct movements tended to merge particularly in recent evangelicalism.[6]

The most direct progenitors of contemporary evangelicalism were those who during the period under consideration basically remained in the major American denominations but who in other ways rejected accommodation to the immanentist, naturalistic, and progressive tendencies of modern thought in favor of exclusivist assertions of the transcendental, supernatural, and fixed factors in Christian teaching. This element, which formed the basis of fundamentalism in the subsequent era, included conservatives in many denominations who made efforts to arrest the new trends and who themselves emphasized especially the supernatural origin of Scripture (often expressed in terms of its "inerrancy" in detail) and the supernatural aspects of Christ's person and work. It also included an influential group of revivalists who were not adverse to some innovation in their reaction to modernist principles. Rejecting the optimistic postmillennialist teachings that were characteristic both of earlier nineteenth-century evangelicals and of liberals, this group taught instead dispensational-premillennialism, a very antinaturalistic and antiprogressive scheme of history based on interpretations positing literal fulfillments of biblical prophecies that were seen as predicting (among many other things) the apostasy of Christendom in the present dispensation, the imminent secret rapture of the saints, and the postponement of most so-

125

cial and political benefits of Christianity until Christ's return and personal reign for a thousand years at Jerusalem.[7] The second stage, which centered in the few years from about 1919 to 1926, was one of the dramatic focal points in the history of American Protestantism and was certainly a decisive experience for much of subsequent evangelicalism. Two important movements, one social and one theological, converged. World War I and its aftermath brought into the open tendencies in American society that seemed startlingly alien to the image of a Protestant America. In response, latent anxieties were marshalled, as in the "Red Scare" immediately following the war and the ironic triumph of prohibition legislation. In this context militant theological conservatives, sensing that they were on the brink of losing control of some major denominations (especially the Northern Baptist and Northern Presbyterian) launched a fierce attack on the Modernists. Beginning in 1920 the term "fundamentalists" was used to describe the somewhat diverse cobelligerents in this anti-Modernist crusade. During this period the term "fundamentalist" had a broad generic meaning roughly equivalent to militant conservative (for its friends) or belligerent reactionary (for its foes), so that it very seldom had any precise reference (as it often does now) to dispensationalist-premillennialists, who in the 1920s were only one of the leading elements in the movement.[8] In the theological debate the best-known spokesman for the fundamentalists (though he accepted the designation only reluctantly) was J. Gresham Machen, a conservative Presbyterian and a respected scholar. In *Christianity and Liberalism* (1923) Machen clearly defined the issue as a test between two logically incompatible religions within the denominations and suggested that the liberals ought to leave. The possibility of carrying on the debate at any restrained level was preempted, however, by the accompanying acrimony of ecclesiastical politics and then totally overwhelmed by the popularity of the social and political aspects of funda-

126

mentalism as an effort to suppress the teaching of biological evolution in public schools. William Jennings Bryan as the acknowledged spokesman for this latter emphasis inadvertently managed to foment the image of the movefent as the final desperate outcry of an outdated and intellectually repressive religious establishment. Within a year after Bryan's last stand at Dayton, it was clear that the fundamentalist battles had been lost on all fronts. Efforts to exclude modernists from the denominations had failed, and fundamentalism was in eccentric disarray as a social force.

The sequel to these defeats was a third stage of withdrawal and regrouping that lasted from around 1926 to about the 1940s. The character of fundamentalism changed remarkably during this period. Whereas in the 1920s fundamentalism had been a movement within the mainstream of American Protestantism aspiring to control not only the churches but the culture generally, by the 1940s it had moved so much in the direction of sectarianism that the doctrine of separation was often a test of fidelity. Characteristically (although not universally) fundamentalists formed or worked through independent denominations, congregations, Bible institutes, and other extra-ecclesiastical organizations. Dispensational-premillennialism, which provided rationales for the apostasy of the church, the demise of the culture, and for a separatist stance toward both, came to be so widely popular in much of fundamentalism that it was now often considered a tenet of orthodoxy. Revivalism remained, however, the chief impetus of the movement so that it flourished best where revival traditions remained alive. During this period the center of gravity of fundamentalism distinctly shifted from the North to the South, where revivalism and a long tradition of dissent from all forms of northern liberalism provided a congenial atmosphere for fundamentalist attitudes both within and without major Southern denominations. In the movement as a whole during this period there

127

were affinities to political conservatism, although political interests were not usually primary. Some fundamentalists, however, increasingly added the threat of a Bolshevik conspiracy to evolutionism as a cause for social alarm.

Not all fundamentalists of the 1920s moved in the separatist direction. Some moderates worked quietly within major denominations and gave up most sense of being part of a distinct national movement.

The fourth period, from the 1940s to the present, was marked by the emergence of a self-conscious new evangelicalism out of the original fundamentalist tradition and hence the clear division of that tradition into two major movements—evangelicalism and separatist fundamentalism.[9]

Those who throughout the entire period persisted in calling themselves fundamentalists were marked by continued militant separatism. They were mostly dispensationalists and maintained a steadfast refusal to cooperate with apostates and even sometimes with friends of apostates. Some of their leading evangelists often preached anticommunism and American patriotism, which paradoxically associated the movement with a social gospel; others were more consistently separatist and apolitical. A well informed count of this type of fundamentalisms estimated its adherents at about four million in 1973.[10]

Much more numerous (perhaps by now seven to ten times so)[11] but less precisely defined were theologically conservative Protestants who no longer called themselves fundamentalists. Many counted in this category had in fact come from traditions that had had little direct contact with organized fundamentalism; but to the extent that persons in this grouping were aware of being part of an evangelical movement they generally were shaped by some conscious ties to the fundamentalist heritage. That heritage, however, was perceptibly modified. Evangelicals maintained separate organizations but did not insist on them. They continued to oppose liberalism in theology but dropped militancy as a primary aspect of their identity. They were willing to reevaluate some of their own theological heritage, often dropping dispensationalism though not usually premillennialism, and allowing debate at least on the question of the inerrancy of Scripture. Aspiring to be a broad coalition of theologically conservative Protestants, they usually tolerated some other doctrinal differences, including Pentecostalism. Evangelism, as epitomized by Billy Graham, remained their central activity, although the forms of presentation now sometimes avoided accentuation of the offensiveness of the gospel. Socially and politically, evangelicals remained predominantly conservative and patriotic, yet since their spokesmen did insist that Christianity had important social aspects, room was allowed for recent demands from within for more radical social applications. Intellectually, evangelicals maintained their own colleges and seminaries that reflected their distinctive stance, yet they emphasized scholarship sufficiently to put aside any image of anti-intellectualism.

In all these areas the basic tension of the new evangelicalism is apparent. On the one hand it has retained the essentials of its separateness that had been so highly developed in its fundamentalist phases; on the other hand its distinctive recent developments almost all have been in the direction of reestablishing its role as a shaper of the culture. These tensions can, of course, be related to various elements in the older heritage of evangelicalism (Calvinist versus Anabaptist and Pietist traditions, for instance), but the more recent dual legacy of the fundamentalist experience of half a century ago and the revivalist heritage of a century ago seem especially pertinent to establishing where things presently stand.

The Fundamentalist Experience: Evangelicals as the Uprooted

Since in some respects fundamentalism was an expression of Christianity unique to America in the twentieth

129

century, one of the legitimate ways for understanding it better is to consider the impact of the cultural revolution that was its context in shaping its distinctive emphases. In brief, the likely effects of such a cultural experience probably can be best described by way of an analogy (which should be regarded more as an extended metaphor than as a formal analysis). The analogy that seems most helpful is to compare the experience of white Anglo-Saxon Protestants to the immigrant experience. Although white Anglo-Saxon Protestants did not experience the shock of crossing the seas during this period, their collective experience of cultural uprooting was somewhat similar. In some basic respects America after 1918 was a new world as compared to America in the latter decades of the nineteenth century. Men who had grown up in a cultural ethos in which their religious views and mores had been dominant found themselves living in a culture where the traditional forms of those beliefs were increasingly being considered quaint and bizarre. As is characteristic of the immigrant experience as well, the community itself divided sharply on how to respond to the new cultural setting. To the modernists who made accommodation of Christian tradition to the new culture, their central principle may be considered analogous to those in immigrant groups who welcome and embrace the new way of life. The fundamentalists, on the other hand, may be considered the white Anglo-Saxon Protestant equivalent to those immigrant elements who resist the assimilation of the melting pot and build rather their own subculture with institutions, mores, and social connections that provide full-fledged alternatives to the dominant cultural ethos. Among those who respond to the tensions of two cultures in such a manner, religious convictions are often basic to their resistance to change. These in turn are usually intertwined with old-world social and political values and mores, and the interrelated aspects of the set of values are held as necessary symbols of separateness from the larger community. Development in these

130

areas is accordingly precluded, so that the forms of beliefs and values are frozen at the point to which they had developed in the old world prior to the migration.[12]

One point at which the analogy is strained (but which accentuates the basic point) is that immigrant normally come to a new land somewhat voluntarily so that their attitude toward it is alienation but not necessarily hostility. Fundamentalists by contrast experienced the transition from the old world of the nineteenth century to the new world of the twentieth century wholly involuntarily. Their reactions to this involuntary transportation were to add to attitudes of separateness a sharp militancy—they had a fondness for military imagery and did not hesitate to describe their cause as a holy war. So the metaphor may be extended to picture fundamentalists not only as sheltered behind an ideological ghetto wall, but the wall itself as heavily fortified and regarded as the very wall of Zion. Behind such a barrier, the potentialities are greatly increased for intellectual isolation, extremism, and conspiratorial views of the world generally. Richard Hofstadter, who describes in terms of loss of "status" the disruptive experience of having one's values displaced and generally repudiated in a society, aptly depicts the mentality that developed among fundamentalists as "Manichaean: it looks upon the world as an arena for conflict between absolute good and absolute evil, and accordingly it scorns compromises (who can compromise with Satan?) and can tolerate no ambiguities." [13] Evangelicals will recognize this description as similar to what Edward J. Carnell characterized in 1959 as "the cultic mentality" in one of the most thoroughgoing repudiations of such aspects of the fundamentalist heritage by a spokesman for evangelicalism.[14]

Despite such repudiations of the extreme effects of fundamentalist isolation and militancy, the whole immigrant-like experience continues to be relevant to understanding contemporary evangelicalism. To return to the cen-

131

tral imagery of this section, the situation for evangelicals today is as though the ghetto walls are still standing but the
armaments have been removed and the gates left open.
This image should not be regarded as a veiled argument
either for dismantling the walls or for shutting the gates.
Rather, taking into account the evangelical position that
there is biblical warrant for some degree of alienation from
the world and that therefore a distinct identity is a source
of evangelical strength, it should be possible to discriminate
between those essential aspects of the heritage that are
properly protected behind the figurative walls and those
that have been preserved there largely because of the ac-
cidents of a particular historical experience.

This general point could be applied to several aspects
of the current evangelical outlook, and some of these
should become apparent in the next section, but the area
where the effects of the developments in relation to American society can be most clearly illustrated is that of evangelical social and political attitudes themselves. There
seems little doubt, for instance, that (analogous to immigrants' rigid preservation of old-world values from the
era when they left) fundamentalist-evangelical social and
political views were frozen at about the point where tensions of the cultural transition began to become severe—
somewhere around 1900.[15] Until that time American evangelicals had generally followed (for better or worse) major
social and political trends, usually providing Christian versions of the prevailing views. Among liberal Protestants
this pattern continued into the twentieth century, but
among fundamentalists it was sharply arrested. This was
due in part to a direct reaction to the liberal Protestant
tendency to make twentieth-century social theory and progressive politics a crucial center of the Christian message in
the form the social gospel. One result was that when after
the fundamentalist era spokesmen for the new evangelicalism endorsed a return in principle to social applications
of the Gospel, their positions were in fact almost identical

to American social and political conservatism. Related in a paradoxical way was the fact that, despite the whole experience of fundamentalist and evangelical alienation from the major trends in twentieth-century America, conspicuously strong attitudes of American patriotism were preserved. By the late 1960s these phenomena began to provoke considerable criticism from within evangelicalism by those who endorsed more liberal or radical social views.[16] This debate can to some extent be understood as a conflict between Christian versions of the conventional political wisdom of two different eras; and the development of a distinctly evangelical stance that transcends, comprehends, or reconciles these differences remains one of the major problems inherited from the past.

In analyzing such social and political dimensions and their roots in the fundamentalist cultural experience it should be kept in mind that exclusive attention to such aspects has the distorting effect of seeming to reduce to social functions the religious impulse at the heart of the movement.[17] To restore the focus, then, it should be observed that the central dynamic of evangelicalism during the last century was the spiritual force found in men of deep convictions. Ultimately fundamentalists were distinguished from modernists (who had similar cultural backgrounds) by their interpretation of the eternal implications of the profound religious issues that were at stake. Such beliefs were of course influenced by their more general cultural experience, so that the patterns of development were inseparable. Yet even in considering the cultural development itself, the distinctly religious motives were central. Fundamentalists were not uprooted in any very unusual ways economically, socially, or geographically; but they were uprooted by what to a religious person is far more crucial—by a culture that seemed to have turned from God. Their responses, whatever their shortcomings, must be credited for preserving not simply an American heritage but the essential message of a vital Christian movement.

133

The Religious Heritage: The Revival

The forms of the Christianity that fundamentalism preserved were basically those of nineteenth-century American revivalism. Since through the first half of the twentieth century there was little internal development in the movement generally, the characteristic emphases and assumptions associated with revivalism survived almost intact. Thus when the new evangelicals moved away from distinctly fundamentalist teachings or attitudes, they were left with religious emphases that had striking continuities with those of a century ago.

The characteristics of revivalism were especially well preserved through the fundamentalist period because revivalism was the basic tradition that determined the character of fundamentalism itself. The eighteenth-century development of pietist revivalism,[18] especially in the Old World, was in the context of Enlightenment infidelity and decline of the traditional churches, so that the evangelical movement that emerged was well equipped with emphases on the Christian life as being basically a battle against worldliness and apostasy. Furthermore the basic assumption in revivalist thought was the radical separation between the converted and the unconverted—a doctrine that was dramatized by very explicit identifications of the nature of the dichotomy between worldliness and spirituality, and was enforced through strict prohibitions of certain notorious personal pleasures the avoidance of which became the chief symbols of separation of the spiritual individual from the world.

In America revivalism flourished in a culture that had already been considerably shaped by dissenting Puritan Calvinism that included some similar emphases, although the Reformed tradition embodied stronger inclinations to dominate and transform a culture than to separate from it. By the first half of the nineteenth century, the revivalist impulse had merged with the Puritan ideal of creating a

134

Christian society, and the resultant evangelicalism had virtually absorbed most other aspects of imported religious traditions. In this context revivalism proceeded with relatively little opposition within the mainstream of the Protestant community and had marked success in shaping the culture generally. Contrary to the popular image, revivalism of this period was not confined to frontier communities. It was the leading motif of the religious life of the East as well as in the West, and its most formidable influence was in its control of American education at every level. "In fact," says Perry Miller in describing the life of the mind, "the dominant theme in America from 1800 to 1860 is the invincible persistence of the revival technique."[19] Presidents Woolsey and Warren, who were encountered at the opening of this essay, anticipated such historical judgments by about a century.

Even though during the ensuing century this influential cultural role was lost, many of the distinctive features of nineteenth-century revivalist-evangelicalism can be seen in evangelicalism today. The forces that helped shape the evangelicalism of the earlier period are therefore relevant to understanding the character, strengths, and weaknesses of evangelicalism today. Some of the outstanding examples of this connection can be classed under two headings— individualism, and other intellectual assumptions.

Individualism. One of the most conspicuous characteristics both of evangelicalism today and of its revivalist predecessors is individualism. Eighteenth- and nineteenth-century American revivalism grew in the same atmosphere that produced the classic individualistic liberalism of popular American political and economic thought. It also shared some of the same assumptions, so that it might be helpful to regard revivalism as in a sense the religious counterpart of democracy and free enterprise. The basic unit in much of American thought was the free individual, so that the revivalists (despite some Calvinistic resistance) came characteristically to seek from individuals voluntary "decisions."

135

Once this personal commitment was made, the process of sanctification was regarded largely in terms of personal purity. Great concern for the welfare of society was often associated with this individualistic scheme,[20] though somewhat as in the free enterprise system the key to collective welfare was to have each individual behaving correctly.

Although some have debated this individualistic premise as it relates to society, evangelicals today still tend to endorse something like a free enterprise system with respect to the primacy of individual religious experience and the relation of individuals to churches. In practice the primary unit of authority has often been regarded as the individual conscience informed by the Bible. Churches and congregations therefore have been viewed essentially as voluntary associations that individuals are free to join and leave. Thus although American evangelicals have inherited some denominational loyalties, they have generally lacked clear principles for such group authority. The strengths of this arrangement (or lack thereof) have been that the dynamic of the movement has always been able to find open channels for expression and that individualistic approaches— particularly as they emphasize individual experience— continue to have great appeal to many types of Americans. The weaknesses are that the idea of the church is amorphous, unity and cooperation within the movement are difficult to maintain, and there is little formal authority for checks on aberrant teaching or individual spiritual pretentions.

Other Intellectual Assumptions. Another side of the individualistic tendencies of American revivalism was that, lacking strong concepts of institutional authority, evangelicals emphasized all the more the Protestant principle of the exclusive and infallible authority of Scripture. This principle is the central feature of the evangelicalism that has survived through fundamentalism and into the twentieth century; it is a crucial factor in defining its current distinctiveness and certainly has something to do with its success. The historical question therefore arises as to why this principle remained so strong among a large segment of American Christians when it diminished in much of the rest of the Protestant world. The answer seems related to the unusual dominance in America of revivalism, which not only made the biblical principle central but also supported it with a set of other intellectual assumptions.

As has already been suggested, revivalism disposed persons to think in terms of fundamental dichotomies—between the saved and the lost, the spiritual and the worldly, absolute truth and error. These tendencies, in turn, were rooted in the Reformation heritage and had been strong in American Puritanism.[21] They were reinforced also by the common sense philosophy that was taught by evangelicals in American colleges through most of the nineteenth century and which was based on the premise of the reliability of common-sense judgments concerning morality and reality generally. With Scripture as the basic guide to reality, evangelicals were confident that they could distinguish between fixed truth and error with a certainty that the most rigorous scientific observation could only confirm.

In combination these intellectual forces provided a sharp contrast to the prevailing trends of Western thought by the last half of the nineteenth century. The emphasis on the fixed antithesis between truth and error allowed little room for historical and developmental views, and the doctrine of the absolute authority of Scripture together with confidence in individuals' judgments concerning reality precluded the growing tentativeness and relativism. These inherited thought patterns, at least as much as rigid reactions to cultural upheaval, determined the character of the fundamentalist thought that arose out of the revivalist tradition. In resisting the dominant twentieth-century trends, fundamentalists were considered obscurantists by everyone else, and indeed their beliefs were often popularized as such in the antiintellectualism of some evangelists. Yet more basically their position was a type of intellec-

137

tualism that reflected at least the assumptions of American Christian scholarship of the previous century and which might be designated as "supernatural positivism." Far from emphasizing the irrational,[22] fundamentalists characteristically presented their faith as being the exact representation of biblically revealed matters of fact for which could be claimed the highest positive standards for scientific objectivity.

Such assumptions, especially when accentuated by the fundamentalist mentality of spiritual warfare and sometimes by a "faith, which could move mountains of evidence," [23] left the movement with some eccentricities even in terms of Christian tradition and certainly isolated it from most of the rest of twentieth-century thought. Yet when recent evangelical scholars began picking up the issues related to historical development that had been largely left on the table since the late nineteenth century, moved away from rigid positivism and extreme fundamentalist conclusions and reestablished cordial contacts with the larger intellectual community, they found themselves with a basic point of view that was both unique and viable. Its uniqueness was that the principle of the reliable authority of Scripture as a starting point for understanding was preserved; its viability was not only that this stance proved reasonably defensible and somewhat adjustable to contemporary thought, but that it appeared particularly strong when compared to the prevailing alternatives. Difficulties, of course, have remained, and it does not seem as though evangelicals have yet attained the maturity of Christian scholarship of some other eras; but the intellectual isolation seems to be past, and isolation itself has had the effect of preserving the principle of biblical authority that is a chief source of evangelical strength.

This estimate is not exclusively that of partisanship— though it is certainly that too. Even from a detached point of view it seems probable that a key factor in current evangelical success is its marked divergence from many prevalent twentieth-century trends in preserving a decisive basis for authority in a culture that has lost most of its other moorings. Contemporary evangelicalism seen in the dual perspective of the revivalist heritage and the fundamentalist experience presents a general mixed picture of dependence on and rejection of American cultural values. Considering primarily its cultural relationships, it is possible to define more clearly certain prominent evangelical traits, but it is difficult to present other than paradoxical (though perhaps valid) reasons for its continuing influence.[24] Yet throughout its history has survived a unifying principle of biblical authority, enthusiastically proclaimed. This factor has not, of course, operated independently of other spiritual and cultural forces, but it can be viewed as a central historical theme. At present the principle of the preeminence of Scripture provides both the basis for critical reevaluation of the culturally-related aspects of the American evangelical heritage and the source for an evangelical proclamation that can challenge the pretentions of both persons and cultures.

Notes

1. *History, Essays, Orations, and other Documents of the Sixth General Conference of the Evangelical Alliance, Held in New York, October 2-12, 1873,* ed. by Philip Schaff and S. Irenaeus Prime (New York, 1874), pp. 527, 249-54.

2. H. L. Mencken, *Prejudices, Fourth Series* (New York: Alfred A. Knopf, 1924), pp. 78-79.

3. Maynard Shipley, *The War on Modern Science: A Short History of the Fundamentalist Attacks on Evolution and Modernism* (New York: Alfred A. Knopf, 1927), p. 4. Willard B. Gatewood, Jr., ed., *Controversy in the Twenties: Fundamentalism, Modernism, and Evolution* (Nashville: Vanderbilt University Press, 1969) presents a fine collection of documents relating to the image of antievolutionary fundamentalism.

4. These suggestions as they relate to the fundamentalist heritage are my tentative conclusions based on research in connection with a projected volume on fundamentalism and American culture; as they relate to the revivalist heritage they are based on my work in

connection with *The Evangelical Mind and the New School Presbyterian Experience* (New Haven: Yale University Press, 1970).

5. See William R. Hutchison, ed., *American Protestant Thought: The Liberal Era* (New York: Harper & Row, 1968).

6. See Vinson Synan, *The Holiness-Pentecostal Movement in the United States* (Grand Rapids: Eerdmans Publishing Co., 1971); and Walter Hollenweger, *The Pentecostals: the Charismatic Movement in the Churches* (Minneapolis: Augsburg Publishing House, 1972). Sydney E. Ahlstrom, *A Religious History of the American People* (New Haven: Yale University Press, 1972), provides the best survey of the relationships and parallels among the various movements.

7. Ernest R. Sandeen, *The Roots of Fundamentalism: British and American Millenarianism 1800-1930* (Chicago: University of Chicago Press, 1970), in the best account of this aspect of the origins of the movement argues that the fundamentalist movement was essentially coextensive with the millenarian movement, which however was influenced by the Princeton Theological Seminary formulations concerning inerrancy of Scripture. I am convinced that fundamentalism, both in its roots and its manifestations in the 1920s, was broader including not only these two most prominent movements but also other aspects of the revivalist-evangelical tradition in America and denominational conservatism, all of which were united as "fundamentalism" essentially by their militant anti-Modernist stance. See my review article, "Defining Fundamentalism," *Christian Scholar's Review* (Winter, 1971) and Ernest Sandeen, "Defining Fundamentalism: A Reply to Prof. Marsden," *Christian Scholar's Review* (Spring, 1971).

8. This change in the precise meaning of fundamentalism (compounded by its more frequent imprecise usages) is a major source of confusion in current historical discussion. Sandeen, for instance, seems to read the contemporary millenarian aspect into the entire past, thus being forced to regard the fundamentalist controversy of the 1920s as a sort of historical parenthesis when many nonfundamentalists were called fundamentalists. George W. Dollar, *A History of Fundamentalism in America* (Greenville, S. C.: Bob Jones University Press, 1973), in a very partisan but informative account, limits the historical meaning even more strictly to standards acceptable to contemporary fundamentalists. Dollar even excludes *The Fundamentals* from historic fundamentalism, p. 175.

9. See Louis Gasper, *The Fundamentalist Movement* (The Hague: Mouton & Co., 1963).

10. Dollar, *A History of Fundamentalism in America*, p. 248. Of these Dollar regards approximately one third as "militant" as opposed to "moderate" fundamentalists (pp. 283-84). Richard Quebedeaux, *The Young Evangelicals: Revolution in Orthodoxy* (New York: Harper & Row, 1974) makes a similar distinction between "separatist" and "open" fundamentalists, pp. 18-28.

11. Forty million seems to be a currently popular estimate of the size of evangelicalism (used broadly to include conservatives and fundamentalists) as reflected in the *New York Times*, June 24, 1974, p. 18.

12. There are, of course, many exceptions to such broad generalizations. Two well known essays where points such as those above are made are: Oscar Handlin, "The Immigrant in American Politics," in David F. Bowers, ed., *Foreign Influences in American Life* (Princeton: Princeton University Press, 1944) pp. 84-98; and Milton Gordon, "Assimilation in America: Theory and Reality," *Daedalus* (Spring, 1961) pp. 263-85.

13. Richard Hofstadter *Anti-intellectualism in American Life* (New York: Vintage Books, 1966) p. 135. Cf: Richard Hofstadter, *The Paranoid Style in American Politics and Other Essays* (New York: Vintage Books, 1967).

14. Edward John Carnell, *The Case of Orthodox Theology* Philadelphia: The Westminster Press, 1959), pp. 113-26.

15. My own argumentation on this point, which others have made as well, is found in "The Gospel of Wealth, The Social Gospel, and the Salvation of Souls in Nineteenth Century America," *Fides et Historia* (Spring, 1973).

16. Quebedeaux's *Young Evangelicals* summarizes most of the recent issues and literature in this debate. Richard V. Pierard, *The Unequal Yoke: Evangelical Christianity and Political Conservatism* (Philadelphia: J. B. Lippincott Co., 1970) and Lowell D. Streiker and Gerald S. Strober, *Religion and the New Majority: Billy Graham, Middle America, and the Politics of the 70s* (New York: Association Press, 1972) are prominent among recent works documenting the ties of establishment evangelicalism to political conservatism.

17. A major school of historical interpreters with little sympathy for fundamentalism has in various ways made social-cultural issues the major explanatory factor. The older standard histories, Stewart G. Cole, *The History of Fundamentalism* (New York: Richard R. Smith, 1931) and Norman F. Furniss, *The Fundamentalist Controversy, 1918-1931* (New Haven: Yale University Press, 1954), the works of Richard Hofstadter cited above, and to some extent Martin E. Marty, *Righteous Empire: The Protestant Experience in America* (New York: The Dial Press, 1970) all tend in this direction.

18. Donald G. Bloesch, *The Evangelical Renaissance* (Grand Rapids: Eerdmans Publishing Co., 1973) emphasizes the importance of irenic pietism in the evangelical heritage. Bernard L. Ramm, *The Evangelical Heritage* (Waco, Tex.: Word Books, 1973) stresses more the Reformation background of the evangelical renaissance.

19. Perry Miller *The Life of the Mind in America from the Revolution to the Civil War* (New York: Harcourt, Brace & World, 1965), p. 7.

20. See especially Timothy L. Smith, *Revivalism and Social Reform: American Protestantism on the Eve of the Civil War* (Nashville: Abingdon Press, 1957).

21. The Ramist logic, for instance, was basically a method for reducing everything to dichotomies. See Perry Miller, *The New England Mind: The Seventeenth Century* (New York: The Macmillan Co., 1939). Perhaps more lasting as an influence was the Puritans' immense concern to distinguish between the regenerate and the unregenerate as a basis for church membership.

22. This is not to say that fundamentalists did not emphasize personal experience, emotion, or "the religion of the heart." None of these emphases, however, is incompatible with a strong sense of the rational and of logical antithesis when it comes to consideration of the intellectual content of faith.

23. This phrase is borrowed from Edmund Gosse who applies it to his father, a member of the Plymouth Brethren and a scientist in nineteenth-century England whose attitudes anticipated those of American fundamentalists, *Father and Son: A Study of Two Temperaments* (New York: W. W. Norton & Co., 1963) pp. 148-59.

24. The difficulties in assessing religious strength on the basis of cultural relationships may be seen by contrasting the conclusions of William G. McLoughlin, "Is There a Third Force in Christendom?" *Daedalus,* 96.1 (Winter, 1967) to those of Ernest Sandeen, "Fundamentalism and American Identity," *The Annals of the American Academy of Political and Social Science,* 387 (January, 1970). McLoughlin, who in *Modern Revivalism: Charles Grandison Finney to Billy Graham* (New York: The Ronald Press, 1959) and many other works presents some of the best accounts of the American revivalist tradition, concludes in "Third Force" that because conservative, fundamentalist, evangelical, and sectarian elements in contemporary Protestantism are so tied to the past they are essentially reactionary in terms of the prevailing trends of American culture and therefore not likely to constitute a lasting formidable "third force." Sandeen, observing the same phenomena, sees the deep roots of the fundamentalist-evangelical tradition as the basic reason for supposing that it will survive as a strong independent conservative force into the future.

Fundamentalists and Evangelicals in Society

David O. Moberg

White evangelicalism is so diverse that it defies simple description. To be sure, reports about evangelicals do appear with relative frequency in news about religion, in speeches and sermons referring to the current religious scene, in theological discussions, and occasionally in social science literature. Such accounts, whether from evangelical or other sources, frequently reflect stereotyped images that would be rejected by some or all of the persons and groups that consider themselves to be evangelicals. To cite but one example, the Christian College Consortium of ten evangelical liberal arts colleges was described as "a union of fundamentalist schools" in a recent interpretive description. Its author suggests that the survival of Wheaton College, one of the ten, may be in jeopardy because of its emphasis upon Christian nurture in an increasingly complex society in which students are likely to be unwilling "to retreat to a sleepy suburb for four years to ponder the pieties of the past." [1]

What Is Evangelicalism?

One difficulty in describing evangelicalism is the question of delimiting its boundaries.

David O. Moberg is Professor of Sociology and Anthropology at Marquette University.

143

One possible social science approach to this problem would be to let people classify themselves whether it be as evangelicals, fundamentalists, neo-orthodox, liberal, etc. Having done so, it would then be possible to identify the bases for their self-classification. Some might apply a particular set of theological beliefs or a cooperative stance toward an evangelistic crusade. While others might base their judgments upon membership in a particular kind of church congregation, denomination, or other group. Still others might assume that any person or group that believes in the need for an explicit conversion experience in order to win the favor of God is evangelical, and some might insist upon certain forms of personal piety and ethics as the essential criteria. Unfortunately, no social scientist has conducted such a study, enlightening as it would be to evangelicals and to the sociology of religion.

Another social science approach to the delimination of evangelicalism would consist of an analysis of persons and groups invited into fellowship or membership in evangelical associations and of the applicants which are rejected. Groups that fulfill the basic "paper qualifications" sometimes are excluded because they have additional beliefs, practices, or criteria for membership which are repugnant to those who hold the balance of power within the evangelical fold. Into some evangelical groups Seventh Day Adventists, Pentecostalists, and Roman Catholics who have an evangelical spirit [2] are accepted with open arms and a warm welcome, while others summarily reject them. Again, analysis of the stated and unstated reasons for acceptance and rejection would contribute a great deal to the understanding of contemporary evangelicalism, but no research on the subject has been concluded.

One of the troublesome aspects of identifying and describing evangelicalism is how to differentiate it from fundamentalism. The complications of this are great because of subtleties of distinctions, so I prefer to view them as blending into and overlapping with each other instead

144

of as absolutely distinct categories. A strictly doctrinal differentiation makes them fellow members of the same religious category. Both evangelicals and fundamentalists are committed to the basic fundamentals of the Christian faith—the deity and virgin birth of Jesus Christ, his vicarious atonement for sin, his bodily resurrection, his personal second coming, and the inspiration and authority of the Bible.

Quebedeaux, partly as a reflection of these problems, has identified several distinctive ideological subgroups: (1) *separatist fundamentalists* who feel it is necessary to separate completely and clearly from every manifestation of liberalism and modernism (as they define them); (2) *open fundamentalists* who are equally dispensational in theology and separatistic in practice but less vocal and extreme about their separatist posture and more open to engage in self-criticism and in dialogue with other theologically orthodox schools of thought; (3) *establishment evangelicals* who consider evangelism—the proclamation of the good news of salvation through Jesus Christ—to be their primary concern but who also have made an honest effort to break away from the separatistic impulses and lack of social concern of fundamentalism; (4) *new evangelicals* whose intellectual transformation has provided a fresh understanding of the message of both the written and revealed Word of God (Jesus Christ), who view a new life in Christ as equally important to correct doctrine, who hold a marked aversion to dispensationalism and its apocalyptic speculations, who are displaying a fresh interest in the social dimension of the gospel and who have reopened dialogue with liberals and representatives of other religious traditions; and (5) *young evangelicals* whose stance is more of a "spirit" than a well defined theology as they advocate an interest in human beings as whole persons (not just as "souls" to be saved) in active Christian involvement in sociopolitical affairs, including the revolutionary struggles of our day, in new forms of worship, in a new spirit in

145

relationship to ecumenism, in reappraising life values, and in opposition to the idolatry of nationalism and the judging of spiritual commitment by external culturally defined appearances and participation. They thus draw close in political, social, cultural, and even theological concerns to many of the priorities of "mainstream ecumenical liberalism." In addition, the transdenominational neo-Pentecostal and charismatic renewal movement, which is unified in its theological diversity by the common experience of the baptism of the Holy Spirit, is a school of thought that overlaps considerably with, but does not nearly fit into, fundamentalism and evangelicalism.[3]

References to evangelicalism in social science literature and research generally are not concerned with the niceties of distinctions between various types of theologically conservative Christians. Some use the term "fundamentalism" to refer to the total scope of the many varieties, while others use "orthodoxy," "conservatism," and other concepts. Furthermore, the primary focus of attention generally is upon subjects other than evangelicalism; consequently nearly all research-based evidence on the subject is a byproduct of other investigations rather than the direct result of studies explicitly designed to explore hypotheses and theories about evangelicals.

The majority of comments concerning evangelicalism in sociological literature are uncomplimentary at best, and many are downright hostile. Lumped as they are with fundamentalists, evangelicals are viewed as out of date, behind the times, relics of a bygone era, cultural surivivals of a preindustrial past, and anachronistic replicas of our ignorant rural ancestors. They are presented as an example of a type of Christianity believed to be dying.[4] At best evangelicalism is alleged to be so out of step with the advanced intellectual achievements of contemporary society, that it will wither like a leaf severed from the stem of its nourishing branch.

The "midcentury revival of religion" in the United

States[5] came as a shock to the many social scientists who believed that traditional forms of religion were breathing their last dying gasps. It stimulated renewed interest in the sociology of religion. In 1961, Lenski postulated that "the religious factor" possessed at least as great significance in its impact upon other sociological variables as social class, which had long been acknowledged as one of the most prominent casual variables. This finding constituted a very important factor in the renewed respectability for sociologists of religion. The subject of their study had not yet died, so why not try to find the reasons for its survival?

Who Are the Evangelicals?

At least one study has been made of the reasons people give for attending a theologically conservative church. In a large independent congregation, informally friendly with and similar to but not affiliated with the Southern Baptists, on the edge of a midwestern industrial city, a stratified quota sample of the members provided interview and questionnaire data, which then were factor analyzed to identify three types of persons. The *authority-seeker* who has a strong and consistent desire for a submissive relation toward authority, particularly desiring a minister who is not afraid to criticize the congregation and "lay it on the line and tell you what you should and should not do." The *comfort-seeker* wants peace of mind and expresses satisfaction that the church provides the way to eternal life, attainment of which he believes to be everyone's primary goal. The *social participator* likes church for its own sake, being satisfied in participation as an end in itself, and is especially prone to fill leadership positions.[6]

One of the leading theoretical orientations to the origin and growth of new religious groups is the deprivation theory developed by Charles Y. Glock, sociologist at the University of California in Berkeley. According to this theory, religion compensates people for economic, social, organismic, ethical, or psychic deprivations for which no

147

direct means of resolution are available; the various organizational forms of religious groups are in part a product of the kinds of deprivation for which compensation is provided.[7]

Possibly in part because every person suffers deprivation of some kind, it is easy to find evidence to substantiate the theory. Research on a random sample of 416 converts in 20 evangelical congregations in a Canadian city revealed that 5 percent exhibited clear external characteristics of *deprivation,* 68 percent were children of evangelical Christians, 4 percent had evangelical relatives, and another 4 percent were converted under the age of 15, primarily while in church youth groups. The predominant social source of religious involvement therefore was *socialization* rather than deprivation. *Accommodation* to social pressures was apparently an important factor also, for 10 percent of the converts were married or engaged to an evangelical Christian at the time of their conversion, and 2 percent more had close evangelical friends who were instrumental in their conversions. *Cognition*—a perception seen as essentially rational—was a dominant factor in the conversions of about 7 percent. It is possible that deprivation is more often associated with problem people and sectarian groups, while socialization is more characteristic of "normal" people and denominational type religious bodies.[8] At any rate, sample evidence in support of the deprivation theory was found in an interpretive study of Jesus People in Washington and Idaho,[9] and the generally lower social and economic position of fundamentalists and members of small sectarian groups is often taken as circumstantial evidence in support of the deprivation theory.

A study comparing Roman Catholics with members of mainline Protestant churches and of sects (roughly equivalent to fundamentalists and evangelicals) revealed that the sect members were more likely than the others to come from blue-collar occupations, to have low incomes, to have less than high school education, to attend church weekly (except Catholics attended most of all), to engage in private prayer daily (slightly exceeded by Catholics), to read the Bible weekly, and to engage in argumentative or persuasive patterns of religious conversation with others. The religious differences could not be accounted for by socioeconomic differences alone.[10]

Some evidence may substantiate the generally lower than average social class position of evangelicals and especially of fundamentalists, but diversities are so great that stereotyped images of evangelicals as low-middle-class people are unwarranted. Entire congregations of predominantly upper-middle-class evangelicals can be identified, and people of high station and wealth are included in their ranks as well as people who are among the poorest of the poor. Evangelicals, like others, tend to reflect their sociocultural positions in society in the stands they take on social, economic, and political issues, so that they are divided among themselves on such matters. Even on questions of belief there are variations. For example, one study among Southern Baptist students in a single theological seminary found that there was not complete agreement on basic statements reflecting orthodoxy.[11]

Since evangelicals come from a broad range of theological, denominational, historical, educational, cultural, ethnic, and other backgrounds, it is no wonder that they do not comprise a homogeneous segment of the population on anything other than the central tenets of faith which give them a distinctive identity in our pluralistic society. Even the faith position may be variously interpreted on the levels of implications for action, internalized subtleties of meaning, and depth of convictions.[12] The wide range of evangelical perspectives on political, philosophical, scientific, social action, and even theological issues is documented in other chapters of this book as well as in the implicit and explicit discussions of numerous important interpretive and exhortative works.[13] Evangelicalism is a broad social movement, not a monolithic, homogeneous group. In seeking to

149

interpret this movement, scholars have found that mass evangelism provides for example, analysis of a random sample of some 20,000 cards filled out by persons who made decisions for Christ at the Billy Graham's New York crusade in 1957 revealed that a large proportion were teen-agers from white, middle-class, suburban areas. Whitam suggested that the crusade provided adolescents with a technique for dealing with problems experienced in the highly competitive status system of the high school.[14] The decision-makers were chiefly of Anglo-Saxon and Northern European ancestry. The majority already had some type of religious identification far exceeding the general population in expressing a religious preference. They were drawn disproportionately from denominational groups with predominantly middle-class orientations rather than from sectarian bodies, and most of them already were attending church regularly at the time of their decision.[15]

Six years later a followup of 290 teen-agers who had made decisions at the 1957 Crusade revealed that various interpersonal factors were very important in the retention of favorable feelings about the decision for Christ, a close personal relationship to God, and regularity of church attendance. Approving reactions of friends, acquisition of new friends as a result of the decision, and favorableness of parents' reactions to the decision were all related (in varying degrees) to the tendency of the decider to stand by the decision.[16]

Similarly, over half of the decision-makers in the 1970 Knoxville Crusade were under sixteen years of age. In contrast to the predominantly youthful character of the decision-makers, people attending the fifth meeting in a series of ten were much more similar to the general Knoxville metropolitan area population distribution. The audience had a higher educational level than the general population, larger family incomes, and (judging from a followup survey a year later) a larger proportion of professional and managerial occupations. It came disproportionately from

Southern Baptist churches, with relatively few from either low status sects or high status churches. Fully half of the followup respondents were officeholders in their churches, and 93 percent of the stadium sample were church members. Four-fifths had attended church the previous week, and only 3 percent had not attended during the past year. A higher level of "orthodoxy" of religious beliefs and of private prayer and seeking God's will in daily life-decisions characterized the Crusade audience than a random sample of the Knoxville area population. The Crusade, therefore, was interpreted as a rite of passage for youth raised in fundamentalist families and as symbolic of the dominant religious, cultural, and political way of life in the South, drawing persons attracted to the old middle-class life-style with an individualistic, nonintellectual, pietistic, and familistic orientation definitely at odds with the cosmopolitanism of corporate and intellectual elites.[17]

Criticisms of mass evangelism are widespread among religious leaders as well as academicians. In his recent interpretation of the subject using Billy Graham as its leading exemplar, Snook points out that the Graham Crusades provide more individual attention, and that on a deeper level, than many people receive from their own ministers.[18] New church members who come as a result of a Graham Crusade are "full of religious energy and ready to work," in contrast to other half-hearted new members who frequently join largely for social reasons.[19]

While it is true that the majority who make decisions already are church members or associated with a church, that is true also of the vast majority of the American population. The old tensions between itinerant and settled clergy, however, still prevail. Some persons may be "spoiled" for their churches by the Crusade.[20] They may become dissatisfied with the nonevangelical orientation of traditional churches and seek congregations which have the spark of "spiritual life" after they have themselves responded to the Holy Spirit through the Crusades. One of the heavy

151

burdens carried by the evangelistic staff is their concern for effective followup to provide nurture that will promote spiritual growth in the new converts. Whitam's study has given empirical evidence of the importance of parents, friends, and peers in the followup process, confirming the experiential impressions of those involved in evangelistic work.[21] Spiritual nurture is essential for those who are "newborn babes" through spiritual regeneration.

The strictly scientific approach to conversion treats it as a natural, human experience rather than as a supernatural phenomenon, for its ultimate spiritual aspects are not directly amenable to empirical observation. As a result of this and the tendency of each discipline to imply that its own interpretations are primary, if not even exhaustive of reality, conversion is more typically looked upon as a dependent variable that is the effect of other influences rather than as an independent variable which causes them. Social psychology views it as involving the development of a new self-identity, and sociological interpretations emphasize socialization, affiliating with a new reference group, and fitting into cultural norms. Numerous social influences affect the nature and number of conversions, and social effects flow out of them. The same applies to the social movements involving large numbers of conversions which commonly are called "revivals."[22] Dike, for example, sees them as only recruiting new members who would have come into the churches anyway.[23]

Although historians have often referred to the social reforms that have followed major revival movements,[24] other social scientists have been skeptical, believing that the observed relationships are the spurious consequences of the association of religion with other traits. Through use of sophisticated statistical techniques, Hammond has demonstrated that the social effects of support for the abolition of slavery following 351 revivals in Ohio between 1825 and 1835 could not be explained by control variables other than the revivals themselves. The revivals transformed world views so that slavery was seen as not only wrong but sinful, and political action to abolish slavery resulted. In contrast to the Glock and Stark hypothesis that a free-will image of man is a root cause of Christian prejudice toward blacks and of negative attitudes toward the civil rights movement,[25] Hammond found that belief in free will "led to a new emphasis on moral obligation; for a change of heart implied a change of conduct" to the nineteenth-century revivalists and their converts.[26]

Key 73 was an evangelistic effort that captured the attention of the nation and obtained the support of a large number of clergy, denominational leaders, and others outside the evangelical movement during 1973. Its success was partly based upon its decentralization—a factor which also was responsible for its failure; each denominational group was free to shape its Key 73 activities in its own way. As a result, many activities under its label were not truly evangelistic, and there was little coordination across denominational and even congregational lines in most communities. Its inclusivistic orientation was an outstanding example of "attitudinal ecumenicity" in contrast to the "organizational ecumenicity"[27] emphasized in the traditional ecumenical movement, and it simultaneously repelled many fundamentalists while attracting increased attention to evangelicals in general. Attempting to work through denominational hierarchies with a very small and loose-knit structure hampered efficiency, and insufficient finances reduced the opportunities for nationwide mass media exposure. At its best it demonstrated the interrelationships between evangelism, the Christian mission, and social action. It also stimulated some liberals to have a more favorable attitude toward mass evangelism and some conservatives to be more amenable to cooperation with others.[28]

Evangelicalism and Its Social Relations

There have been some studies which have revealed statistical relationships between conservative or orthodox

153

Christian theological positions and such characteristics as political, social, and economic conservatism;[29] race prejudice;[30] a tendency toward anti-Semitism;[31] authoritarianism and dogmatism;[32] and a lack of social compassion or weak social ethics.[33]

On the other hand, research also has shown that among church people, those who are the most deeply committed and intrinsically involved in their religious life so that it has a high level of salience to them personally are less prejudiced than persons with a superficial, extrinsic kind of instrumental religiosity that uses it to gain other goals.[34] The relationships between religion, prejudice, and personality are very complex.[35] The instruments used to identify and measure their various characteristics, the hidden assumptions that underlie the analytical work, the indicators or dimensions of religion that are the focus of attention, the samples of persons studied, and many other details influence the result to such a high degree that research on most aspects of the consequences of religious commitment is still in its infancy. The results to date must, therefore, be taken with considerable caution.

Fundamentalist clergymen differ sharply in their perspectives on civil rights, civil liberties, welfarism, and internationalism from those who are self-classified as conservative, neo-orthodox (moderate), and liberal, so the lumping of them together with other evangelicals may account for some of the antisocial views attributed to all theological conservatives.[36] Research among the constituents of the LaSalle Street Church in Chicago revealed a constituency that is highly orthodox in doctrine but also strongly concerned about the social implications of their faith.[37] They and numerous other individuals and groups are a living demonstration of the fact that there is no necessary antithesis between theological conservatism and genuine social concern for human welfare.

The surprising finding of Campbell and Fukuyama that those members of the United Church of Christ who had a devotional orientation (which emphasized the personal pieties of daily prayer and Bible reading) were more generous toward minorities and expressed greater sympathy for civil rights than others[38] supports the conclusion that evangelical commitment at its best can help people transcend the cultural pressures that tend to mold them in anti-Christian directions of social conformity.

The complexity of relationships between doctrinal beliefs and positions on social issues has been demonstrated through various studies, several of which taken all alone appear at first glance to cover the subject adequately and reach clear conclusions suggesting a close linkage of evangelicalism with other conservatisms. Wuthnow's review of sixty-six recent articles dealing with aspects of the relationship between religious commitment and conservatism found 266 relationships that were explored in research reports. Social conservatism, in most cases focusing upon racial prejudice, was the most related to doctrinal orthodoxy (46 percent of the relationships observed), political conservatism next (36 percent), and economic conservatism (20 percent) the least. In only two-fifths (39 percent) of the relationships covered was conservatism positively related to religious commitment. He concluded that "until more systematic evidence is available, the relationship between religion and conservatism must be considered problematic." [39]

In an effort to elaborate relationships between doctrinal beliefs and social issues more clearly, Driedger conducted a survey of Protestant, Catholic, and Orthodox clergy in Winnipeg, Manitoba, classifying them into "absolutist" and "evolutionist" types on the basis of four doctrinal items related to the nature of God. The clergy agreeing with at least three of four "orthodox" doctrines (belief in the virgin birth of Christ, his physical resurrection, the Bible as God's Word and all it says is true, and belief that some will be punished in life after death) were classified as absolutists because they "perceived a transcendent God in a closed system," while those agreeing with two or fewer were termed evolutionists who "believed in an immanent God in a less rigid system." A high level of association was found between concerns for personal morality and absolutism (*i.e.,* doctrinal conservatism, believing in at least three of the doctrines). The evolutionists were more open to change and focused upon such issues as civil liberty, minority rights, and welfare support, while absolutists were reluctant to change society and supported governmental social control, considerable use of force by the power elite, and personal morality. Doctrinal orthodoxy differentiated the attitudes of the clergymen toward social issues considerably more than social class and education.[40]

A study of roles of the clergy in relationship to a protest orientation toward social action found, among a sample of Protestant ministers in five major U. S. cities, that the community problem-solving role was linked with both theological and political liberalism. Theological conservatives scored particularly high on the traditional role which sees the minister as a soul-winner, man of prayer, shepherd and example to his members, and one who fights for what is right and helps his members overcome evil.[41]

The Rising Strength of Evangelicalism

In his appraisal of anticipations for evangelicals in 1974, Dr. Ronald J. Sider flatly states that a majority of Protestants today are evangelicals.[42] Evangelical Protestantism beyond all doubt has been the dominant religious orientation of the South.[43] The relative growth and increasing strength of evangelicalism is increasingly recognized and commented upon as one of the unanticipated trends of a modern age. Evangelicals were violating the principles that had been established as guides to action in mainline denominational bodies, yet they grew while followers of the guidelines diminished in strength.[44]

From a position of disdain and contempt, evangelicals

156

nationwide have risen to one that is envied in this decade by many bureaucratic leaders and clergy in mainline denominations. While most of the latter have been declining in membership and financial strength, many evangelical congregations and denominations have been growing, some at unprecedented rates. Analysis of this phenomenon led Dean Kelley to conclude that the basic reason was that theologically conservative bodies had not forgotten their first priority, that of explaining the meaning of life in ultimate terms.[45] Quebedeaux adds several more reasons for growth: the compatibility of the values of "Middle America" with the beliefs and concerns of establishment evangelicals and thus the lack of challenge to its social and political values, the mounting anxiety and pessimism about the future of mankind to which an apocalyptic religion appeals, provision of the answer to the search for authenticity in living, the mounting acceptance of experiential and emotional religiosity within middle-class society, and the rediscovery of the supernatural in our era.[46] At least within Protestantism, the groups that have done the best are those that have stood for something clear and positive, however old-fashioned it seemed to the sophisticated. The "old-time religion" draws people in new ways but with little if any loss of the power of the old revivals. New life has been breathed into the older forms that modern ways seemed to have doomed.[47]

Shortly before Kelley's study of church growth, a survey of New England churches of all varieties was made to identify factors in the growth and development of churches. Most churches were declining, but the majority of key pastors, denominational leaders, and executives of councils of churches who were questioned were able to identify at least a half a dozen churches they knew to be growing. A profile of the growing congregations revealed that nearly all were evangelical.[48]

The relative growth of the religious groups in Canada from 1961 to 1971 show a similar pattern. Pentecostals grew by 52.9 percent, the Salvation Army by 30.4 percent, Roman Catholics by 19.6 percent, Baptists by 12.4 percent, and other dominant bodies at a lesser rate, with the United Church (possibly the most liberal) at the bottom with only a 2.8 percent increase. A number of smaller "conservative evangelical" groups also grew at a faster rate than the general population increase of 18.2 percent during the decade.[49]

Only indirect and circumstantial evidence is available on the strength of evangelicalism within the mainline Protestant denominations. In their 1964 survey of members of the United Church of Christ, one of the theologically most liberal bodies in the United States, Campbell and Fukuyama included an Index of Belief Orientation, which was constructed from twelve traditional statements on the content of Christian theology. Twenty-six percent ranked high, agreeing with ten to twelve of the statements, and an additional 31 percent were moderately high, agreeing with seven to nine.[50]

In their 1964 sample of the national adult population, Glock and Stark found that the proportion of "orthodox persons" (those with high scores on belief in God, in the devil, and in life after death) was 32 percent among persons with Protestant self-identifications and 29 percent among Catholics, with a range from zero for Unitarians and five percent for Congregationalists to 44 percent for Southern Baptists and 52 percent for "sects." Among California church members the range was from 4 percent of the Congregationalists and 10 percent of the Methodists to 88 percent of the Southern Baptists. Those who said belief in Jesus Christ as Savior is absolutely necessary for salvation ranged from 38 percent in California Congregational members to 97 percent of the Missouri Synod Lutherans and Southern Baptists for a total of 65 percent of all Protestants and 51 percent of the Roman Catholics.[51]

No question about self-classification as "evangelical" or other theological orientations was asked in these studies;

with the increasing level of awareness of such distinctions, it is probable that today many of the members would accept, or even seek, the label of "evangelical."

In a massive 1970 survey of Lutherans from the three leading synods (American Lutheran Church, Lutheran Church in America, and Lutheran Church–Missouri Synod) it was found that 44 percent of the clergy and laity identified their theological position as conservative and an additional 14 percent as fundamentalist. Ten percent professed to be neo-orthodox and 26 percent liberal. The liberal self-classification, however, was based upon the descriptive statement, "I am willing to change some aspects of the faith in the light of new understanding (Liberal)," so it is possible that many respondents who chose it are not thoroughgoing theological liberals. The proportion of Lutherans in the conservative half of the theological spectrum therefore may exceed 58 percent. A thirteen-item fundamentalism-liberalism scale supports the conclusion that most Lutherans are theologically conservative.[52]

To some extent, the resurgence of evangelicalism can be viewed as verification of the thesis of Greeley, who has argued that the basic religious needs and functions of mankind have not changed notably since the late Ice Age. Although secularization may have advanced considerably more than he gives it credit, much of its apparent triumph may have come from the fallacy of accepting the perspectives of the intellectual community as if they were those of the entire society. The need for commitment to provide meaning and the need for community still characterize the human condition.[53] These are not ignored in evangelicalism.

The recognition of evangelicalism's new strength may represent primarily an emerging awareness among religious leaders and social scientists of what has been quietly present in Christianity for some time. Members who are theologically conservative participate more in worship and other church activities and contribute more generously financially than those who are liberal.[54] If it were not for theological conservatives sustaining them, many congregations might have toppled long ago. The growing self-consciousness among evangelical laity and clergy constitutes a significant source of strength for the movement just as it has among other American minorities.

Another possibility is rarely mentioned, however. Birth rates in the United States have been dropping in recent years. Fewer births mean fewer accessions into membership among the churches which baptize infants and count all "baptized souls" as members. Eventually reduced birth rates also will affect the number of baptisms and confirmations in groups which receive members only after they reach age ten, puberty, or some other point in the life cycle. Since most evangelicals are in the latter category, it is possible that they simply have not yet suffered the effects of reduced population growth rates which already have influenced mainline religious bodies.

Consequences of Evangelical Strength

As a result of present trends, it is conceivable that evangelicalism soon may become if it is not already the dominant religious orientation in Protestant America.

> Evangelicalism is doing very well numerically and financially, and it gives every indication of further growth and success along its separate path, while Liberalism seems to be slowly dying. Before long, in fact, it may be more appropriate to speak of mainstream Evangelicalism rather than mainstream Ecumenical Liberalism.[55]

If evangelicalism becomes the "new religious establishment," it will catch the brunt of criticisms from forces both within and outside organized religion for its actions and failures to act. Much of the condemnation now vented upon mainline denominations could be redirected toward evangelicalism.

160

One reflection of the evangelical resurgence is the rise of powerful organizations dominated by evangelicals within the major denominations, like the Presbyterian Lay Committee which counterbalances the bureaucratic power structure in the United Presbyterian Church. Explicit attention now is being given to the evangelical perspective in appointments to boards and committees, denominational resolutions, and the distribution of funds for projects and programs as a result. These viable suborganizations aim at internal revitalization, not withdrawal. Their cooperative approach stands in sharp contrast to controversies earlier in this century which often led to schisms and the establishment of new competing denominational bodies by fundamentalist leaders.

The "evangelical establishment" correspondingly needs to recognize more fully that their fellowship in Christ is shared by millions of people in mainline denominations. The North American Interchurch Study of Church members from fifteen denominations, most of which were members of the National Council of Churches, revealed that, in contradiction to

> A virtual axiom of modern churchmanship that classic doctrines of Christianity need to be reinterpreted in contemporary terms, American Protestants today overwhelmingly affirm the traditional concepts of faith and insist that these be preached and taught, along with a vigorous effort to persuade others of Christ's saving truth.[56]

While upholding faith in the "classic fundamentals" and asserting that the first and foremost task of the local church is evangelism to "win others to Christ" [57] are not necessarily automatic indicators of evangelical identity in and of themselves, these findings lend credence to the conclusion that a substantial proportion of the membership of mainline denominations is evangelical.[58] They also reveal the high regard for evangelism in American Christendom outside the boundaries of Establishment evangelicals.

161

The high priority which members give to evangelism in the North American Interchurch Study does not mean, however, that antagonism toward church action on social issues characterized the members surveyed. Serving as the "social conscience to the community" was sixth in order of priorities for the work of the local church. It came after evangelism, worship, religious instruction, the sacraments, ministerial services, and help to the needy; and ahead of foreign missions, fellowship, providing facilities for congregational activities, support to the denominaton, support for minority groups, influencing legislation, and building low-cost housing (in order of priorities from high to low). The lay people were not as strongly in favor of social involvement as the clergy, but neither were they as threatened by it as the clergy tended to believe they were. What they wanted most was the "cultivation of the Gospel" and its "application to personal growth and orientation in life." [59]

Although fallacies that emerged during the fundamentalist-modernist controversies early in this century have misled many into believing that social concern is incompatible with evangelism, the combined testimony of the teachings of the Bible, the experience of past Christian history, the rise of new evangelicalism, and many other evidences demonstrate that the personal and social implications of the gospel are not incompatible.[60] In innovative Christian communities[61] as well as in mainline denominations, among the radical Christians [62] and among the young evangelicals,[63] there is an increasing demand for church ministries to the whole person while also focusing upon the central issues related to the ultimate meaning of life. Involvement in secular social change organizations leads many laymen to value a "fundamentally quietistic and comfort-oriented view of the role of the church" and to seek in it relief from the pressures and conflicts of life.[64] Each emphasis needs the other.

As its future becomes more promising in terms of numerical strength and ecclesiastical recognition, evangelicalism stands even more exposed to the danger of becoming conformed to sinful worldly aspects of the social system. Already prone to capitulating to the civil religion,[65] to giving an uncritical blessing to political and industrial power structures,[66] to sanctifying the social and cultural system,[67] and to blessing materialism, which is the contemporary form the worship of mammon against which Jesus so clearly spoke,[68] evangelicals, if impressed by their own new status, will become even more susceptible to the temptation to bow their knees before the economic and political Baals of modern society.

With increased influence and power comes increased responsibility. Will the cause of justice and righteousness be furthered by increased evangelical power, or will it be set back to lower levels, allowing even more social evils than now prevail? The greater the power and the longer it is held, the more difficult will it be for evangelicals to plead innocent for the collective sins of the nation, including those pertaining to the economic, political, educational, legal, health, and communications systems.

The more conscientiously evangelicals work to keep close to the roots of their faith—Jesus Christ and the Bible—the less likely they are to become a mirror image of corrupt society and the more likely they are to be a redeeming influence upon the social system as well as individual persons. Going back to the roots of the faith, instead of to time- and culture-bound interpretations which were appropriate for a past age but now are enshrined only by tradition, will make evangelicalism a vibrant and alert means for Christ-honoring social change. The future of the new evangelicals is hard to predict, but it is certain that the comfortable relationship between the evangelical churches and the political and economic status quo is being seriously challenged by the growing evangelical insurgency.[69]

As the awareness of Christian social responsibility flows to all evangelical groups[70] like undammable floodwaters of a mighty river of righteousness and justice, the evangelical resurgence can become a refreshing stream revitalizing society as well as its individual members.

Notes

1. Sharon Johnson, "The Harvard of the Bible Belt," *Change,* (March, 1974), pp. 17-20.

2. See Harry E. Winter, "Evangelical and Catholic?" *America,* (Aug., 1972), pp. 63-68; Kilian McDonnell, "A Catholic Looks at Evangelical Protestantism," *Commonweal,* (Aug. 21, 1970), pp. 408-13; Paul W. Witte, "Can Catholics Learn Anything from Evangelical Protestants?," *Christianity Today,* (Dec. 18, 1970), pp. 268-70.

3. Richard Quebedeaux, *The Young Evangelicals: Revolution in Orthodoxy* (New York: Harper & Row, 1974), pp. 18-45, 53-54.

4. A notable example of this perspective is Harry Elmer Barnes, *The Twilight of Christianity* (New York: Vanguard Press, 1929).

5. For a brief summary and references to other resources see David O. Moberg, *The Church as a Social Institution* (Englewood Cliffs, N.J.: Prentice-Hall, 1962), pp. 40-43.

6. Robert R. Monaghan, "Three Faces of the True Believer," *Journal for the Scientific Study of Religion,* (Fall, 1967), pp. 236-45.

7. Charles Y. Glock, "On the Origin and Evolution of Religious Groups," *Religion in Sociological Perspective,* ed. by Charles Y. Glock (Belmont, Cal.: Wadsworth Publishing Co., 1973), pp. 207-20.

8. Reginald W. Bibby and Merlin B. Brinkerhoff, "Sources of Religious Involvement: Issues for Future Empirical Investigation," *Review of Religious Research,* (Winter, 1974), pp. 71-79.

9. Donald W. Peterson and Armand L. Mauss, "The Cross and the Commune: An Interpretation of the Jesus People," *Religion in Sociological Perspective,* ed. by Charles Y. Glock (Belmont, Cal.: Wadsworth Publishing Co., 1973), pp. 261-79.

10. T. Edwin Boling, "Sectarian Protestants, Churchly Protestants and Roman Catholics: A Comparison in a Mid-American City," *Review of Religious Research,* (Spring, 1973), pp. 159-68.

11. Robert C. Thompson, "A Research Note on the Diversity among American Protestants: A Southern Baptist Example," *Review of Religious Research,* (Winter, 1974), pp. 87-92.

12. For pregnant thoughts relevant to this subject see Sanford M. Dornbusch, "Two Studies in the Flexibility of Religious Beliefs," *American Mosaic: Social Patterns of Religion in the United States,* ed. by Phillip E. Hammond and Benton Johnson (New York:

Random House, 1970), pp. 100-10. For empirical evidence of variations in beliefs, background, attitudes, etc., see Paul M. Lederach, *Mennonite Youth* (Scottdale, Pa.; Herald Press, 1971); Paul F. Barkman, Edward R. Dayton, and Edward L. Gruman, *Christian Collegians and Foreign Missions* (Monrovia, Cal.: MARC, 1969); Roy B. Zuck and Gene A. Getz, *Christian Youth: An In-Depth Study* (Chicago: Moody Press, 1968).

13. Examples include Richard Bube, ed., *The Encounter Between Christianity and Science* (Grand Rapids, Mich.: Eerdmans Publishing Co., 1968); Robert G. Clouse, Robert D. Linder, and Richard V. Pierard, eds., *The Cross and the Flag* (Carol Stream, Ill.: Creation House, 1972); Charles Y. Furness, *The Christian and Social Action* (Old Tappan, N. J.: Fleming H. Revell Co., 1972); Melvin Gingerich, *The Christian and Revolution* (Scottdale, Pa.: Herald Press, 1968); Arthur G. Gish, *The New Left and Christian Radicalism* (Grand Rapids, Mich.: Eerdmans Publishing Co., 1970); Vernon C. Grounds, *Revolution and the Christian Faith* (Philadelphia: J. B. Lippincott Co., 1971); Erling Jorstad, *That New-Time Religion: The Jesus Revival in America* (Minneapolis: Augsburg Publishing House, 1972); David O. Moberg, *The Great Reversal: Evangelism Versus Social Concern* (Philadelphia: J. B. Lippincott Co., 1972); Richard J. Mouw, *Political Evangelism* (Grand Rapids, Mich.: Eerdmans Publishing Co., 1973); Richard V. Pierard, *The Unequal Yoke: Evangelical Christianity and Political Conservatism* (Philadelphia: J. B. Lippincott Co., 1970); Gary R. Collins, ed., *Our Society in Turmoil* (Carol Stream, Ill.: Creation House, 1970).

14. Frederick L. Whitam, *Adolescence and Mass Persuasion: A Study of Teen-Age Decision-Making at a Billy Graham Crusade* (unpublished Ph.D. Dissertation, Indiana University, 1965); *Dissertation Abstracts,* vol. 27, no. 2.

15. Frederick L. Whitam, "Revivalism as Institutionalized Behavior: An Analysis of the Social Base of a Billy Graham Crusade," *Social Science Quarterly* (June, 1968)), pp. 115-27.

16. Frederick L. Whitam, "Peers, Parents, and Christ: Interpersonal Influence in Retention of Teen-Age Decisions Made at a Billy Graham Crusade" (unpublished paper presented at annual meeting of Southwestern Social Science Association, circa 1970).

17. Donald A. Clelland, Thomas C. Hood, C. M. Lipsey, and Ronald Wimberley, "In the Company of the Converted: Characteristics of a Billy Graham Crusade Audience," *Sociological Analysis* (Spring, 1974), pp. 45-56.

18. John R. Snook, *Going Further: Life-and-Death Religion in America* (Englewood Cliffs, N. J.: Prentice-Hall, 1973), p. 40.

19. *Ibid.,* p. 44.

20. *Ibid.,* pp. 45-48.

21. Whitam, "Peers, Parents, and Christ."

22. Moberg, *Church as a Social Institution,* pp. 421-43.

23. Samuel W. Dike, "A Study of New England Revivals," *American Journal of Sociology* (Nov., 1909), pp. 361-78.

24. For examples see Timothy L. Smith, *Revivalism and Social Reform in Mid-Nineteenth-Century America* (Nashville: Abingdon Press, 1957); and Whitney R. Cross, *The Burned-Over District: The Social and Intellectual History of Enthusiastic Religion in Western New York, 1800-1850* (Ithaca, N. Y.: Cornell University Press, 1950).

25. Rodney Stark and Charles Y. Glock, "Prejudice and the Churches," *Prejudice U.S.A.,* ed. by Charles Y. Glock and Ellen Siegelman (New York: Praeger Publishers, 1969), pp. 70-95.

26. John L. Hammond, "Revival Religion and Antislavery Politics," *American Sociological Review* (April, 1974), 175-86.

27. Harry H. Hiller, "Communality as a Dimension of Ecumenical Negativism," *Review of Religious Research* (Winter, 1971), pp. 111-14.

28. Editorial Comment, "Key 73 and Constantine," *Christian Century* (Jan. 2, 1974), pp. 4-5; "What Went Wrong with Key 73?" *Evangelical Newsletter* (Nov. 19, 1973), p. 1.

29. Benton Johnson, "Ascetic Protestantism and Political Preference," *Public Opinion Quarterly* (Spring 1962), pp. 35-46; Benton Johnson, "Theology and Party Preference among Protestant Clergymen," *American Sociological Review* (April, 1966), pp. 200-208; Lawrence L. Kersten, *The Lutheran Ethic* (Detroit: Wayne State University Press, 1970); Gene F. Summers, Richard L. Hough, Doyle P. Johnson, and Kathryn A. Veatch, "Ascetic Protestantism and Political Preference: A Re-Examination," *Review of Religious Research* (Fall, 1970), pp.17-25; Jeffrey K. Hadden, *The Gathering Storm in the Churches* (Garden City, N. Y.: Doubleday and Co., 1969).

30. Hadden, pp. 110-18, 254-55; Glenn D. Wilson and Christopher Bagley, "Religion, Racialism and Conservatism," *The Psychology of Conservatism,* ed. by G. D. Wilson (New York: Academic Press, 1973), pp. 117-28; see also Stark and Glock, "Prejudice and the Churches."

31. Charles Y. Glock and Rodney Stark, *Christian Beliefs and Anti-Semitism* (New York: Harper & Row, 1966); and Rodney Stark *et al., Wayward Shepherds: Prejudice and the Protestant Clergy* (New York: Harper & Row, 1971). Numerous critical discussion of deficiencies and weaknesses of this research, however, indicate that the data do not demonstrate a causal connection between Christian beliefs and anti-Semitism. See Donald R. Ploch, "Religion as an Independent Variable: A Critique of Some Major Research," *Changing Perspectives in the Scientific Study of Religion,* ed. by Allan W. Eister (New York: John Wiley & Sons, 1974), pp. 275-94; William Silverman, review of *Wayward Shepherds, Contemporary Sociology* (May, 1972), p. 261.

32. T. W. Adorno, E. Frenkel-Brunswik, D. J. Levinson, and

R. N. Sanford, *The Authoritarian Personality* (New York: Harper and Brothers, 1950); Milton Rokeach, *The Open and Closed Mind* (New York: Basic Books, 1960); R. DiGuiseppe, "Dogmatism Correlation with Strength of Religious Conviction," *Psychological Reports* (Feb., 1971), p. 64.

33. Milton Rokeach, "Religious Values and Social Compassion," *Review of Religious Research* (Fall, 1969), pp. 24-39; Rodney Stark and Charles Y. Glock, *American Piety: The Nature of Religious Commitment* (Berkeley: University of California Press, 1968), pp. 213-21. For critical appraisals, see David O. Moberg, *et. al.*, "Religious Values and Social Compassion: A Critical Review of the 1969 H. Paul Douglass Lectures by Dr. Milton Rokeach," *Review of Religious Research,* (Winter, 1970) pp. 136-62; and David O. Moberg, review of Stark and Glock, *American Piety, The Christian Scholars Review,* vol. 3, no. 3, (1972), 267-68.

34. Gordon W. Allport, *The Nature of Prejudice* (Cambridge, Mass.: Addison-Wesley, 1954); Gordon W. Allport and J. Michael Ross, "Personal Religious Orientation and Prejudice," *Journal of Personality and Social Psychology,* (1967), 5, 432-43; Richard A. Hunt and Morton King, "The Intrinsic-Extrinsic Concept: A Review and Evaluation," *Journal for the Scientific Study of Religion* (Winter, 1971), pp. 339-56; Charles H. Anderson, *White Protestant Americans* (Englewood Cliffs, N. J.: Prentice-Hall, 1970), pp. 162-63; E. D. Tate and G. R. Miller, "Differences in Value Systems of Persons with Varying Religious Orientations," *Journal for the Scientific Study of Religion* (Winter, 1971), pp. 357-65; James J. Vanecko, "Religious Behavior and Prejudice," *Review of Religious Research* (Fall, 1966), pp. 27-37; James J. Vanecko, "Types of Religious Behavior and Levels of Prejudice," *Sociological Analysis* (Fall, 1967), pp. 111-22.

35. James E. Dittes, "Religion, Prejudice, and Personality," *Research on Religious Development,* ed. by Merton P. Strommen (New York: Hawthorn Books, 1971), pp. 355-90.

36. Jack O. Balswick, "Theology and Political Attitudes Among Clergymen," *Sociological Quarterly* (Summer, 1970), pp. 397-405.

37. David O. Moberg, James Bobzien, Michael R. Leming, and John Zylak, "Interrelationships Between Christian Social Concern, Evangelism, and Orthodoxy," paper presented at the joint annual meeting of the Religious Research Association and Society for the Scientific Study of Religion, Boston, Oct., 1972.

38. Thomas C. Campbell and Yoshio Fukuyama, *The Fragmented Layman: An Empirical Study of Lay Attitudes* (Philadelphia: Pilgrim Press, 1970).

39. Robert Wuthnow, "Religious Commitment and Conservatism: In Search of an Elusive Relationship," *Religion in Sociological Perspective,* ed. by Charles Y. Glock (Belmont, Cal.: Wadsworth Publishing Co., 1973), pp. 117-32.

40. Leo Driedger, "Doctrinal Belief: A Major Factor in the

Differential Perception of Social Issues," *Sociological Quarterly,* (Winter, 1974), pp. 66-80. One weakness of the study is that only 26 of the 130 clergymen had low scores (agreeing with 0, 1, or 2 of the four beliefs) on the doctrinal index; 53 believed three, and 51 all four of the items.

41. Hart F. Nelson, Raytha L. Yokley, and Thomas W. Madron, "Ministerial Roles and Social Actionist Stance: Protestant Clergy and Protest in the Sixties," *American Sociological Review* (June, 1973), pp. 375-86.

42. Ronald J. Sider, "What's in Store for '74?: Evangelical Churches," *Christian Century* (Jan. 2, 1974), pp. 12-13.

43. Samuel S. Hill, Jr., *et al., Religion and the Solid South* (Nashville: Abingdon Press, 1972), p. 22.

44. Dean M. Kelley, *Why Conservative Churches Are Growing* (New York: Harper & Row, 1972).

45. *Ibid.,* pp. 36-55.

46. Quebedeaux, *The Young Evangelicals,* pp. 50-51.

47. Snook, *Going Further: Life-and-Death Religion in America* pp. 4, 5.

48. Personal correspondence dated June 25, 1974, from Donald H. Gill, Executive Director, Evangelistic Association of New England.

49. Charles A. Tipp, "The Religious Complexion of Canada," *Yearbook of American and Canadian Churches 1974,* ed. by Constant H. Jacquet, Jr., (Nashville: Abingdon Press, 1974), pp. 254-57.

50. Campbell and Fukuyama, *The Fragmented Layman,* pp. 70-72.

51. Stark and Glock, *American Piety,* pp. 58-64, 42-44.

52. Merton P. Strommen, Milo L. Brekke, Ralph C. Underwager, and Arthur L. Johnson, *A Study of Generations* (Minneapolis, Minn.: Augsburg Publishing House, 1972), pp. 107-8, 378-82. Variations between the three denominations are not reported for these items, but Kersten's research found the highest proportion of theological conservatives in the Wisconsin and Missouri Synods and the lowest in the LCA (Kersten, *The Lutheran Ethic,* pp. 32-39).

53. Andrew Greeley, *Unsecular Man: The Persistence of Religion* (New York: Schocken Books, 1972).

54. Stark and Glock, *American Piety,* pp. 81-107.

55. Quebedeaux, *The Young Evangelicals,* p. 137.

56. Douglas W. Johnson and George W. Cornell, *Punctured Preconceptions: What North American Christians Think about the Church* (New York: Friendship Press, 1972), p. 13.

57. *Ibid.,* pp. 63, 79, 188.

58. The findings of the study are not reported separately by denomination. Evangelical bodies like the Church of God (Anderson, Indiana), Cumberland Presbyterian Church, Lutheran Church—Missouri Synod, Mennonite Church, and Seventh-day Adventist

Church are included among the fifteen denominations, so a bias favoring evangelical orientations is introduced. If the sample was selected randomly in proportion to denominational membership, those five would account for 12.5 percent of the membership sample of the fifteen bodies as of 1972 (Jacquet, *The Yearbook of American and Canadian Churches*), but if each denomination was given an equal-sized sample, they would account for 33.3 percent. Substantial proportions of the congregations of the American Baptist Churches, American Lutheran Church, Reformed Church in America, and United Presbyterian Church also are basically evangelical in orientation.

59. Johnson and Cornell, *Punctured Preconceptions,* p. 34.

60. David O. Moberg, *Inasmuch: Christian Social Responsibility in the Twentieth Century* (Grand Rapids: Eerdmans Publishing Co., 1965); Moberg, *The Great Reversal;* Klaas Runia, "Evangelical Responsibility in a Secularized World," *Christianity Today* (June 19, 1970), pp. 851-54.

61. Ron E. Roberts, *The New Communes: Coming Together in America* (Englewood Cliffs, N.J.: Prentice-Hall, 1971), p. 80.

62. For example, the People's Christian Coalition; see its significant periodical, *The Post American.*

63. Quebedeaux, *The Young Evangelicals.*

64. Joseph C. Hough, Jr. "The Church Alive and Changing," *Religion American Style,* ed. Patrick H. McNamara (New York: Harper & Row, 1974), pp. 316-21 (from *Christian Century,* Jan. 5, 1972).

65. Robert N. Bellah, *Beyond Belief: Essays on Religion in a Post-Traditional World* (New York: Harper & Row, 1970), pp. 168-89.

66. Lowell D. Streiker and Gerald S. Strober, *Religion and the New Majority; Billy Graham, Middle America, and the politics of the 70s* (New York: Association Press, 1972); Wesley Pippert, "What Watergate Means to Me," *Evangelical Newsletter* (Nov. 19, 1973), p. 4.

67. Hill, *et al., Religion and The Solid South;* George H. Shriver, "When Conservatism Is Liberalism," *Christian Century* (Aug. 6, 1969), pp. 1040-41; James R. Dolby *et al.,* "Cultural Evangelicalism: The Background for Personal Despair," *Journal of the American Scientific Affiliation* (Sept. 1972), pp. 91-101.

68. R. H. Fuller and B. K. Rice, *Christianity and the Affluent Society* (Grand Rapids: Eerdmans Publishing Co., 1967).

69. Jim Wallis, " 'New Evangelicals' and the Demands of Discipleship," *Christian Century* (May 29, 1974), 581-82.

70. Even Pentecostalism, which many believe to be "incurably individualistic and escapist" in orientation, is awakening to its social responsibility. See Larry Christenson, *A Charismatic Approach to Social Action* (Minneapolis: Bethany Fellowship, 1974).

Tensions Within Contemporary Evangelicalism: A Critical Appraisal

Martin E. Marty

American Protestant evangelicalism considers itself to be simply an expression of classic orthodox Christianity. So also do several hundred million worldwide Roman Catholic, Eastern Orthodox, Lutheran, Anglican, and other Christians who are not part of conventional evangelicalism. None of these agree with any other of these so far as the content and substance of Christian doctrines are concerned. No councils of the church and no set of theologians have successfully determined which complex of Christian churches are in most direct continuity with orthodoxy, nor is anyone likely ever to do so. But evangelicalism finds it important to engage in acts of self-definition that would satisfy its own clientele at least.

Most of the energies expended recently by evangelicals have been directed chiefly to the cause of demarking or delineating boundaries between themselves and American Protestant liberals on one hand or fundamentalists on the other. While the debates have to do with twenty centuries of Christian argument, the most interesting and perhaps the only resolvable element in these concerns the question of continuity with nineteenth-century American evangelical Christianity. In their own ways, all three Protestant clusters

Martin E. Marty is Professor of Modern Church History and Associate Dean at the Divinity School, University of Chicago.

regard this as their special ancestral faith and culture, though no liberals are more ready than are their two counterparts to distance themselves from many features of nineteenth-century faith and life.

These debates could be regarded as nothing more than the kind of "we're truer than you" controversies with which theologians idle away their days. But they take on a certain importance for anyone who tries to understand today's power alignments in American religion, and they have attracted many people who are busy making up their minds about affiliations and loyalties. Social philosopher Ernest Gellner has observed that each society tends to regard the ideology with which it has "passed the hump of transistion" to its present status with special regard. Indeed, that ideology remains its "nominal doctrine," the "symbol of that overcoming of the painful hump, of the achieved satisfactory order which is now the true 'social contact.' " [1] Nineteenth-century Protestantism serves as such an ideology in the eye of most twentieth-century American Protestants, and thus the controversy as to who are the best custodians of its lore has religious and social consequences.

The earlier evangelicalism was shaped by the First and Second Great Awakenings, with their accent on revivalism and personal conversion. In the process a distinctive doctrine of God and man became normative: God was not a remote sovereign potency but a benevolent loving Father who normatively addressed the human situation in Christ. Man was indeed a sinner, but he was capable of responding to the revivalists' appeals, and once converted, he acquired great potency for doing good. A benevolent empire, full of errands of mercy and agencies of reform and welfare, emerged out of the company of the converted. Most of them found their spiritual home in a cluster of competing but sometimes cooperating denominations.

By the time of the revival of 1858 one could still speak of this evangelical empire as a kind of unity,[2] but in the subsequent half-century, by the time of the formation of the old Federal Council of Churches in 1908, that unity had been broken. One segment of Protestantism regarded the other as liberal; the two divided not only over doctrinal emphases but also over social policy, with the conservatives stressing individual salvation and their counterparts being more ready to make a public address to corporate problems of society.

During the half-century of progressive division the conservatives alone came to cherish mass evangelism: many of them also adopted premillennial views. The liberals were more positive toward evolutionary and critical biblical thought and more adaptive to social and intellectual change. After the publication of *The Fundamentals (1910-1915)*, the conservatives came to be called fundamentalists. By the 1920s they had set up their own network of organizations, Bible schools, and publishing ventures; they had also grown in militancy. During that decade Protestantism was torn by political and power disputes; portions of the two emphases went their separate ways.

By the 1940s conservatives were themselves clearly divided. A symbol of the fundamentalist reorganization was the formation of the American Council of Christian Churches, "militantly pro-Gospel and anti-modernist," on September 17, 1941. On October 27-28, 1941, another group met to discuss organizing what became the National Association of Evangelicals. Its spokesmen were "determined to break with apostasy but . . . wanted no dog-in-the manger, reactionary, negative, or destructive type of organization." They had fundamentalism in mind. Instead they sought one that was "determined to shun all forms of bigotry, intolerance, misrepresentation, hate, jealousy, false judgment, and hypocrisy." [3]

In the late 1940s and early 1950s the second party of evangelicals took clearer shape under the leadership of Harold Ockenga, Billy Graham, Carl F. H. Henry, and others. They shared in the benefits of the religious revivals

172

of the 1950s and have survived in the 1970s in better shape institutionally than have either the liberals on their left or the fundamentalists on their right.

On the cognitive level and insofar as a religion is represented by assent to the substance of dogmas, evangelicalism has more in common with fundamentalism's heirs than it does with the children of the liberals. Even in the midst of heated polemics, evangelicals and fundamentalists then tried to remind themselves that they agreed on "the fundamentals." More often than not they have boiled down to five "doctrines that were declared to be essential" by several conservative gatherings: "the inerrancy of Scripture, the virgin birth of Christ, the atonement of Christ, the resurrection of Christ, and the miracle-working power of Christ." [4] Ernest Sandeen's recent researches have turned up lists as long as the fourteen doctrines set forth by the Niagara Bible Conference of 1895; he contends that these all have found widespread support as being basic or fundamental.

During the recent debates it has become clear that new power alignments have emerged, and that these do not all follow the lines of nominal assent to five or fourteen fundamentals. The modernist or liberal parties that gave battle to fundamentalists in the 1920s have largely disappeared as effective forces. The radical theology of American Protestants in the mid-1960s never was regarded as having had much ecclesiastical consequence, however exciting it appeared in the media and in certain academic elitist circles. Contemporary usage more frequently speaks of the predominance of a more moderate and chastened refinement of the liberal party in the form of "mainstream" or "mainline" Protestantism, most of which coexists reasonably creatively with many kinds of evangelicalism but with no kinds of fundamentalism. Most of these mainliners would probably recognize themselves as being in continuity with nineteenth-century evangelicalism. They might well be at home with the kind of Christocentric liberalism that

Henry Pitney Van Dusen found worthy of vindication in 1963,[5] a liberal theology far removed from either old modernism or new radicalism.

Ernest Gellner had pointed out that through the passage of time "the effective content" of an earlier successful ideology might be "eroded, becoming even more selective, symbolic, 'spiritual,' etc." In politics and religion demythologizers arise to reinterpret their faith in such a way that it cannot come into conflict with anything at all. (Extreme sophisticated fundamentalism achieves the same end, by a route only slightly different from extreme theological liberalism. It *also* brutally disconnects Faith from what one really and normally believes)." [6] Christians, Gellner says, have found that "the modernism of one generation is doubly dated in the next." The same is also the case for fundamentalism, which was its own kind of overreactive counteraccommodation or adaptation. For that reason evangelicals today progressively distance themselves also from fundamentalists and see them also as a deviation from the nineteenth-century Protestant *Gestalt*. (Needless to say, fundamentalists return the compliment to the two other parties!)

However important cognitive assent to demarking dogmas may be, particularly among intellectual articulators of the faith, in *praxis* and action and in the eyes of virtually every believer and beholder other elements besides substantive doctrinal ones must be taken into account when the shape and prospects of a religious emphasis are being considered. Chief among these would be the expressions of social and collective behavior, the characteristics and even nomothetic behavior patterns of the three groups. Fundamentalism's are most intact and predictable; mainstream Protestantism's are least so; evangelicalism has enough coherence to make generalization possible.

Behavior relates to faith and even to doctrine. If ideas have consequences, consequences also have ideas. If what Ortega y Gasset calls *vigencias,* the binding customs, manners, morals, mores, habits, and expressions of a social group are sufficiently reflexive, sufficiently profound and sustained, one must look for the "real" beliefs and ideas of that group to coexist or to transcend the nominal dogmas that normally are conceived as being delineating. On few Protestant subjects is more ink spilled than in discussion of these *vigencias*.[7]

In *The Evangelical Renaissance* Donald Bloesch, an advocate of thoughtful evangelical theology, speaks of "the new evangelicalism [as] a mood and not a theological system." [8] But he outlines so many differences between fundamentalism and evangelicalism that "mood" overwhelms commonly agreed upon system. A spokesman for *The Young Evangelicals,* Richard Quebedeaux, complains that "for too long it has been the fault of mainstream Ecumenical Liberalism to lump together with pejorative intent *all* theological conservatives into the worn Fundamentalist category. In general, Evangelicals resent being called Fundamentalists, and Fundamentalists likewise do not usually appreciate the Evangelical designation." Both these "varieties of Orthodox Christianity have undergone modification to some degree in the finer points of theology and, more profoundly, in their attitudes toward culture." [9]

Carl F. H. Henry earlier had noted that "by mid-century, fundamentalism obviously signified a temperament as fully as a theology." Some evangelicals courageously stayed with fundamentalism, remembering its contribution to Christianity's age-old battle against unbelief, but others "weary of the spirit of strife" declared that "fundamentalism is dead." Henry argued that evangelicals should admit the excesses of fundamentalism just as neo-orthodox leaders admitted the excesses of the prevailing liberalism. A new "mind-set and a new method in ecclesiastical life" were needed.[10]

Gellner constantly compared Christian revisionist debates to those of Marxism. The fundamentalists and the evangelicals today fight over the character of the Christian

175

deposit just as Russian and Chinese Communists contend over the appropriateness of each one's claim to legitimacy in Marxian succession. Both may be perpetuating the substance of the dogmas, but the context, character, and ethos of behavioral patterns have diverged so much that two different faiths come to predominate.

By the 1970s, evangelicalism had permanently parted company with the shapers of the fundamentalist *Gestalt*. Its leaders could not go the fundamentalist way; their organization, cognition, intention, and behavior now differed so vastly that they would have to desert evangelicalism itself to take the fundamentalist course. Yet evangelicals also had difficulty moving further toward the mainline Protestants, who also had much claim on the nineteenth-century lineage. While many elements of their behavior patterns were increasingly converging, they honestly differed too much on the appropriation of doctrine to be at ease with each other. The younger evangelicals sometimes found pragmatic alliances with mainline church people to be advisable. But Carl F. H. Henry, doughty warrior for the original restatement of modern evangelicalism and a man who made more than most of the intellectual formulation of the movement, demurred. Even in the ethical realm, because of differences in motivation, goals, and ethics, "it would be naïve to argue . . . that liberals and evangelicals need each other for complementary emphases." Alliance could mean that the biblical view of God would be destroyed and the welfare state produced.[11]

Insofar as Henry is representative, it would seem that evangelical leadership is enjoying its evident majority status and, in a way, "going it alone" in its claim on the heritage, however blurred its boundaries may be becoming. If, in effect, it is turning out to be *the* Protestant mainstream, it will increasingly take on the burdens of typicality and of cultural predominance. Indeed, its self-critics are regularly pointing to just such tendencies. Evangelicals are ecumenical under the banner of "cooperation without compromise."

By this they mean that none of their churches will compromise their distinctive and separating dogmas. Yet in practice and behaviorally they cooperate with nonevangelicals, including mainstream Protestants and Roman Catholics in some of their most prized ventures, including evangelism—witness the effort called Key 73—and are perceived by the public as creatively compromising cooperators.

Evangelicals' increasing cultural openness leads them to an embrace, albeit a critical one, of intellectual and artistic currents that subtly alter the character of faith's expression.

They also, their internal critics contend, too often uncritically embrace some of the practices of popular culture that their fathers and mothers had shunned. Donald Bloesch is not alone in stating this, and he is certainly mild in his comment:

> This brings us . . . to the carnality and frivolity in much modern-day popular evangelical religion. This can be seen in the glorification of beauty queens and athletes who happen to be Christian. It is also noticeable in the fascination of many evangelicals with public relations and showmanship. In some schools and churches technique and method are valued more highly than right doctrine, and group dynamics is given more attention than prayer and other spiritual disciplines. The popularity of gospel rock groups that appeal to the sensual side of man is yet another indication of accommodation to worldly standards. Culture-religion is also evident in the camaraderie between some evangelical leaders and right-wing politicians.[12]

He quotes A. W. Tozer on this tendency toward culture-religion: evangelicalism is "fascinated by the great, noisy, aggressive world with its big name, its hero worship, its wealth and garish pagentry." Millions of disappointed persons who never found worldly glory could through evangelicalism have a shortcut to their heart's desire in the realm of social acceptance, publicity, success in sports or business or entertainment. "All this on earth and heaven

177

at last. Certainly no insurance company can offer half as much." [13]

If evangelicalism has drifted, perhaps irretrievably, into much affirmation of and some accommodation to culture-as-it-is, its future life will also be complicated by the presence of vital critical groups within it. These are counterparts to the liberals' social gospel and Christian realist voices that in the early 1900s and in the 1930s and 1960s troubled the peace of mainstream Protestantism. Influenced by men like Jacques Ellul, Helmut Thielicke, and William Stringfellow or issuing in numbers of evangelically radical groups like the Christian World Liberation Front and publications like the *Post-American,* these forces are beginning to disrupt evangelicalism's uncritical bond with the social status quo. They will, if they survive, make it possible for a biblically prophetic note to be heard with more consistency—at great expense to evangelicalism's popularity and its sanctioning by the powers that be.

In short, while fundamentalism and evangelicalism both defer to each other and show some respect for the way each retains at least nominal assent to the old nineteenth-century Protestant symbols, their behavior patterns show such divergences that we must be alerted to the possibility of needing to say that their similarities have "died the death of a thousand qualifications." On the levels of social behavior and, presumably, of the ideas that motivate such behavior, evangelicals often show more similarities with and affinities to mainstream Protestants, with whom they disagree more openly on the cognitive level but with whom they have more profound similarities so far as world views are concerned. Brief comments on the evangelical-*versus*-fundamentalism polemics in four areas will illustrate particularly the first half of this thesis.

Not necessarily in the matter of the doctrine of the church itself, but rather in that of the *ecclesia-in-praxis,* qualitatively different ideas are finding expression in the patterns of social behavior of evangelicalism as against

178

those of fundamentalism. The evangelicals would seem to have more rightful claim on the nineteenth-century heritage. For all the denominational competition, the fathers of that century were ecumenical in outlook. Europeans complained that Americans were not enthusiastic partners in the Evangelical Alliance (after 1846), not because they were not ecumenical or cooperative but because cooperation came so instinctively and naturally to them that they did not need the international organization. Yet these evangelicals who were cooperating were by no means wholly agreed cognitively or substantively with each other.

The fundamentalists of the twentieth century have parted company with the nineteenth-century policy-makers. They are separatist and schismatic and proud of it. They cooperate with each other simply on pragmatic and on quasimilitary joint-defense and joint-aggression grounds. But they make no claims of spiritual union of any sort where there is not total agreement on doctrine. Virtually all fundamentalists sound like each other on this topic, and almost any of them could be taken as typical. Thus Thomas E. Baker in his manual on fundamentalism says that "new evangelicalism . . . violates the plain teaching of scripture," for example in its understanding of "the last days" or in its "departure from the truth of separation from unbelief." Thus the new evangelicalism "brought a major 'division' in the ranks of fundamentalism as well as a minor division in the philosophies of Liberalism and Neo-Orthodoxy." Yet for Baker the difficulty the fundamentalist has with the new evangelical is found in that "he is not dealing with an unbeliever, but one who believes most of the basic fundamental truths of scripture."

Nominal agreement on these basics always has to be asserted. Baker goes on to criticize evangelicals for dealing with pentecostals, non-Calvinists, clergy from communist countries, but not with fundamentalists. "This . . . revealed the same attitude that prevailed in Liberalism." Fundamentalists warned evangelicals that "cooperation of belief

179

with unbelief in Ecumenism would produce ecumenical babylon. . . . This is exactly what took place." Fundamentalists dare not allow evangelicals to share their pulpits. Such practice is unscriptural. It causes confusion. It is not necessary. There is no benefit. "The invisible line must be drawn and kept drawn at all times between fundamentalist and New Evangelical, even when the fundamentalist feels strong enough through growth spiritually, numerically or financially." [14]

From the evangelical side, the early leader Harold Ockenga set a tone and the terms that remain consistent. "Fragmentation, segregation, separation, criticism, censoriousness, suspicion, solecism, is the order of the day for fundamentalism." [15] Over against fundamentalism, evangelicals assert, says Millard Erickson, that "there are only two justifiable grounds for separation from an existing denomination: eviction or apostasy." Yet fundamentalists split "on the basis of personality or minor creedal items." "The new evangelicals are not separatists in the sense of seeking to withdraw from any slight taint of heterodoxy or worldliness." [16] Bruce Shelley, speaking for evangelicals, complained of fundamentalism's "wowser' worship, its cultural isolationism, its sectarian separatism, its monastic ethics, its theological hair-splitting." [17]

In the face of such sharp and consistent lines of definition and attack, the Christian observer who is not part of either movement can be forgiven if he or she is bewildered about the claims of some sort of kinship on the basis of cognitive assent to basic tenets. Thus both evangelicals and fundamentalists insist on the "inerrancy of scripture" as being the most basic of all their fundamentals. Since they do not agree with each other or among each other on the basis of it, what does this nominal agreement on a substantive category mean? The larger world feels much more the effect of the two social behavioral patterns than it does the professed dogmatic agreements.

A second area, and one that gave rise to much of the

demarcation between the two, has to do with the social and ethical realm. Here again evangelicalism would seem to have the more rightful claim on the nineteenth-century lineage, and fundamentalism would be the "modernist" deviation. It is hard to account for fundamentalism's departure from the older evangelical concern for Christianity as it relates to the whole social fabric. No doubt premillennialism's rise in the late nineteenth century had much to do with this withdrawal into purely private and personal moral discourse on the part of fundamentalism. Premillennialism, the belief in God's forthcoming intervention to inaugurate a millennium of Christ's rule, has characteristic but not inevitable behavioral corollaries. Many evangelicals are also premillennial, but not all segregate themselves so consistently from efforts to participate positively as the church in the social sphere. (Fundamentalists are not removed from some kinds of participation, but these tend to be restricted to supporting legislation having to do with private vices—gambling, liquor, pornography—or to advocacy of the conservative status quo on the grounds of biblically based injunctions to undergird civil authority.)

Millard Erickson typically criticizes fundamentalism on this point. "During its long history orthodox, or conservative, Christianity had stressed the application of its message to social ills . . . As the twentieth century moved on, however, fundamentalism neglected this emphasis. . . . The fundamentalist seemed to be . . . passing suffering humanity." [18] Carl F. H. Henry, Harold Ockenga, Sherwood Eliott Wirt, and Leighton Ford among the older evangelicals have persistently concurred in this judgment. Positively, asserts Ockenga in one of the most famous passages in this literature:

> The new evangelicalism embraces the full orthodoxy of fundamentalism, but manifests a social consciousness and responsibility which was strangely absent from fundamentalism. The new evangelicalism concerns itself not only with

181

personal salvation, doctrinal truth and an eternal point of reference, but also with the problems of race, of war, of class struggle, of liquor control, of juvenile delinquency, of immorality, and of national imperialism. . . . The new evangelicalism believes that orthodox Christians cannot abdicate their responsibility in the social scene.[19]

The younger evangelicals, led by Richard V. Pierard, Richard Quebedeaux, Richard J. Mouw, the editors of *The Reformed Journal,* the Southern Baptist Convention's Christian Life Commission, the authors of the Chicago Declaration of Social Concern, and others have taken up this theme with a vengeance and totally part company with the fundamentalist pattern. Each side is as proud of its stand as it is rejective of the other's. Each accepts the general depiction of its own stand by the other. Meanwhile, evangelicalism distances itself somewhat from at least the position of official elites (though by no means necessarily of the majority of constituents) on the mainstream Protestant side. It remains critical of simple liberal-church-liberal-social policy syndromes, of the leadership's presumed speaking for the clienteles, of liberal Protestantism's tendency to bureaucratize social programming, of its readiness to take legislative routes reflexively. But while differences with fundamentalism are differences in kind, with the mainstream they have come more and more to be matters of degree. In the case of the prophetic criticism and occasional radicalism of the new evangelicals, it is often possible to see the mainline forces actually being eclipsed.

Once again, in the face of these obvious, profound, enduring differences concerning the *polis,* one of the most decisive spheres in theology and social life, what is the outsider to make of professed agreements between fundamentalists and evangelicals on, say, belief in Christ's second coming? Why should the two be seen as united in belief, when there is little agreement on other doctrines on what the vast majority of Christians—Roman Catholic, Orthodox, Lutheran, and Anglican—have always regarded as fundamental (for example, the sacraments)? Social behavior ought at least to be regarded as indicative or emerging theological flaws and faults in what was once a settled conservative Protestant landscape.

Historically of less significance but now gaining in prominence are differing a third set of behavioral responses. Fundamentalists have not been antiintellectual. The name of J. Gresham Machen is regularly invoked to show that their school was not always antiacademic and rationally roughshod. A kind of seventeenth-century scholastic philosophical approach has provided intellectual structure for much fundamentalism. Yet fundamentalists have been nervous about universities and colleges—even under their own auspices. Instead they have cherished more focal and more easily controlled Bible schools and institutes. Not all of them shun the arts. Bob Jones University has notable art collections, and other fundamentalist organizations make much of music. But little attempt is made to integrate theologically the aesthetic vision and Christian faith.

The evangelicals want to be known as favoring both intellectuality and arts in the service of faith. In H. Richard Niebuhr's familiar typology, fundamentalism tends to represent "Christ against culture," while evangelicalism wavers between "Christ transforming culture" or "Christ and culture in paradox" but not in mutual negation. Carl F. H. Henry long ago set the terms for criticism when he accused fundamentalism of having narrowed "the whole counsel of God," becoming other-worldly in spirit, neglecting the exposition of Christian philosophy, and even being distrustful of such interests. It degenerated, to use Dr. G. B. Wurth's phrase, into "a morbid and sickly enthusiasm." It embodied "an uncritical antithesis between the heart and the head . . . belittling . . . the intellect." Fundamentalism "neglected the production of great exegetical and theological literature," and reprinted works from the past.

183

Therefore, "if modernism stands discredited as a perversion of scriptural theology, certainly fundamentalism in this contemporary expression stands discredited as a perversion of the biblical spirit." [20]

Evangelicals have supported colleges more than Bible institutes; they have reached into more and more areas of culture, though without yet having made a significant contribution to modern art or literature; they have built seminaries that allow for some internal pluralism in approach to philosophy and arts; they have made much of authors like C. S. Lewis when these embody orthodox Christianity; they have even tolerated moderate appropriations of biblical critical methods—George Ladd is usually cited as an examplar[21]—though the exemplars usually reply in haste that they in no way depart from their belief in complete biblical authority. The evangelicals pursue doctorates at prestigious European and American theological schools; their scholarly societies have become more and more sophisticated, even though they may require creedal assents not expected elsewhere in the American academy.

Individual fundamentalists may not find fault with all these tendencies and may occasionally pursue some of these themselves. But as a movement, fundamentalism rejects them all. The Christian who belongs to neither party has difficulty seeing why the two should be considered a single expression of Christian faith, again, for example, because of belief in both the atonement and the resurrection of Christ, when the majority of mainstream Protestants share these beliefs and have views of intellect and culture more congruent with evangelicalism's intentions than either of them have with fundamentalism's.

A fourth area that receives perhaps the most attention in evangelical-fundamentalist polemics is the more subjective and elusive sphere of manners, mores, habits, and customs. These may be seen as adisphoral or peripheral to true dogmatists, but biblical religion and centuries of tradition count these as being extremely revelatory of the character and actual content of personal or group beliefs. The lines are clearly drawn here. The fundamentalists regard evangelicals as suave, accommodating, too genteel, too worldly.[22] To the militants such postures are indicative not merely of wrong manners but of wrong commitments and beliefs.

Evangelicals are just as consistent in their rejection of fundamentalism's militancy, belligerency, uncouthness, prescriptive legalism, and ad hominem argumentation. They spend enormous amounts of energy distancing themselves from contemporary fundamentalists who manifest these traits and sorting out earlier fundamentalists who did not possess them. Virtually every commentator from the evangelical side has treated fundamentalism's moral taboos against dancing, card playing, mixed swimming, and the like as being normative and nomothetic expressions of that faith. They often believe that these taboos shroud complex problems, as in the area of sex. Daniel Stevick quotes and agrees with Carl Henry:

> The Fundamentalist catalogue of "sins" is small and specific: commercial movies, dancing, gambling, card-playing, drinking beer or wine or liquor, and smoking. No "spiritual Christian" will presumably do any of these things, and generally will have little to do with anyone who does do them. Everyone who grows up in this tradition finds that it has a vise-like grip on him. His conscience has been made sensitive to these things by the never-ending tirade against them.

The evangelicals are not exactly libertarian or antinomian, but they feel that instead of "a childish reaction into a uniformly opposite pattern of behavior," there should be a "variety of practice that indicates life, color, and the freedom for each person to be himself." [23] Since the fundamentalist believes his or her practices to be grounded completely in the only possible scriptural interpretation of

185

ethics, he sees such evangelical "variety" as being world-liness and apostasy.

Along with personal morals, the two clusters part company over the manner and manners of denominational fighting. Carl F. H. Henry even goes so far as to say that "the real bankruptcy of fundamentalism has resulted not so much from a reactionary spirit—lamentable as this was—as from a harsh temperament, a spirit of lovelessness and strife contributed by much of its leadership in the recent past." "It is this character of fundamentalism as a temperament, and not primarily fundamentalism as a theology, which has brought the movement into contemporary discredit." Historically it was a theological position. Only gradually did it become a mood and disposition as well.[24] Yet in separating from that mood and disposition, evangelicalism takes on the risks of mainstream Protestantism. "When evangelicalism becomes respectable and even fashionable," writes Donald Bloesch, "then the temptation to accommodate to the values and goals of the world becomes almost overwhelming." Such accommodation, he says, is present and brings dangers.[25]

One could carry these comparisons into numerous other fields; for example, differing attitudes toward the study and use of the Bible could be enlarged upon as manifesting other qualitative differences between the two conservative claimants to rightful lineage of American nineteenth-century Protestantism. These illustrations should suffice for present purposes, however. It is clear from what has been indicated that fundamentalism and evangelicalism are now at the stage where they should begin to explore at what point drastic behavioral differences reveal and represent actual substantive differences, opposing grasps of biblical and traditional Christian teaching.

The intent has not been to show that evangelicals and mainstream Protestants now will find either simple theological or social behavioral agreement or that alliances between them can easily come about. They do have more

186

in common than they have recognized; this will become even more evident as evangelicals come increasingly to the conclusion that modernist-liberal Protestantism of the 1920s was a deviation from nineteenth-century continuities and syndromes on the left just as the older fundamentalism was on the right. Most important, this thesis or interpretation suggests that evangelicalism is taking on and will increasingly take on the burdens of interpretation and accommodation that have created numerous troubles for the mainstream groups. Evangelicals will have to be especially alert to the ways in which they can replenish and revitalize their theological tradition through the passing years. They cannot expect a serene life as they try to remain a "cognitive minority" while they have become a kind of social behavioral majority far beyond the borders of middle America.[26]

Notes

1. Ernest Gellner, *Thought and Change* (Chicago: The University of Chicago Press, 1965), p. 123.

2. See Timothy Smith, *Revivalism and Social Reform in Mid-Nineteenth Century America* (Nashville: Abingdon Press, 1957).

3. Quoted in Louis Gasper, *The Fundamentalist Movement* (The Hague: Mouton & Co., 1963), pp. 23, 25, in his account of the formation of these two organizations.

4. Ernest R. Sandeen, *The Roots of Fundamentalism: British and American Millenarianism 1800-1930* (Chicago: The University of Chicago Press, 1970), p. xiv; see also Appendix A for the Niagara Bible Conference's fourteen points.

5. See Henry P. Van Dusen, *The Vindication of Liberal Theology* (New York: Charles Scribners Sons, 1963).

6. Gellner, *Thought and Change*, p. 124.

7. The concept of *vigencia* appears frequently in Ortego's work; for succinct definition see Harold C. Raley, *Jose Ortega y Gasset: Philosopher of European Unity* (Tuscaloosa, Ala.: University of Alabama Press, 1971), p. 218.

8. Donald Bloesch, *The Evangelical Renaissance* (Grand Rapids: Eerdmans Publishing Co., 1973), p. 41.

9. Richard Quebedeaux, *The Young Evangelicals: Revolution in Orthodoxy* (New York: Harper & Row, 1974), p. 19.

10. Carl F. H. Henry, *Evangelical Responsibility in Contemporary Theology* (Grand Rapids: Eerdmans Publishing Co., 1957), pp. 45 ff.

11. Carl F. H. Henry, *The God Who Shows Himself* (Waco, Tex.: Word Books, 1966), pp. 59 ff.

12. Bloesch, *The Evangelical Renaissance*, p. 24.

13. *Ibid.*

14. Thomas E. Baker, *Christ and the Even Balance: a Manual on Fundamentalism* (Millersburg, Pa.: Bible Truth Mission, 1968), pp. 72-74, 76, 85.

15. Ockenga is quoted in Daniel B. Stevick, *Beyond Fundamentalism* (Richmond: John Knox, 1964), p. 28.

16. Millard Erickson, *The New Evangelical Theology* (Westwood, N.J.: Fleming H. Revell, 1968), pp. 165, 164.

17. Bruce L. Shelley, *Evangelicalism in America* (Grand Rapids: Eerdmans Publishing Co., 1967), p. 112.

18. Erickson, *The New Evangelical Theology*, p. 178.

19. Quoted by Lowell D. Streiker and Gerald S. Strober, *Religion and the New Majority: Billy Graham, Middle America, and the Politics of the 70s* (New York: Association Press, 1972), p. 112.

20. Henry, *Evangelical Responsibility in Contemporary Theology*, pp. 33 ff., 47.

21. Quebedeaux, *The Young Evangelicals*, p. 74 ff.

22. George W. Dollar, *A History of Fundamentalism in America* (Greenville, S.C.: Bob Jones University Press, 1973), p. 207 ff.

23. The first quotation is Henry's; the second is Stevick's, *Beyond Fundamentalism*, p. 206.

24. Henry, *Evangelical Responsibility in Contemporary Theology*, pp. 43 ff.

25. Bloesch, *The Evangelical Renaissance*, p. 18.

26. For comment on the ties to middle America, see Streiker and Strober's *Religion and the New Majority*.

Part III. Where Evangelicals Are Changing

The Resurgence of Evangelical Social Concern (1925–75)

Robert D. Linder

Something is happening among American evangelicals.[1] This seems to be the consensus of a growing number of students of the American religious scene, of friends and foes of the evangelicals alike. A marked change of attitude on the part of millions of evangelical Christians in America toward social issues is under way.[2]

As recently as 1967, noted historian William G. McLoughlin accused evangelicals of being "the spiritual hardcore of the radical right" with relative impunity.[3] And many contemporary historians writing for college undergraduates have passed off the religious resurgence following World War II with an intellectual shrug and characterized it as "in harmony with a patriotic, moderately conservative, and notably consensus-minded era in modern American history."[4]

But today things are different. Evangelicals have become their own best critics. McLoughlin and others have overlooked the growing number of evangelicals who honestly have reassessed their position vis-à-vis society and who currently are seeking biblical and historical guidance as they, like millions of other Americans, struggle to discover

Robert D. Linder is Professor of History at Kansas State University.

their real heritage. In short, many of America's millions of evangelicals agree with Canadian Inter-Varsity Christian Fellowship Secretary Samuel Escobar's evaluation of the current scene:

> The evangelical community in the Anglo-Saxon countries has money, influence, and numbers that could really make a decisive force for the reform of their society. By creating a false dichotomy between evangelism and social action, by closing their eyes to the example of evangelicals in England in the nineteenth century, and by spiritualizing the Gospel to heretical extremes, they have let secularism take the initiative in education, politics, the media, and international relations.[5]

Concomitant with this development—and in some ways because of it—there has been in recent years in evangelical circles a shift away from a position of indifference or hostility to Christian social concern toward a serious interest in the social implications of the gospel.[6]

It is the purpose of this essay to examine the historical background of this resurgence and to analyze the factors which have helped to bring it about. My discussion draws heavily upon the work of others who have preceded me while at the same time it makes use of my own research. My procedure will entail a study of developments within evangelical Christianity in the United States since the end of World War I, and especially during the 1920s when the evangelical social conscience was blunted. I will touch on the evangelical social conscience during the generation between 1930 and 1960 when the foundations were laid for the present resurgence before pointing out signs of social reawakening since 1960. Finally, I will draw some conclusions concerning the prospects for a new era in evangelical social ministry. This analytical framework will allow for a discussion of the main reasons for the current resurgence of social concern.

Historical Background: The Blunting of the Evangelical Social Conscience, 1918–29

The end of World War I was a watershed for Americans in general as well as for American evangelicals in particular. It marked the close of one era of American history and the opening of another. For the war and its aftermath— especially the fight over the League of Nations and the Red Scare—bruised the American spirit and dampened American optimism. The happily secure world which Americans knew before 1914 had disappeared. Their prewar problems seemingly paled in significance when compared with those of the twenties.[7]

In her poignant novel *Not Under Forty,* Willa Cather wrote that "the world broke in two in 1922 or thereabouts."[8] She may not have correctly identified the exact year but there is no question that the decade of which 1922 was a part was one of extraordinary change for the American nation. The 1920s was not an age of "normalcy" for the churches. It was a time of crisis for both the Protestant establishment and for historic evangelicalism which undergirded it. As Sydney E. Ahlstrom correctly observed concerning the twenties: "Furious controversies, great debates, and wild fulminations were the order of the day. And nearly all of this conflict is part of the nation's religious history, either because the churches were active participants or because events impinged on their lives."[9] It seems clear in retrospect that the period from the Armistice to the Crash marked a crucial transition in American religious history which had especially important implications for evangelical social concern.

Most important for evangelicals, the "social and moral crisis" produced by the war seriously challenged the preeminence of orthodox Christianity in American life. The formerly ascendant moral beliefs were attacked as never before. Main Street craved a safe understandable religion as of old upon which to continue to base its wounded idealism while the intellectual elite proceeded to formulate a new morality resting upon the premise that religion should defer to science. The eventual result was a confrontation between the defenders of orthodoxy and the champions of the new science which would have many ramifications.[10]

Equally important was the fact that the 1920s marked the end of rural America and the beginning of the urban era. The 1920 census revealed for the first time that more Americans now lived in cities and towns than on farms. The cities bulged with new immigrants who settled by choice or by force of circumstances in ethnic enclaves thus creating new problems of assimilation. The enormity and complexity of the evils created by urbanization and industrialization overwhelmed the efforts of evangelical philanthropists and led many to disillusionment. Combined with other factors, urbanization temporarily sapped the *élan* of Christians who supported reform, and many retreated from active social involvement into private prayer and personal evangelism as the primary means of coping with the problems of the cities.[11]

Ironically, while some in the slums of the cities did not prosper enough, many other Americans prospered too much. The most salient feature of the 1920s was the new prosperity, and as Leuchtenberg points out, it was fraught with perils.[12] Even though the country was infused with a benevolent materialism, most Americans lacked experience in handling this new life-style. Money became too important, for it provided the measure of achievement, the level of social status for men. The new prosperity desiccated Christianity, undermined the American character, and encouraged an anxious concern for social approbation among the newly prosperous. Most, including many evangelicals, assumed that the new age of affluence would last forever. When it collapsed like a house of straw in a puff of financial wind in 1929, it was psychologically devastating.

The spectacular development of science and technology in the decade following World War I formed both the basis of this new prosperity and the means for expressing it. The impact of technology on the average American was staggering and fundamentally altered his life-style. Automobiles, radios, and the movies changed the way most Americans had lived, and the gadget became god. It is difficult for those who did not experience this era to comprehend the enormous impact it had on the psyche of most Americans, not to mention their morals. Evangelicals did not have time to work out a theology of the car, wireless, or cinema, and consequently produced a fragmented, rag-tag social response to these new developments.

Some Protestant thinkers tried to accommodate modern scientific thought to theology, which resulted in the popularization of theological liberalism in some circles in the 1920s. Other Protestants, mostly evangelicals, steadfastly refused to come to terms with the scientific world, especially in the realms of biology and anthropology. This led to a major confrontation between those who accepted and taught the possibility of evolution—mostly theological liberals and assorted non-Christians—and those who rejected any possibility of the evolutionary development of man—mostly evangelicals and their fellow-travelers—in the public schools and state legislatures of America.[13]

This was also a period of increasing cultural, ethnic, and religious diversity. All of the foregoing stimulated social heterogeneity. Moreover, during the 1920s new immigrants tended not to "melt" in the famous American melting pot; science and technology challenged older institutions for the social leadership of the nation; the Protestant establishment fell apart as Protestant turned against Protestant in the theological debates of the period; and the "lost generation" appeared to lead a literary and cultural revolt against the materialism, smug hypocrisy, and middle-class mores of their elders. Ironically, the concerns of the young rebels coincided with a new emphasis on individualism and a deemphasis on social reform which so characterized the age in which they lived.[14]

These, plus a number of lesser factors, led to the polarization of the American people in the decade following World War I. Science versus religion became one of the dominant themes. But this polarization expressed itself in other ways as well: a generation gap, rural against urban, the hostility of the old Americans to the new immigrants, business versus bolshevism, and, of paramount interest for this essay, fundamentalist versus modernist.[15]

In the context of the subject under discussion, the fundamentalist-modernist controversy was the most important event of the decade. During this period fundamentalism became the most vocal, if not the most numerous, segment of evangelical Christianity in America. Although fundamentalism was an extremely complex movement which defies easy generalization, several developments related to its rise are important for an understanding of why evangelical social concern was blunted during the 1920s.[16] For better or for worse, the fundamentalist-modernist row helped shape the attitude toward social concern of a whole generation of evangelicals.

Central to the fortunes of fundamentalism in the twenties was the Scopes Trial of 1925. This case gave the fundamentalists worldwide notoriety and brought the issue of evolution to the attention of Main Street, America. The trial in Dayton, Tennessee, also dramatized the nature of the conflict between the two religious movements fighting for the soul of America: fundamentalism and its friends on the one hand and modernism and its allies on the other.

A study of the affair yields valuable insights into the question of how fundamentalism came to be stamped with the negative image it has had to bear, in part, to the present day.

The ostensible reason for the confrontation between the forces of fundamentalism and modernism at Dayton from July 9-21, 1925, was the case of a local high school teacher, John T. Scopes, who was accused of violating a new Tennessee law which forbade the teaching of the

194

theory of evolution in the public schools. Scopes freely admitted that he had taught the questionable doctrine in his biology class but, through his lawyers, challenged the constitutionality of the law.

But legal niceties aside, the real protagonists in the trial were the older Protestant America on the one hand and the newer, increasingly secular America on the other. By 1925, evolution had succeeded prohibition as the focal point of evangelical social concern. The Dayton trial provided a forum for a great debate between two of the leading spokesmen for the two sides: William Jennings Bryan for the old Americans, that is, Protestants in general and evangelicals in particular; and Clarence Darrow for the new Americans, that is, theological liberals, many scientists, and a growing body of people with no religious preference at all.

As indicated before, the story of the Scopes Trial is the saga of the making of a negative image for fundamentalism. By 1925, fundamentalism represented evangelical Christianity to the popular mind, and Bryan was its prestigious leader. But the Bryan of 1925 was not the vigorous, dynamic Bryan of 1896 or even 1916. His defense of the faith he loved so well was neither sophisticated nor particularly relevant. On the other hand, Darrow was ruthless in his dealing with Bryan and left no avenue unexplored which might cast his opponent in the light of religious fanatic and crank. In effect, Darrow put Bryan on trial at Dayton and focused attention on him rather than the hapless Scopes.

Darrow was abetted in his manueverings by a hostile press.[17] This subject needs further research, but preliminary studies indicate that the majority of those who reported the Dayton trial in the newspapers and over the radio went out of their way to cast Bryan in the role of an ignorant fanatic and bigot. He was misquoted, jeered, and villified in the pages of many of the nation's leading newspapers and magazines by H. L. Mencken, Frank R. Kent,

195

Dudley Nichols, Heywood Broun, Joseph W. Krutch, and Russell D. Owen, to name a few. A study of the *New York Times* coverage of the event reveals how far this hostility toward Bryan extended. The champion of fundamentalism was strategically misquoted by a *Times* reporter on the front page on the opening day of the trial, and its correction, published at Bryan's insistence, appeared days later on page two. During the course of the trial, the *Times* ran several editorials severely criticizing Bryan and referring to him as "prodigiously ignorant" and a man with a "poorly furnished brain-room." Even when Bryan died shortly after the trial, the *Times* editors could find little good to say about him except for a few backhanded compliments.[18]

Bryan officially "won" the trial but lost the larger contest for the hearts and minds of America. The spectacle of a man on trial for teaching new scientific doctrines in Bible-belt Tennessee was inflated by the press and reported in sensationalist terms to the world at large. This had a sobering effect on many Americans who were embarrassed and repelled by what they read in the papers. Fundamentalism was henceforth associated in the popular mind with bigotry, ignorance, and intolerance.

The upshot of all of this was a loss of status and morale among fundamentalists. They suffered a further setback only a few days after the trial when on July 26, 1925, Bryan unexpectedly died. The evangelical world thus lost its key leader, and without his prestige, eloquence, and dynamism the fundamentalist movement fragmented and floundered.

More important, Bryan and the movement he championed left Dayton with a negative image. This stereotype given the fundamentalists was in part deserved because of their own failure to take seriously the need to cultivate the press since they so strongly felt they had truth and God on their side. Relations with the press continued to degenerate during the next decade as various fundamentalist leaders dueled with the media over a multitude of matters. With the negative image came an increasing negativism within the movement itself. In the face of building hostility from a formerly amicable world, the fundamentalists began to withdraw from the mainstream of American society. Gradually, they became defensive and exclusivist, defining the "good life" as the "separated life" and developing a negative code of ethics. Most important, they began to concentrate less on the theology which they originally championed and more on fighting their now mortal enemy, modernism, and its social gospel.[19]

A final result of the Dayton debacle which affected the future of evangelical Christian social concern was a growing disillusionment with political and social activism. Evangelicals had thrown themselves with great vigor into earlier crusades of a progressive nature: women's suffrage, prison reform, prohibition, and finally the "war to end all wars." Now, their latest great crusade against evolution had fizzled. Attempts to legislate evolution out of existence had failed except in a few areas, and even in friendly Tennessee they had met with a psychological defeat at Dayton. After 1925, many evangelicals grew wary of social involvement. This view received crucial support from the unfortunate confluence of Protestant theological liberalism and the social gospel in the early twentieth century.

In many ways, the fundamentalist-modernist controversy was the climax of a struggle that had begun as early as 1865 with the coming of the Industrial Revolution with all of its concomitant social stress, and the introduction of new theological ideas from Germany later in the century which led to the rise of theological liberalism—later popularly called modernism—in America. The social gospel actually was born out of theological considerations as evangelical Christians struggled to meet the needs of industrial society and as they worked out the logic of their evangelical quest for "a Christian America." At first, they took the lead in social ministry, especially in the nineteenth century.[20] However, in the twentieth century, the social gospel was detached from its evangelical roots by theological liberals looking for a *raison d'être* as they watched their young men leave the ministry and their constituency drift away because of the theological sterility of their position.[21]

The modernists interpreted the gospel in terms of social thrust. At first, evangelical reaction to this was rather mild but after World War I it became more encompassing. Thus when W. B. Riley, speaking at the opening of the newly organized World Christian Fundamentalist Association in Philadelphia in 1919, called for mobilization against such modern subversion as "social service Christianity," it struck a responsive chord.[22] After the great evolution controversy of the twenties, the terms modernist and social gospel became synonymous in the minds of most fundamentalists.[23]

This denunciation of the social gospel should not obscure the fact that many evangelicals, including a number of fundamentalists, continued to maintain a social witness. In fact, recent research has discovered numerous instances of evangelical social concern in the 1920s and 1930s, including the activity of such organizations as the rescue missions and the Salvation Army, and of such individuals as John Roach Straton and Russell H. Conwell.[24] Bryan, himself, possessed a highly developed sense of social Christianity.

But these examples aside, the majority of evangelicals appeared to forget their own heritage of social concern and ministry in this period. Evangelical Christians in other eras previous to the twentieth century had been extremely active in the social realm. One of the most damaging myths perpetrated by those evangelicals and pseudoevangelicals committed to the status quo is that orthodox Christianity has always been the ally of the establishment. Not so, and current research has demonstrated the incorrectness of this position. It has been only in the twentieth century, and especially after 1925, that large numbers of evangelical Christians have been enslaved by the radical right.[25]

The *"Kulturkampf* of American Protestantism,"* as Richard Hofstadter called it, left an ugly scar on the soul of American evangelical Christianity.[26] The fundamentalist movement which had attracted such a large number of American Protestants now became more a sociological movement than a theological one. As noted before, negativism became its hallmark after its bruising encounter with militant secularism at Dayton. In what was a gradual alienation from its roots, the movement became more doctrinaire, rigid, and cultic, and more preoccupied with its struggle against modernism and the social gospel.

In their search for allies against modernism, many evangelicals made strange bedfellows: big business, right-wing politicians, and super patriots. In many cases the fundamentalists' genuine love of country and fear of communism was used by their new-found friends for their own ends. Sometimes this alliance became shocking and unchristian.[27]

A combination of events now led to what Timothy L. Smith and David O. Moberg have called the "Great Reversal" in the attitude of most evangelicals toward the social dimensions of the gospel. More and more over the years after 1925, it became the habit to separate evangelism from social concern and to emphasize the individual and private at the expense of the corporate and public aspects of Christianity. Consequently and ironically, after dominating numerous aspects of American society and culture in the nineteenth century, evangelical Christians now took on many of the earmarks of an unimportant and despised subculture. Like blacks in America, they were given little notice in history textbooks and they virtually disappeared from the mass media's considerations during the generation following Bryan's death.[28]

The evangelical reaction against social concern and involvement resulted from the experiences of the twenties:

increasing identification of the social gospel with theological liberalism, growing disillusionment with legislative initiative, an expanding alliance with big business and the status quo, and mounting disgust with a hostile press which seemed to ally itself with secularism and the religious left. By 1929 the evangelical image to the outside world—deserved or not—was one of negativism, intolerance, and status quoism in all areas of life.

The Slumbering Giant Finally Reawakes: The Evangelical Social Conscience, 1930–1975

The 1930s were years of economic and spiritual depression for most Americans, a depression which inevitably affected the evangelical churches as well. Most people in the United States in this decade expended their best energies simply trying to meet the problems of daily living with little time to spare for other matters. With the 1940s came World War II when the nation gave its full attention and resources to the fight against fascism. The 1950s found the American people weary of war and the heavy responsibilities of world power. Most, including evangelicals, welcomed the low-key presidency of Dwight Eisenhower and were content to bask in the sunlight of his warm smile and the gigantic postwar economic boom.

These were years when evangelical Christianity institutionalized its suspicion of ecumenism and the social gospel, continued to struggle with modernists for control of several denominations, and made a number of unsuccessful attempts to form broadly based evangelical organizations to stem the twin tides of theological liberalism and moral nihilism. It was also the era when evangelicals were most fully coopted by the forces of the status quo. In addition, it was a period of leadership crisis when the giants of the previous generation disappeared from the scene with only a few men of equal stature to succeed them. Consequently, this generation best fits the perceptive analysis which

200

Edward J. Carnell made in 1959 of the fundamentalist evangelicals in America:

> When the Fundamentalist develops his ethical code, he is somewhat prompted by a quest for status in the cult. Consequently, he defines the *good* life as the *separated* life—separated, that is, from prevailing social mores. Whereas Christ was virtuous because he loved God with all his heart and his neighbor as himself, the Fundamentalist is virtuous because he does not smoke, dance, or play cards. By raising a scrupulous demur over social mores, the Fundamentalist can divert attention from grosser sins—anger, jealously, hatred, gossip, lust, idleness, malice, backbiting, schism, guile, injustice, and every shade of illicit pride.[29]

But there were prophets and pioneers among the evangelicals in this period as well—men and women who insisted that believers ought to do more than attack personal sins and public corruption. These were the individuals who helped pave the way for a resurgence of evangelical social concern and ministry in America after 1960. Most of their influence was exercised through literature, the teaching ministry, and a few key organizations.

Prominent among these were T. B. Maston[30] and J. B. Weatherspoon,[31] whose prolonged and vigorous efforts in writing and teaching were rewarded in 1954 when the Southern Baptist Convention voted overwhelmingly, despite grassroots opposition, to support the Supreme Court's decision ordering the racial integration of schools. Richard Caemmerer,[32] among the Missouri Synod Lutherans, stands out as an early prophet for social justice, too, as does Carl Henry, whose book *The Uneasy Conscience of Modern Fundamentalism,*[33] exploded in the fields of evangelical thought in 1947 like a bombshell. Henry's concern for a new reformation in evangelical social attitudes was soon hastened by his appointment as the editor of the journal, *Christianity Today*. From that position he continued to prod evangelical Christians on social issues as he made

Christianity Today the most formative influence on social ethics in the evangelical world.

In 1947 evangelicals also started World Vision International, an organization dedicated to childcare, social ministry, and medical missions in Asia. Also in this period, the National Association of Evangelicals, founded in 1942, became much more conscious of social dimensions of the Gospel. During the 1950s, Henry and others organized a commission on evangelical social action in the NAE, and it held a number of important panel discussions on race, economics, and social justice. Many NAE leaders called for the application of Christianity to every aspect of life, including the social.[34]

By 1960 there were definite signs of a genuine revival of the evangelical social conscience in America. But there was also widespread opposition to any such development from hardcore fundamentalists and their right-wing allies.[35] It remained to be seen what the next decade would bring: a resurgence or a relapse of evangelical social concern?

In 1960 Harold J. Ockenga, writing in *Christianity Today* ("Resurgent Evangelical Leadership"), felt the pulse of American Christendom and correctly observed that, after a period of eclipse, the evangelical star was once again near ascendancy as the country poised on the brink of an evangelical revival. Also with accuracy, Ockenga pointed out that in its vanguard was a new generation of evangelical leaders who were interested in making Christianity the mainspring of social reform as well as the means of personal regeneration for millions of Americans. And finally, Ockenga noted that the new evangelicals of 1960, even as they sensed that the wave of the religious future in America was with them, were still groping for a plan of action.

Events following 1960 validated Ockenga's prognosis of the religious climate, and more. There was a steady buildup of evangelical interest in the social aspects of the gospel throughout the 1960s which carried over into the

1970s. Much of this was based on work begun in the preceding 20 years by the precursors of the present resurgence and upon the ongoing work of older evangelical organizations and groups, like the rescue missions and the Salvation Army.

David Moberg, for example, in his *The Great Reversal* cites a number of recent developments in the evangelical community which are helping to reverse the Great Reversal. These include both an increasing crescendo of voices calling for social action and a number of new evangelical social ministries which are attempting to implement biblical principles by linking social action with evangelism.[36] But beyond this there are a number of less publicized evangelical efforts in the field of social ministry: the new Bread for the World organization based in New York City and spearheaded by Missouri Synod Lutheran pastor Arthur Simon; the multifaceted program of the Lutheran Human Relations Association of America with headquarters in Valparaiso, Indiana; and, the work of the Christian Life Commission of the Texas Baptist Convention and its daughter agency, Texas Baptist Urban Strategy Council.[37]

At the interdenominational level, World Vision International under the direction of W. Stanley Mooneyham provides a model of evangelical cooperation in the realm of social ministry. WVI cares for more than 51,000 homeless children in Asia. Most impressive, the work of WVI is enthusiastically supported by evangelicals of such diverse political viewpoints as Mark Hatfield, W. Maxey Jarman, John B. Anderson, and Art Linkletter.[38]

Locally, an increasing number of evangelical congregations have inaugurated programs of social ministry. One of the first among Missouri Synod Lutherans was the Immanuel Lutheran Church in Chicago where Ralph L. Moellering was pastor from 1953 to 1958. Moellering and his congregation made extensive and fairly successful efforts to minister to the needs of the inner city and to a multiracial constituency. Other Missouri Synod Lutheran churches currently involved in vigorous programs of community social ministry include St. John the Evangelist in Brooklyn, Cross Lutheran in Milwaukee, and the Church of the Redeemer in St. Paul, Minnesota.[39]

The Christian Life Commission of the Southern Baptist Convention, since 1960 under the able leadership of Foy Valentine, has stimulated the initiation of social programs in many Southern Baptist churches and associations. By 1974 several hundred local congregations had initiated social ministries. Some of the best examples of this are the First Baptist Church, the Trinity Baptist Church, and the Temple Baptist Church, all of San Antonio, Texas; the First Baptist Church, Decatur, Georgia; the South Main Baptist Church, Houston, Texas; and the Wieuca Baptist Church, Atlanta, Georgia. Numerous Baptist associations have moved in the direction of social involvement including the Baptist Association of Louisville, Kentucky; and the Union Baptist Association, the Tarrant Baptist Association, and the Dallas Baptist Association, all of Texas.[40]

This blossoming of social ministries at the local level gives credence to several recent important pronouncements of social concern adopted by various evangelical bodies. In the case of the Missouri Synod Lutherans, it was the "Affirmation of God's Mission" approved at the Synod's annual meeting in Detroit in 1965. For Southern Baptists their 1968 "Statement Concerning the Crisis of Our Nation" was a key document in which they confessed past failures in dealing with social issues and pledged to bring biblical principles to bear on national problems in the future. Two important interdenominational gatherings which gave escalating expression to renewed evangelical social concern were the Wheaton Declaration of the Congress on the Church's Worldwide Mission in April, 1966, and the United States Congress on Evangelism held in Minneapolis, Minnesota, in September, 1969.[41]

But the climax to growing evangelical social concern came with the Thanksgiving Workshop on Evangelical

Social Concern held in Chicago in November, 1973, and the Declaration of Evangelical Social Concern subsequently issued by its participants. Taken in context and remembering how difficult it has been in the past to secure agreement among evangelicals on controversial issues, the promulgation of the Declaration was nothing short of a miracle. In brief, the 473-word social action statement made clear the evangelical faith of the signers, confessed past sins, emphasized that God requires both love and justice, pointed out that the Christian life demands total discipleship, and proclaimed: "So we call our fellow evangelical Christians to demonstrate repentance in a Christian discipleship that confronts the social and political injustice of our nation." [42] The only question that remains is: For how many of the country's more than 40 million evangelicals did the 45 original signers speak?

The giant who slept during the years of painful schism and reorientation in evangelical faith has now reawakened. The new social emphasis which is appearing is not, however, really new. It may seem novel and innovative following the period of its relative absence from 1930 to 1960 but the truth of the matter is that this relative absence was the novelty and innovation. An evangelical faith which is whole is what is normative, and it is this which characterized many evangelicals during the nineteenth century. The last fifteen years, therefore, can be seen best as a return to normality after a period of aberration. The reappearance of evangelical social concern is a "dusting off of the heritage." [43] It involves, therefore, a return to a faith that is more biblical, authentic, and true to itself. And what has been gained is not merely a social element but also a faith once again confident enough to sustain a social conscience.

Notes

1. A theological definition of "evangelicals" is discussed elsewhere in this book. I am well aware of the continuing debate over

the exact meaning of terms like "evangelical" and "fundamentalist," that honest men differ on this matter, and that some would like to drop the use of the term "evangelical" altogether. My own working definition is biblically based and includes all Christians who regard a return to the gospel documents as essential to the faith. Thus evangelicals are those who accept biblical authority, the saviorhood and lordship of Jesus Christ, and the necessity of spiritual regeneration as the very essence of Christianity. In this essay I have excluded theological liberals who have departed from historic biblical Christianity on the one hand and ultrafundamentalists who have remained "unspotted" by the world—in both senses of that word—on the other. It seems to me to be necessary to do this in order to make my discussion meaningful and coherent. Finally I regret that most of my essay must of necessity center upon the activities of white evangelicals in the United States because until very recently both Christian and non-Christian scholars have neglected the story of the development of nonwhite American evangelicals. Robert T. Handy, "Fundamentalism and Modernism in Perspective," *Religion in Life* XXIV (Summer, 1955), pp. 381-394; Harold J. Ockenga, "Resurgent Evangelical Leadership," *Christianity Today* (Oct. 10, 1960), pp. 11-14; and William G. McLoughlin, Jr., ed., *The American Evangelicals, 1800-1900* (New York: Harper & Row, 1968), pp. 5-6.

2. Carl F. H. Henry, "Evangelical Social Concern," *Christianity Today* (March 1, 1974), pp. 99-100, and "Revolt on Evangelical Frontiers," *Christianity Today* (April 26, 1974), pp. 4-8; "The New Evangelicals," *Newsweek* (May 6, 1974), p. 86; Michael McIntyre, "Religionists on the Campaign Trail," *Christian Century* (Dec. 27, 1972), pp. 1319-22; "Evangelical Protestants Turn Political," *Washington Post* (Dec. 28, 1973). p. C13; and Richard Quebedeaux, *The Young Evangelicals* (New York: Harper & Row, 1974).

3. William G. McLoughlin, Jr., "Is There a Third Force in Christendom?" *Daedalus* (Winter, 1967), p. 61.

4. Gilman M. Ostrander, *A Profile History of the United State:* (New York: McGraw-Hill Book Co., 1972), p. 327.

5. "Conditions for World Evangelism," *The Times* (May 13, 1974), p. 18.

6. When I speak of evangelical Christian social concern, action, and ministry I do not mean to equate these terms with the social gospel of theological liberalism. Although the social gospel movement had evangelical roots, during the 1920s it was coopted by the theological liberals and thus became anathema to most evangelicals. By social concern, I mean a general interest in society's problems, especially those relating to biblical commandments dealing with human relations and social issues. By social action, I mean organized effort at any level—personal, nonpolitical, and political —which seeks to change social and economic conditions to con-

form more closely to principles laid down in the Bible. By social ministry, I mean the specific efforts of Christians—individually and collectively—to help those individuals harmed by adverse social conditions. Social action is more concerned with the causes of harmful social conditions; social ministry is more concerned with their effects. For further discussion of this subject, see William M. Pinson, Jr.'s, excellent books *The Local Church in Ministry* (Nashville: Broadman Press, 1973); and, *A Program of Application for a Local Church* (Nashville: Christian Life Commission, 1974).

7. William E. Leuchtenberg, *The Perils of Prosperity* (Chicago: University of Chicago Press, 1958), pp. 1-11.

8. Willa Cather, *Not Under Forty* (London: Cassell, 1936), p. v.

9. Sydney E. Ahlstrom, *A Religious History of the American People* (New Haven: Yale University Press, 1972), p. 896.

10. Leuchtenberg, *The Perils of Prosperity*, p. 8. Frederick L. Allen, *Only Yesterday* (New York: Harper & Brothers, 1931), pp. 196-97; and, Willard B. Gatewood, Jr., *Controversy in the Twenties: Fundamentalism, Modernism, and Evolution* (Nashville: Vanderbilt University Press, 1969), pp. 7, 12.

11. Leuchtenberg, *The Perils of Prosperity*, pp. 10-11, 120-39; and Richard V. Pierard, *The Unequal Yoke* (Philadelphia: J. B. Lippincott Co., 1970).

12. Leuchtenberg, *The Perils of Prosperity*, pp. 1-11.

13. Allen, *Only Yesterday*, pp. 196-99; and David O. Moberg, *The Great Reversal: Evangelism Versus Social Concern* (Philadelphia: J. B. Lippincott Co., 1972), pp. 14-15, 37.

14. Ahlstrom, *A Religious History of the American People*, pp. 895-917; and James D. Hart, "Platitudes of Piety: Religion and the Popular Modern Novel," *American Quarterly*, VI (Winter, 1954), 315-16.

15. Gatewood, *Controversy in the Twenties*, pp. 24-25; and Paolo E. Coletta, *William Jennings Bryan* (Lincoln, Neb.: University of Nebraska Press, 1964-69), III, 270-74.

16. The history of the conflict between fundamentalism and modernism in the 1920s is an intricate chronicle, a detailed study of which is not the purpose of this essay. Most accounts of fundamentalism in general and of the movement in this period in particular are too simplistic or too inconclusive to be of much help. In my judgment the most sensitive analyses of fundamentalism in this context are the following: Robert T. Handy, "Fundamentalism and Modernism in Perspective," *Religion in Life* (Summer, 1955), pp. 381-94; Handy, "The American Religious Depression, 1925-1935," *Church History* (March, 1960), pp. 3-16; and Paul A. Carter, *The Decline and Revival of the Social Gospel: Social and Political Liberalism in American Protestant Churches, 1920-1940* (Ithaca, N.Y.: Cornell University Press, 1954). Also helpful are Louis Gaspar, *The Fundamentalist Movement* (The Hague: Mouton, 1963), especially for the years following 1931; and George W.

Dollar, *A History of Fundamentalism in America* (Greenville, S.C.: Bob Jones University Press, 1973), a work which is not particularly objective but which provides valuable insights into the movement by an insider.

17. David F. Brod, "The Scopes Trial: A Look at Press Coverage After Forty Years," *Journalism Quarterly* (Spring, 1965), pp. 219-26.

18. The Scopes Trial dominated the front page of the *New York Times* from July 9, to July 22, 1925. See especially the editorials of July 19, p. 16; July 13, p. 16; July 21, p. 20; and, July 22, p. 18. Also see Joseph W. Krutch, *More Lives Than One* (New York: William Sloane, 1962), pp. 143-61. The stereotype of Bryan and the fundamentalists as vicious and bigoted hypocrites was further perpetrated by a popular Broadway play of the 1950s which was made into a movie in 1960: *Inherit the Wind*. The play and movie make Bryan out to be an ignorant fanatic and Darrow a showcase liberal, neither caricature supported by the facts. Jerome Lawrence and Robert E. Lee, *Inherit the Wind* (New York: Samuel French, 1955).

19. For a further discussion of this development and its implications for evangelical Christianity, see Edward J. Carnell, *The Case for Orthodoxy* (Philadelphia: The Westminster Press, 1959), pp. 113-26.

20. Timothy L. Smith, *Revivalism and Social Reform in Mid-Nineteenth- Century America* (Nashville: Abingdon Press, 1957); and Norris A. Magnuson, "Salvation in the Slums: Evangelical Social Welfare Work, 1865-1920" (unpublished Ph.d. dissertation, University of Minnesota, 1968).

21. Carroll E. Harrington, "The Fundamentalist Movement in America, 1870-1921" (unpublished Ph.D. dissertation, University of California, Berkeley, 1959); George H. Betts, *The Beliefs of 700 Ministers* (Nashville: Cokesbury Press, 1929); and Robert T. Handy, "The Protestant Quest For a Christian America," *Church History* (March, 1953), pp. 8-12.

22. W. B. Riley, "The Great Commission," in *God Hath Spoken,* 25 addresses delivered at the World Conference on Christian Fundamentals, Philadelphia, Pa., May 25-June 1, 1910. (Philadelphia: Bible Conference Committee, 1919), pp. 427-43.

23. Carter, *The Decline and Revival of the Social Gospel;* and Robert M. Miller, *American Protestantism and Social Issues, 1919-1939* (Chapel Hill: University of North Carolina Press, 1958).

24. For example, see Frederick L. Coutts, *The Better Fight: A History of the Salvation Army* (London: Hodder & Stoughton, 1947-1973), VI, covers 1914-1946; Hillyer H. Straton, "John Roach Straton: Prophet of Social Righteousness," *Foundations* (Jan., 1962), pp. 17-38; and Clyde K. Nelson, "Russell H. Conwell and the 'Gospel of Wealth,'" *Foundations* (Jan., 1962), pp. 39-51.

25. Pierard, *The Unequal Yoke*. The material for this discussion is taken primarily from Smith, *Revivalism and Social Reform;*

Magnuson, "Salvation in the Slums;" Carter, *The Decline and Revival of the Social Gospel;* Earle B. Cairns, *Saints and Society* (rev. ed., Chicago: Moody Press, 1973); and Charles I. Foster, *An Errand of Mercy* (Chapel Hill: University of North Carolina Press, 1960).

26. Richard Hofstadter, *Anti-Intellectualism in American Life* (New York: Alfred A. Knopf, 1963), p. 123.

27. This aspect of evangelical Christian history is often over-emphasized, especially by critics. However, even politically conservative evangelicals today are startled by the crudeness of a work like Bruce Barton's *The Man Nobody Knows: A Discovery of the Real Jesus* (Indianapolis: Bobbs-Merrill, 1925), which made Jesus out to be a capitalist and the founder of modern salesmanship and advertising. Barton's book was a bestseller in the late twenties.

28. Moberg, *The Great Reversal: Evangelism Versus Social Concern,* p. 11.

29. Carnell, *The Case for Orthodoxy,* p. 120.

30. Vance C. Kirkpatrick, "The Ethical Thought of T. B. Maston," (unpublished Th.D. dissertation, Southwestern Baptist Theological Seminary, 1972). See T. B. Maston to R. D. Linder, Nov. 28, 1973, p. 1; Foy D. Valentine to R. D. Linder, Nov. 29, 1973, pp. 1-2; William M. Pinson, Jr., to R. D. Linder, Dec. 13, 1973, p. 4; and the following books by Maston: *Of One* (Atlanta: Home Mission Board, 1946); *The Christian in the Modern World* (Nashville: Broadman Press, 1952); *Right or Wrong?* (Nashville: Broadman Press, 1955); *Bible and Race* (Nashville: Broadman Press, 1959); and, *Christianity and World Issues* (New York: The Macmillan Co., 1957).

31. J. B. Weatherspoon, "Ethical Note in Preaching," *Review and Expositor* (Oct., 1930, pp. 392-406. See also C. Welton Gaddy, "The Christian Life Commission of the Southern Baptist Convention: A Critical Evaluation," (unpublished ThD dissertation, Southern Baptist Theological Seminary, 1970); *Annual of the Southern Baptist Convention* (Nashville: SBC, 1954), pp. 56, 403-4; and, Roy Jones to R. D. Linder, March 1, 1974, p. 1. Jones, a student at Southern Baptist Seminary, is currently writing a ThD dissertation on Weatherspoon.

32. Richard Caemmerer, "Lutheran Social Action," Thirty-Seventh Annual Convention of the Associated Lutheran Charities, 1938, pp. 48-54. See also his *The Church In The World* (St. Louis: Concordia Publishing House, 1949). For other examples of Missouri Synod leaders who worked for social concern in this period, see F. Dean Lueking, *A Century of Caring: The Welfare Ministry Among Missouri Synod Lutherans, 1868-1968* (St. Louis: The Board of Social Ministry, LCMS, 1968).

33. Carl Henry, *The Uneasy Conscience of Modern Fundamentalism,* (Grand Rapids: Eerdmans Publishing Co., 1947).

34. James DeForest Murch, *Cooperation Without Compromise*

(Grand Rapids: Eerdmans Publishing Co., 1956); and, Harold J. Ockenga, "Resurgent Evangelical Leadership," pp. 11-15.

35. John L. Eighmy, *Churches in Cultural Captivity* (Knoxville: University of Tennessee Press, 1972), pp. 179-99; and Dollar, *A History of Fundamentalism*, pp. 204-6.

36. Moberg, *The Great Reversal*, pp. 150-79.

37. See "Bread For the World" *Newsletter*, (July, 1973–Feb., 1974); Arthur Simon, *Faces of Poverty* (St. Louis: Concordia Publishing House, 1966); Thomas Coates, *The Lutheran Human Relations Association of America: A Historical Summary* (Valparaiso: LHRA, n.d.); and, "Baptists in Texas Take to Lobbying," *The New York Times* (Aug. 26, 1973), sec. L, p. 48.

38. World Vision International *Newsletter*, 1974, p. 4.

39. Martin E. Marty, "Renewal in the Inner City" *Christian Century*, (Dec. 5, 1956), pp. 1417-1420; and, Ralph L. Moellering to R. D. Linder, March 16, 1974, p. 1.

40. For further details, see the entire issue of *Home Missions*, (Oct., 1973).

41. *Proceedings of the 46th Regular Convention of the Lutheran Church—Missouri Synod*, Detroit, Michigan, June 16-26, 1965, pp. 165-72, and addenda "Affirmation of God's Mission;" *Annual of the Southern Baptist Convention* (Nashville: SBC, 1958), pp. 67-69; *The Wheaton Declaration*, Congress on the Church's Worldwide Mission, April 9-16, 1966, Wheaton, Illinois, pp. 23-24; and, "Much Given—Much Required," *Christianity Today* (Sept. 26, 1969), pp. 40-41.

42. For the text of the Declaration and an Analysis of this historic gathering, see Ronald J. Sider, ed., *The Chicago Declaration* (Carol Stream, Ill.: Creation House, 1974).

43. George Marsden, "Evangelical Social Concern—Dusting Off the Heritage," *Christianity Today* (May 12, 1972), pp. 8-11.

Evangelicals: Society, the State, the Nation (1925–75)

George H. Williams and Rodney L. Petersen

Introduction

Evangelicalism, generally defined in this volume as that broad ellipse of Protestant Christianity, of which the two foci are the all-sufficiency of the Bible as God's word unto salvation and such salvation received as by faith alone, allowed already in the classical period of Protestantism for quite disparate views towards the state. Luther, for example, held to a doctrine of the Two (profoundly separated) Kingdoms, united, however, to a practical extent in his other doctrine of the priesthood of all believers and the various vocations in the world. Calvin established a biblical theocracy in Geneva. Cranmer obsequiously implemented almost every whim of national Catholic Henry VIII and yet in the end held steadfast to his national Protestant convictions in a self-deprecatory martyrdom at the hands of Catholic Mary. And not to be overlooked is the radically separationist, often eschatologically oriented church-state viewpoint of various groupings within the Radical Reformation, of whom the Mennonites (and *mutatis mutandis* the Baptists) are the present-day American descendants.

Given this diversity of belief, it should not be surprising that American evangelicals, heirs of the Reformation and subsequent developments, have assumed differing attitudes

George H. Williams is Hollis Professor of Divinity at Harvard Divinity School. Rodney L. Petersen is on the staff of Intervarsity Christian Fellowship.

towards the state in the United States in the period from 1925 to 1975.

In the following discussion of the evangelical attitude toward the state we have in mind those persons and groups and that thrust in Protestantism on the conservative side in the succession of controversies or alignments of our period, 1925–1975 (or during the antecedent fifty years): Progressive (Social Gospel)—conservative; modernist—fundamentalist; the Federal (1908) National (1950) Council of Churches and the National Association of Evangelicals (1940-42). It will not be overlooked that there have been also extreme fundamentalists and groupings further to the theological and the political right than the National Association of Evangelicals.[1]

There are three introductory generalizations about Evangelicals and the state. It makes a great deal of difference whether the persons or groupings under consideration stress the evangels and the apostolic writings of the New Covenant, or whether, like Calvin (and Luther), they understand the Bible as the setting forth of a single covenant of the elect. Clearly the Old Testament has both a larger place than the New for the state (the judges and the kings of Israel and Judah) and also a greater place for the prophetic criticism of the God-ordained state (the king, the Lord's anointed) by a God-summoned Nathan or Amos.

By the end of the nineteenth century there had developed, largely unarticulated, a common view of the American Federal Republic as constitutive of a "sifted" people with a special mission among the nations. Although the Republic was clearly a secular covenant with a Constitution grounded in the separation of church and state, there had developed first among the Protestants a feeling for what would eventually be called the "American Way of Life." However long the phrase had been in use prior to Franklin D. Roosevelt's elevation of it to a slogan (1936), it is indeed distinctive in suggesting not only the American political and economic system, but also the American experience of fair play, upward mobility, and cultural pluralism, and finally a distinctive American mission among the nations (in the nineteenth century more often referred to as American Manifest Destiny).

The "American Way of Life" also connotates a special feeling for the Federal government of limited powers all backed by the great national covenant: the Constitution. The fact that immigrants and natives are frequently called upon to pledge allegiance (1892) to that Constitution and to the flag, symbolic of the nation, enhances the religio-political connotation of the "American Way of Life," the more so for the reason that about midway in our period, namely in 1954, the phrase "under God" was inserted into the Pledge by a House joint resolution. The important point for our fifty-year survey is that in an ever-enlarging consensus, which first included only evangelicals, then all Protestants, then Catholics, and finally the "three [established] religious communities" (as defined by Will Herberg, *Protestant-Catholic-Jew, 1955*), there is embedded in the concept of the American Way of Life, a kind of civil religion and a special feeling for the American state and nation and the presidency, even though there might be a wide divergence of conviction as to what constitutes that "true" Americanism. And more important still, in the aftermath of World War I, during which almost all "preachers (and priests and rabbis) presented arms" (cf. the book of similar title, 1933),[2] modernist/liberals and fundamentalists/evangelicals have not essentially disagreed about the American state as having a special place in their theology of history or theodicy if not in their systematic theology.[3]

However, it should be added, as a third introductory generalization, that a number of sectarian groups and then, in the fractured and breakaway denominations consequent upon the fundamentalists/modernist controversy, an increasing number of fundamentalists/evangelicals, when adopting premillenarian views, could never wholly again

213

identify the American state and nation with the emergent Kingdom of God—a motif in the earlier social gospel and even of earlier American evangelicalism (cf. Lyman Beecher). Thus within fundamentalism/evangelicalism millenarianism and the general stress on the Second Advent among the fundamentals tended to create a paradoxical strain in evangelical attitudes towards even the American state: both extreme, even militaristic nationalism and individualistic indifference to public life in anticipation of imminent catastrophe.[4]

With these initial observations we shall now attempt to clarify the church-state and related issues partly in terms of a succession of major figures whom all readers, within and without evangelical Protestantism, would recognize as representative embodiments of that community within Protestantism central to this volume. These figures are sufficiently eminent to provide the clues and pointers to what appears, in fact, to be a shift of stance among evangelicals toward the state, from a nearly uncritical identification of evangelical Protestantism with "true" Americanism in 1925 to a more critical view, as the nation approaches the bicentennial of the Republic.

William Jennings Bryan: The End of an Era 1925-29

Under the presidency of Calvin Coolidge (1923-29), amid fears that the American way of life would soon be lost in the face of perceived moral disintegration or radical influence from abroad, Fundamentalism emerged as a distinctive, organized force dividing itself from mainstream liberal-conservative Protestantism, although both wings of Protestantism (except for the Episcopalians and Lutherans) as recently as 1920 had jointly brought about the Nineteenth Amendment on Prohibition. No figure better embodies this initial phase of our period and so well illustrates the complexity of Christian and national concerns than the "Great Commoner," William Jennings Bryan (1860-

214

1925),[5] who suddenly regained national prominence as the antievolutionist lawyer pitched against benign atheist Clarence Darrow in the Scopes Trial. Bryan, who had written *In His Image* (1922) and other pieces on religion and nation, had stirred the hopes of fundamentalists by appearing in 1924 at the Minneapolis convention of the World's Christian Fundamentals Association (formed at the Moody Bible Institute in Chicago, 1919).

Bryan represented the end of a long line of evangelicals who maintained a theologically conservative stance still allied to a social gospel with hopes for legislative implementation. A Jeffersonian democrat and a spokesman for the populist protest against the drift of federal, state, and municipal government from the popular will, Bryan viewed social problems as essentially moral problems. Yet the Jeffersonian motto which he often quoted, "Equal rights to all and special privileges to none," summarized a social policy which transcended a narrow concern with prohibition that formed so singularly the legislative preoccupation of most other contemporary fundamentalists/evangelicals.

When, after the Scopes Trial, he was asked by the Chicago *Tribune* how he could hold such seemingly disparate points of view on politics and religion, he responded: "People often ask me why I can be a progressive in politics and a fundamentalist in religion. The answer is easy. Government is man-made and therefore imperfect. . . . If Christ is the final word, how may anyone be progressive in religion? I am satisfied with the God we have, with the Bible and with Christ." [6] Bryan might not have been aware that in this statement he was wholly in accord with *The Fundamentals,* one of which, written by Professor Charles Erdman of Princeton, "The Church and Socialism," [7] recognized that an evangelical could be a socialist, that Christianity was tied to no particular system—a breadth of social view that would now be much narrowed in fundamentalist/evangelical circles well into the sixties.

215

Bryan had a conception of the Republic that he once expressed thus: "A man can be born again; the springs of life can be cleansed instantly . . . if this is true of one, it can be true of any number. Thus, a nation can be born in a day [Isaiah 66:8] if the ideals of the people can be changed." He also believed that the American civilization was "time's noblest off-spring." [8]

Bryan was the populist hero for most issues which have been clarified by subsequent historians as the conflicting agrarian-urban values of his era. Not to be placed in the agrarian-urban context was Bryan's failure, alas, to include Negroes in his evangelical or democratic embrace. Yet Bryan had advocated "a regulated individualism" which would maintain and restore true economic competition, arguing that such quasisocialistic measures as municipal ownership of utilities, government ownership of railroad, telegraph, and telepgraph companies, government guarantee of bank deposits, and a system of old-age pensions would, in fact, stop the spread of political socialism and protect the essentials of the American way of life. Bryan's interest in the peaceful settlement of international affairs, an issue advocated by many social gospelers, had been underscored by his resignation as Secretary of State in 1915. When Wilson's policy seemed to risk war with the Central Powers Bryan had hoped this act would rally the country to the cause of peace in isolation from Europe's agony. Bryan continued to make suggestions for world peace during the last years of his life, and he vigorously supported the League of Nations, saying it was "the greatest step towards peace in a thousand years." But by 1925 his interests increasingly centered upon the advocacy of prohibition and evangelical orthodoxy.

Although Bryan was the best known figure of our period who combined a commitment to evangelical faith and to the social reforms implemented through political means, he was not alone in his concerns. Dr. John Roach Straton, Baptist pastor of New York's Calvary Church from 1918 until his death in 1929, commonly called "the Pope of Fundamentalism," attempted to bring about municipal reform and economic and social equality for all men and women.[9] He continued into our period to attack Tammany Hall with an impressive coalition of evangelical forces, urging amelioration of slum conditions and also municipal censorship of stage and entertainment in New York City (*Shame of the Cities,* 1904, directed against party machines; *The Menace of Immorality in Church and State,* 1920; and *Church Against State,* 1921). Precisely in our opening year, 1925, Straton published *The Gospel at the Heart of the Metropolis.*

Both mainline and fundamentalist successors of nineteenth-century evangelicalism in their separate ways followed the example of Bryan and Straton and developed organizations to press for legislation against unbridled thought and undesirable practices which were felt to be detrimental to national life and purpose. The fostering of prohibition and antievolution teaching were two rallying points for most evangelicals, two symbolic issues of great emotional scope and intensity, which had also the advantage in terms of support from big business so they constituted no threat to the basic economic structure. A plethora of fundamentalist groups grew up to help turn the current in America, as well as scores of tiny charismatic sects. But it should be pointed out that some groups specialized only in revivalist preaching. E. Howard Cadle in Indianapolis and the Pentecostalist Aimee Semple McPherson viewed any social action other than soul winning as basically a waste of time as they established their first tabernacles in 1927. Other fundamentalists, such as the Defenders of the Christian Faith under the leadership of Gerald Winrod of Kansas, discredited the theologically conservative movement through their open fascist teachings (cf. Buzz Windrip in Sinclair Lewis' *Elmer Gantry,* 1929). The new Ku Klux Klan, 1915, but especially active from 1920 to 1928, enjoyed evangelical support and participation, as did

Edgar Young Clark's Supreme Kingdom founded in Georgia.

From the Stock Market Crash to the Beginning of World War II
1929-39: "The Last Years" of Billy Sunday

Billy Sunday (1863-1936), the baseball player ordained Presbyterian minister, a major evangelical revivalist in the line of Moody, was roughly a contemporary of Bryan, featured in the previous period, and he might well therefore have already drawn our attention.[10] But Sunday, at least, lived a decade further into the twentieth century than Bryan. Precisely in this final phase of his career, he was pushed to the margins of mainstream Protestantism. Though once recognized in a poll sponsored by *The American Magazine* as one of the greatest Americans of his day, Sunday represented the tone and stance of evangelicalism, as it had become ever more intensely fundamentalist in its self-conscious and programmatic dissociation from the mainline Protestant denominations in the course of numerous and rancorous schisms.

Sunday had absorbed the premillenarian eschatology of John Darby (d. 1882) as modified by former lawyer and Congregationalist minister Cyrus I. Scofield (d. 1921), who annotated the Scofield Reference Bible (1910) widely used in fundamentalist circles. The relevance of this eschatology in interpreting a widespread evangelical view of the state is that it anticipated the rapture of the elect (I Thess. 4:13-17), the collapse of the world order (Matt. 24:21), the emergence of a world ruler/dictator who would arrogate to himself the honor due to Christ (Rev. 13:1, 2), whereupon—after a fleeting period of world peace (3 1/2 years shown in Rev. 13:5)—a world conflagration would set in (Rev. 16:19) to be followed by the Second Coming of Christ (Rev. 20:4-6, Point V of the essential fundamentals).[11]

218

Yet with fears for the world order, Billy Sunday loved his country chauvinistically in the nineteenth-century tradition.[12] He offered the following solution for America's postwar ills: "If I had my way with these ornery wild-eyed socialists and IWW's [International Workers of the World], I would stand them up before a firing squad and save space on our ships [deportation had been suggested]." [13]

Conversion, despite the stress on a personal faith commitment to Jesus Christ, for Sunday also meant everything from patriotism to prohibition. Revivalistic conversion was the guarantee of heaven and of success both in the American economy and the American way of life. His appeal for conformity in belief and acceptance of the status quo was significant in the precedent it set for defining what a true American was to believe and how such a one was to act.[14] The uncritical acceptance of nineteenth-century *laissez-faire* capitalism on the part of so many conservative and fundamentalist evangelicals led some of the more socially minded heirs of nineteenth-century evangelicalism in the direction of an American form of Christian socialism.[15]

The Stockmarket crash of 1929 with its worldwide repercussions shattered the confidence of mainline Protestants, evangelicals, Catholics, and all other citizens in the American way; but of these groups the evangelicals were least affected theologically, even though this same grouping may well have suffered the most in terms of personal hardship because of their relatively more exposed position sociologically and economically; and this was because they had already developed a rather pessimistic, often premillenialist view of history, despite its incongruity with their uncritical Americanism.[16] In any case the crash left no traumatic indentation in the steady line of ascent of evangelicalism, while it was a major blow in terms of theology and theodicy for the mainline progressivist Protestants. About this time the term "modernist" slips away from the Protestant vocabulary. Therefore the crash tended to make mainline Protestants look more and more to the federal government for succor, while the fundamentalists/evangelicals turned more to the states, reemphasized self-reliance, and many prayed for an immediate Second Advent.

Nevertheless, according to Sunday and other fundamentalists, the fate of a secure world was still seen to hinge on how Americans behaved morally. Loyalty to the American system and values was increasingly called for. By "loyalty" Sunday meant adherence to the Republican party and its platform, called "the party of grand moral ideas." [17] Communists and "Reds" were seen in the Civil Liberties Union and even in the Democratic Party and the Federal Council of Churches (1908). Bolshevism, evolutionism, and atheism were seen as taking over the schools of the land.

Under Franklin Delano Roosevelt (1933-45), in the prewar period of his four terms as president, prohibition was repealed and an extensive federal program of public works and social welfare was instituted under the slogan "New Deal," in part challenged by the Supreme Court. The economy and the ominous success of Hitler became the major preoccupations of the nation. Evangelicals seemed to become politically reactionary and even cryptofascist and sometimes anti-Semitic[18] in an attempt to defend the Christian faith and American way of life. Many were even supportive of the strident, anti-Semitic Father Charles E. Coughlin of Detroit, founder of the Union of Social Justice and its associated radio program (1930-42). "America must turn to God to avoid a revolution," Sunday wrote in his "Autobiography" for *Ladies' Home Journal*.[19]

Increasingly pessimistic social views developed in Sunday along with a heightened adventist aura in the Darby-Scofield premillenarian line. One of Sunday's last sermon revisions in 1934 was entitled "The Coming Dictator" (an allusion to Roosevelt as much as to Hitler). Here all faith and hope in the American heritage began to be rejected. The year 1935 was set by him for the end of the world.

Only sweeping revival could possibly save the world. In a quite different social setting the same thing was being said by pietist Keswick—converted Lutheran Frank Buchman and his Oxford movement (1929), leading to Moral Rearmament (1932) and an attempt to convert Hitler.

The Evangelicals and the State at War Under Roosevelt and Truman; and Under Eisenhower 1939/41-61: The American Council, the National Association of Evangelicals; Supreme Court Decisions on Church and State; Billy Graham

Out of several decades of increasing controversy among fundamentalist/evangelicals/holiness groups, new organizations of conservative Protestants emerged in the period surrounding World War II. First came the exclusive American Council of Christian Churches formed in 1941 by Bible Presbyterian Carl McIntire, sometime associate of J. Gresham Machen (of Princeton, then Westminster), but who had since formed his independent seminary, Faith, in Wilmington, Delaware. The association was politically very reactionary and provocatively antiecumenical. McIntire had been putting out the weekly *Christian Beacon* since 1936 and wrote about his Council in *Twentieth Century Reformation* (1944), the title of his radio hour on some five hundred stations.

The National Association of Evangelicals, 1942, a neo-evangelical group, was founded by those dissatisfied with both McIntire's Association and the Federal Council of Churches. Although agreeing with McIntire that a unified counterforce to the Federal Council was needed, many evangelicals desired a less divisive and theologically, as well as politically, more constructive association. While all three of these organizations can be seen as continuing *mutatis mutandis* the Evangelical Alliance of 1846, the National Association of Evangelicals seems to have been most conscious of itself as the authentic American residual

221

heir.[20] The National Association gave almost denominational status to many of the independent fundamentalist/ evangelical and pentecostal/holiness churches—"the third force" in American Christianity, alongside mainline Protestants and Catholics. The phrase "third force in Christendom" (1958) stems from President Henry Pitt Van Dusen of Union Seminary.

Another reason for the founding of the National Association seems to have been as much political as religious. On the one hand there was an increasing tendency on the part of conservative Protestants to distrust the Federal Council, which seemed even more ready to resort to political pressure in Washington in what appeared to many evangelicals to be an outright socialist platform.[21] Indeed, by the founding of the National Association the Federal Council had proven to be theologically or sociopolitically unacceptable to 176 out of some 200 Protestant denominations.[22]

Fear of undue Roman Catholic influence upon federal and state government policies was another motivation of the National Association.[23] Evangelical (indeed Protestant) anxiety with respect to Roman Catholicism was especially evidenced in the reaction to the appointment of Myron C. Taylor (1939) as a personal envoy of Roosevelt and then of President Harry S. Truman (1945-1953) to the Vatican.[24]

Of other major wartime church-state issues we must mention the fact that Christians in general and evangelicals were conspicuously silent or even fully supportive when the government interned on the western seaboard American citizens of Japanese ancestry (Nisei), many of whom (quite incidentally, as far as civil liberties go) were Christians.

Also during the war there were two religiopolitical issues that reached the Supreme Court. The first issue concerned the refusal to salute the flag on the scripturally motivated principle of no oaths, the Gobitis case 1940, which was reversed by the Supreme Court in *West Virginia State*

Board of Education v. Barnett, 1943. The second related to the civil liberty of Jehovah's Witnesses to disseminate religious literature without a license, then their right to solicit funds (upheld 1940), and ending with their not being subject to a special tax *(Murdock v. Pennsylvania,* 1943). Although the Federal Council of Churches took an interest in these religiopolitical civil libertarian adjudications, neither individual evangelicals as such nor evangelical groups, except insofar as Mennonites were beginning to come under this heading, sided with the extreme millenarians and pacifists in the maintenance of the civil liberties of the Witnesses.

After World War II evangelicals were confronted by many developments about which they were none too pleased. Whereas most mainstream Protestants were enthusiastic about the formation of the United Nations in 1945, evangelicals were reluctant to see so close and working relationship with the "second world" of Joseph Stalin, and they were disturbed by UNESCO's penchant towards working for a single world culture which would implicate eclectically all religions in a "universal atheism." [25]

In 1948, Christians, Jews, and all other believers were confronted with a landmark decision of the Supreme Court, *McCollum v. Board of Education,* which struck down the most convenient form of "released-time" religious education, namely that which permitted school pupils on a voluntary basis to receive instruction in religion during regular school hours and on school property with private teachers. In *Zorach v. Clauson,* 1952, the Supreme Court allowed a variant of released-time religious instruction off school property but during school hours. In the agitation, some evangelicals began thinking of a constitutional amendment which would, in effect, prevent "the establishment of secularism" as the pseudoreligion of public education.

When in 1948 the State of Israel was established by the

223

U.N. largely under American leadership, many evangelicals, despite an earlier anti-Semitism, descried in this event the fulfillment of prophecy portending the Second Advent. Fear of atheistic communism and radicalism in the United Nations and around the world was intensified among evangelicals by the "fall" of China (1949) to the communists, the closing of this field to Western missionaries, and the extension of Soviet influence in Eastern Europe. Not only did the National Association of Evangelicals almost every year include a resolution condemning atheistic communism, but evangelical Congressman Walter H. Judd of Minnesota (formerly a congregationalist missionary-physician) spearheaded an effective lobby against the admission of Communist China to the United Nations.[26] The World Evangelical Fellowship (1951) mirrored the dissatisfaction of American evangelicals concerning the political, theological, and ecclesiological position of the National Council of Churches (as of 1950) and the World Council of Churches (1948), thought to be too lenient to communism, Romanism, liberalism, paganism, atheism.[27]

Under the leadership of Dr. Clyde W. Taylor of the National Association, a theology and tactic of evangelical relations with the federal government began to emerge. A permanent Commission on Government Chaplaincies was established as well as other new services and policies headed by Dr. Harold Ockenga. The idea of a dual citizenship was seen by Taylor as the operating principle for evangelicals (Phil. 3:20 and 2:15 were frequently cited). Particular abuses of the principle of separation were seen to persist or reassert themselves in the United States. Adhering in principle to the separationist principle, many evangelicals now sought to relate their confessional views to the state and society at large. Particular dangers considered were the "efforts of the Roman Church to promote Church-State union with the Church dominant." A second abuse in the opinion of the evangelicals was the effort of "agnostics, atheists, and misguided zealots," attempting

224

"to take all religion out of government and public education." Other abuses mentioned were those committed by communists and socialists in the government as well as "government ownership of resources, industry and property which would make U.S. citizens wards of the State." [28]

Relations of the National Association with the federal government improved under Dwight D. Eisenhower (1953-61). President-elect Eisenhower asked Billy Graham to supply him with appropriate scriptural texts in his inaugural in which Eisenhower used the expressly religious term "sin." In July, 1953, a delegation of the Association was received at the White House. The need for moral and religious ideals was seen to underlie American freedoms, and the President affixed his signature to a document which called for "a national reaffirmation of faith in God, the Author of man's freedom, repentance from sin, and a new dedication to the task of bringing freedom to the world." [29] This event is important in that from 1953 on it can be said that evangelicals had outgrown their minority paranoia.[30]

Evangelicals strongly supported the Bricker Amendment to the Constitution (1953) designed to protect American sovereignty in all relations with foreign powers.[31] The Republican Party platform had espoused such an amendment. Later disavowed by President Eisenhower, it failed of passage by a single vote. Evangelicals not only feared "world government" and the United Nations' genocide convention as interference in the internal affairs of the nation but also sought "to protect us from the schemes and subtleties of those who are working for a One World Church." At the same time, many evangelicals found themselves seeking to protect the American way of life through making a common cause with Catholic Senator Joseph McCarthy of Wisconsin,[32] who had abandoned the anti-Semitism of Coughlin and the Klan.

With the founding of *Christianity Today* in Washington, D.C., in 1956, a periodical of fortnightly news and opinion, much of the neoevangelical movement was given a nationally needed news outlet, under the able and foresighted editorship of sometime theology professor Carl F. H. Henry, who as early as 1947 had sounded a new note for Evangelicals, *The Uneasy Conscience of Modern Fundamentalism.*

The new move into a majority-consciousness was furthered through the return to mass revivalism under Southern Baptist Billy Graham.[33] No other figure better embodies the postwar renascence of evangelicalism. Just as the late careers of Bryan and Sunday helped summarize two earlier phases in our period, so the career of Billy Graham can be a focus for the evangelical understanding of the relationship of church and state following World War II.

William Bell Riley, head of the World's Christian Fundamentals Association, had chosen Graham as his successor to the presidency of the Northwestern Schools in Minneapolis. Graham would maintain this position until the burden of his crusades made it impossible for him to function effectively there.[34] Graham, in his assumption of leadership in Minneapolis and through his ever growing crusades, began to be looked upon as the most popular and visible spokesman of the neoevangelical movement, centered in the National Association, and developed theologically and religiopolitically by such thinkers as Henry and Edward John Carnell of Fuller Seminary.

In New York and Boston in 1950, nine weeks before the United Nations and American military action in Korea (1950-53), Graham saw America as a backsliding people like that of the Old Covenant in the days of Isaiah and spoke of "our crusade to bring America to her knees in repentance of sin and faith toward God." [35] In August, President Truman invited him to the White House. This was the first of many such conversations with presidents throughout the remainder of our fifty-year period.

With a five-week crusade in Washington, D.C., in 1952,

226

following an invitation extended to the evangelist by Democratic and Republican senators and representatives, Graham's involvement with high-level political figures became ever more visible. Speaking on the steps of the Capitol, Speaker of the House Sam Rayburn said, "This country needs a revival, and I believe Billy Graham is bringing it to us." The Capitol service, permitted by an unprecedented act of Congress, was carried on radio and television across the nation. During it Graham read Lincoln's 1863 proclamation for a day of humiliation and prayer. In a time of war, social corruption, and unrest he called the nation to "return to God, Bible, and the Church." [36] The Capitol crusade brought Graham into association with Senators Lyndon Johnson and Richard Nixon. He was also asked to run as senator from his home state of North Carolina but declined. That Christmas, 1952, Graham, with a staff like Cardinal Spellman, addressed the troops in Korea. On social and racial issues, evangelicals north and south were much less activist than their liberal counterparts within the older denominations; and none of the fully evangelical or fundamentalist organizations took an early stand on the implicit scriptural principle that in Christ there is neither Jew nor Gentile, black nor white. However, already a year before the landmark Supreme Court decision of May 17, 1954, on desegregation of the races in public schools, Graham began the first deliberate integration of crusades at Chattanooga, Tennessee (although he was temporarily forced to revert to segregated seating in Dallas). Issues of peace, of race, and of other domestic policies were still seen to be resolved only through the transformation of individuals (cf. Graham's *Peace With God)* who could and would therefore exert themselves to bring about social reform. With a strong pointer at personal sin, a skepticism toward all plans and programs which purport to deal with the corporate or governmental amelioration of evil, Graham believed that only

227

the repentant and converted individual could transform the institutions of society.

This conviction was carried abroad by Graham in his crusades in London and Berlin in 1954. In East Berlin the crusade was seen as the spiritual arm of American imperialism. Secretary of State Dulles had been attempting to create a European Defense Community (abbreviated in German as EVG and Graham's activity was referred to as *EVGelismus)*. A cartoon pictured Graham flying over Berlin, Bible and bomb in hand, with Dulles cheering him on.[37]

Breaking into our outline of the first national phase of the evangelically representative career of Billy Graham, we at this point take note of the rise of the John Birch Society, organized in Belmont, Massachusetts, by Robert H. Welch in 1958 in memory of a fundamentalist Baptist missionary who was a captain in the American army and was killed by the Red Chinese shortly before V-J Day. He is identified by Welch, who did not know him personally, as the symbol of the "struggle from which either communism or Christian-style civilization must emerge with one completely triumphant and the other completely destroyed." [38] Birchers, regarding Chief Justice Earl Warren and President Eisenhower as dupes of the communists, gained substantial support among two groupings: recently affluent Eastern and California suburban Republicans and the evangelical or fundamentalist extremist fringe of various economic classes and political antecedents.[39]

Reacting perhaps to the extremism of the American Council and other right-wing fundamentalist groups, Dr. Ockenga, Graham's close ally, stated significantly in 1960: "The Evangelical intends that Christianity will be the mainspring in many of the reforms of the societal order. It is wrong to abdicate responsibility for society under the impetus of a theology which overemphasizes the eschatological." [40]

Evangelicals Under Kennedy and Johnson,
1961-68: Graham, Phase II

The year 1960 brought new challenges to Graham and
to the evangelical forces as well as predictions of Graham's
eclipse in the midst of new sociopolitical problems.[41] Although as a Southern Baptist Graham at first had political
friends mostly among Democrats, ever since he and Richard
Nixon had met in 1953 they were close. Despite continuously guarded attempts to remain neutral in the presidential
campaign between Nixon and Catholic Democrat John Kennedy, many felt Graham to have at least covertly endorsed
Nixon.[42] A good number of evangelicals and Protestants
in general were still profoundly fearful of the election of a
Roman Catholic to the nation's highest office. Extreme
evangelical groups and leaders opposed Kennedy in a
crusading spirit, including Carl McIntire, Bob Jones, and
the cowboy evangelist of the Rockies, Harvey Springer. The
last even boasted that he had a secret weapon which
would defeat Kennedy on election day.[43] Warnings of
sinister events to come even surfaced from the headquarters
of the National Association of Evangelicals and *Christianity
Today*.[44] However, most of the strident anti-Catholic
propaganda came from those politically further to the right
of Graham and the main body of evangelicals. Graham,
himself, was able to avoid excessively close contact with
the supporters of Nixon or with the anti-Catholic evangelical and economico-political rightist propaganda. Kennedy, through the clarity of his pronouncement at the
strategic meeting with Texas Baptist ministers in Houston,
was able to allay most Protestant and, to a large extent,
evangelical fears, on the issue of church and state. Following his narrow victory over Nixon, Kennedy called Graham
to a conference on January 16, 1961, at Palm Beach, and
cordial relations developed between the two men.[45] Graham backed Kennedy in the Cuban missile crisis of 1962
but criticized the Peace Corps as completely "materialistic."

229

Soon the recurrent problematic of religion and the public schools reasserted itself. In 1962, in *Engel v. Vitale,* the Supreme Court, considering a New York State Board of Regents optional prayer for the public schools, held that "it is no part of the business of government to compose official prayers to be recited as part of a religious program"; and in *School District of Arlington Township v. Schempp* in 1963, the Court ruled out in public schools any daily Bible reading (even without comment) and the Lord's Prayer. Although the National Council and most affiliated denominational headquarters favored these decisions, sometimes with briefs *amicus curiae,* most evangelicals felt alarmed. Graham for his part favored a referendum on Bible reading in the public schools.[46]

Relations between Graham and President Johnson were friendly, though at times strained, Johnson (by background of the Churches of Christ) was the first President to attend a Graham crusade, he and Lady Bird being present in the Astrodome in Houston in 1965.[47] As early as 1965 Graham was being called the "Chaplain of the White House." Under Johnson, in reaction to the series of Supreme Court decisions that completely secularized the public schools (from *McCollum* in 1948 to *Schempp* in 1963), agitation was strong among evangelicals for a return to an "older" America, understood to have grown out of Puritan-evangelical principles as further molded in the course of the nineteenth century.

Strong in its own way in the belief in the separation of church and state, the National Association of Evangelicals insisted that the spheres of influence might "overlap but they do not coincide" (1963). It resolved:

> Whereas, the resulting revolutionary changes in long-established practices are beginning to create a moral and religious vacuum in our educational system in which secularism, humanism, practical atheism and amorality are beginning to take root and thrive; thus threatening the very foundations of our society and the welfare of the nation,

Therefore. . . . [six courses of action should be endorsed, among them:] 1. The enactment . . . of an amendment. . . . 2. The affirmation of the public school's duty to do full justice to the large place of the Judeo-Christian tradition in our American heritage. There should be in all areas of subject matter an objective presentation of the contribution made by the Christian faith to the development of that heritage.[48]

Out of this kind of evangelical resolution an amendment would indeed soon be proposed.

Precisely what the association meant by "responsibility for society" was to be a continued cause of consternation for evangelicals who, in large part, were critical of the 1964 Civil Rights legislation begun under Johnson in that it seemed to take responsibility away from individuals and local government and place it in the hands of an ever increasingly omnicompetent federal bureaucracy.[49]

Evangelicals were not on the whole conspicuous in the desegregation of buses and lunch counters and in the freedom marches and demonstrations (Lincoln Monument, 1963; Selma, 1965) for the equalization of blacks. Nonetheless, editors of several major publications commented that Graham, through his integrated evangelistic rally (Birmingham, 1964), left a deep impact in bettering race relations in the South; and he received the George Washingtion Carver Award in June, 1964.

Evangelicals, as largely uncritical heirs of the tradition of a Christian manifest destiny for America, especially as it moved ever westward, even into Asia, were also conspicuously out of sympathy with the university-based resistance to the war in Southeast Asia (1961-1973)—a resistance shared, however, by wide sections of the National Council of Churches and the constituent denominational leadership, and eventually the Catholic hierarchy.

Sympathizing with Barry Goldwater, against whom Johnson ran in 1964, was a whole congery of radical right leaders: Australian Baptist Dr. Frederick C. Schwarz

231

(originally sponsored by McIntire's American Council, who organized the Christian Anti-Communism Crusade; Billy James Hargis of the Churches of Christ, who, based in Tulsa, Oklahoma, published the monthly *Christian Crusade* (and who would be publically endorsed by Governor George L. Wallace in his third-party presidential campaign in 1968); George Washington Robnett, a Chicago advertising agent, later overtaken in leadership by former Air Force officer Edgar C. Bundy, who directed the Church League of America; Meyers C. Lowman of the Circuit Riders of Cincinnati; Gerald L. K. Smith, the successor of Winrod, and many others. Many moderate evangelicals also urged Graham to come out for Goldwater.

It was in the Johnson period that evangelicals, against the contrary persuasion of the National Council of Churches and the Jewish community, found in Dutch Reformed Senator Everett Dirksen the effective advocate for their long besought constitutional amendment that would undo the secularizing Court decisions from *McCollum* (1948) to *Schempp* (1963). Dirksen introduced the resolution in 1966 thus: "I do not intend to let nine men tell 190 million Americans where and when they can say their prayers."

Toward the end of the Johnson administration civil rights for blacks had suffered the recoil of white backlash and black separatism ("Black Power," 1966; "the long hot summer," 1967). Johnson in the face of mounting opposition to the Vietnam War had to give up seeking a second full term.

The Nixon Presidency, 1969–74:
The Increasingly Uneasy Conscience of
Critical Evangelicals; Graham, Phase III

After the close November, 1968, election of Richard Nixon over Vice President Hubert Humphrey with what seemed to be overwhelming evangelical support, criticism again began to develop, especially on the part of those concerned with the stalemate in Vietnam, as to whether evangelicals and Billy Graham were calling for a return to biblical Christianity or the American way of life variously interpreted. That Graham himself had great hopes for the law-and-order administration of Nixon is evident in his lengthy prayer at the inauguration in January, 1969. Later in 1969 Graham met with representatives of SDS and attempted to grasp their moral concerns but came away fearful that "in our search for new freedom, we are in danger of losing what little freedom we have left." [50]

But our antiestablishment, evangelical movement, critical of American involvement in Vietnam and related policies, especially after the Kent State and Jackson State massacres (1970) and the Cambodian incursion, began to grow. This was due in part to general disillusionment and in part to the rediscovery of the rigorous separation of church and state among the seventeenth-century English Baptists and the earlier continental evangelical Anabaptists in contrast to the classical Protestant Reformers. A consequent repudiation of merely cultural Protestantism or folk evangelicalism soon followed.[51] Much of this new thinking within evangelicalism appealed to the teachings of Jesus, to Old Testament prophets and their criticism of society under the Covenant, but now in the mid-twentieth-century context of a premillennial theology that was accommodating itself to the current needs of secular society under a separationist Constitution.

In the minds of evangelical critics, two events served to link Graham and the establishment evangelicals closely to the administration and the American way. The first was Graham's participation in the Honor America Day, July 4, 1970. Hobart Lewis, president of *Reader's Digest,* asked Graham to work with Bob Hope on a happening which would pull all Americans together despite the Vietnam War and the racial and student crises. Although Graham offered grudging admiration for many of the protesters at the rally,

233

he seemed to be more a spokesman for middle-American values than for Christianity.[52] Graham's address at the Honor America Day cannot be analyzed here, although it is probably one of the most important evangelical statements on church-state relations in our fifty-year period. Speaking before the Lincoln Memorial, Graham outlined what America is and should be.[53] In a manner reminiscent of Billy Sunday, he took as his text I Peter 2:17, "Honor all men . . . Fear God. Honor the King." Graham praised the country, its perceived evangelical foundations, and its Christian faith. He criticized all extremists, whether on the right or the left. The second event which placed Graham firmly within the ranks of those who seemed to hold an almost uncritical view of America was his role as Grand Marshal in the New Year's Day 1971 Tournament of Roses Parade in Los Angeles.[54]

It is evident from what has been adduced thus far for our fifty-year period that the "myth" of America has been induced through a combination of biblicism, moral righteousnes, nationalism, and patriotism. The editor of *Christianity Today* in 1969 found it consistent with his Christianity and American citizenship to write: *"Christians ought to be the best citizens and the finest patriots. Certainly they have a prior allegiance to God Almighty. But this can only make them better Americans."* [55] A particular kind of nationalist evangelical piety, a "civil religion," is seen as the foundation and continuing spirit of the Republic.[56]

It is of interest that evangelicals as disparate as the faith healer turned university president, Oral Roberts; Methodist evangelist and charismatic healer Kathryn Kuhlman; and the scholar-publicist Presbyterian Rousas John Rushdoony have all in one form or another strong residues or even quite articulate formulations of the interpenetration of American and Christian virtues. A pervasive patriotism in song and other illusions is evident in the great healing assemblies of both Roberts and Miss Kuhlman. Rushdoony, editor of the Chalcedon Press in California (and in his several books *This Independent Republic,* 1964, and *The Nature of the American System,* 1965), bases his religio-political views on Mosaic legislation as still valid in many cases in the Christian dispensation and upon Calvin's "common grace" (cf. Cornelius Van Til), even though he expressly acknowledges the separation of church and state: "All law rests on God's fundamental [revealed] law, so that true laws must be oriented to this higher law" (one of his five basic religiopolitical propositions).

"To be an American is to belong to a pietistic sect." This phrase probably ties up more of the history of evangelical thought in America on church-state relations than any other.[57] In recent years it has been seen most conspicuously in institutions like the White House prayer services and the Nixon Sunday worship. Throughout the country there are also state legislative prayer breakfasts with the governor present.

The antiestablishment evangelicals have raised a strong voice against the implications of such practices. Moreover, they have rightly questioned whether the Republic ever in fact was Protestant or even in any profound sense Christian at its foundation. Many today point to the genocide of Indians and the oppression of the black peoples carried over to this country as slaves. The views of most founding fathers were, in fact, looked upon by the leading Protestant divines of their own day as rank "infidelity." Not Christianity in its evangelical sense but rationalism, deism, and natural religion are now being understood by many evangelicals as having been at least equally foundational to this country. "Nature's God," not the God of "Abraham, Issac, and Jacob," interpreted in terms of the scientific revolution then occuring in England, is being seen as the ultimate sanction of many of the founding fathers of the Republic at a time when, in fact, only a very small percentage of the population were strongly identified with church life.[58]

The ambiguity at the heart of America and sometimes

in the heart of individual citizens between the conception of the nation as chosen of God with a unique destiny and as merely one nation among many is mirrored in American foreign policy, which has oscillated even in our fifty-year period between isolationism and what is understood to be America's responsibility for other nations including what was once also called America's manifest destiny to extend its influence particularly ever further west, even to Asia.[59] The second thrust in this tension contributed to the development in American militarism following World War II. Critical evangelical Richard V. Pierard points to strong evangelical participation in this militarization.[60]

Throughout the sixties and seventies, along with extraordinary advances in social justice, there has been also a severe erosion of American values. American society was brutalized by violence on streets and campus, by an Asian war fought out almost daily on television screens, and by resorts to political assassination, from that of President Kennedy in November, 1963, to that of the elder Mrs. Martin Luther King in June, 1974.

In these parlous times evangelicalism seemed to speak with two voices. Great works of philanthropy and evangelizing zeal flourished alongside often callous disregard for those different from one's own church, confession, party, class, race, or nation. And just as one can document evangelical participation in the growth of American militarism and unwarranted criticism of organizations like the League of Nations and the United Nations, so can one find a strong countervoice as well, a growing reaction to what seems to many evangelicals an all too easy truce between "evangelicalism made respectable" and the state.[61] Looking back to the days when nineteenth-century evangelicalism was linked to the most progressive issues of the day, evangelicals like Sherwood Wirt, Richard Pierard, David Moberg, and Richard Quebedeaux, among others, have attempted to illustrate the "unequal yoke" which seems to have existed between evangelical Christianity and political conservatism, at least since the death of William Jennings Bryan in 1925.

With the "uneasy conscience of modern fundamentalism" first articulated by the evangelical book of that title in 1947 and intensified by disenchantment, especially since the Watergate break-in, with conservative presidential leadership conspicuously bemantled in religion, an alternative antiestablishment evangelical view of American politics and social action has become a significant force, at least within evangelicalism itself, if not in the country at large.[62]

Evangelical disaffection with American society increased following the Supreme Court's sweeping decision on January 22, 1973, on abortion *(Roe et al. v. Wade)*. An editorial in *Christianity Today* criticized the Court's appeal to "ancient religion" meaning paganism, rejection of the Hippocratic Oath, and lack of "established medical fact." The editorial asserted that the Court "clearly decided for paganism and against Christianity." [63] The National Association —along with the Missouri Lutheran Synod and the Mormons—was one of the few ecclesiastical organizations to take any formal stand against abortion. At the thirty-second annual convention in Boston in 1973, the National Association stated that the issue at hand was much broader than the issue of the freedom of a woman to control her own body. And they deplored "in the strongest possible terms the decision . . . which has made it legal to terminate a pregnancy for no better reason than personal convenience or sociological considerations." [64]

What seems to be occurring is that "the great reversal" is itself being reversed in a growing sector of evangelicalism. At the 1966 Wheaton Congress on the Church's Worldwide Mission, the evangelical establishment itself took up the call for renewed and increased social awareness.

At the 1969 United States Congress on Evangelism, social responsibility was again underlined by Leighton Ford of the Billy Graham Evangelistic Association. Ford challenged the church to match its profession of faith with its deeds. Dr. Myron S. Augsburger, a Mennonite, called for a recommitment to the Lordship of Christ in all areas of social evil. Senator Mark Hatfield of Oregon, a Baptist, called for an end to the polarization between the social gospel and the emphasis upon conversion. Dr. Richard Halverson, minister of the Fourth Presbyterian Church in Washington, D.C., pointed out that witness "by presence and performance as well as proclamation, is the product of the Spirit filled life." [65] Speaker after speaker at the United States Congress on Evangelism appealed for ever more evangelical social concern.

This growing political awareness and renewed sense of social responsibility are evidenced by the pronouncements of other evangelical groups including the following: the April 1973 conference "On Christianity and Politics" convened at Calvin College in Grand Rapids, Michigan;[66] the "Thanksgiving" workshop on Evangelical Social Concern which met in November of 1973;[67] the last two trienniel Inter-Varsity Fellowship Mission Conventions (1970, 1973), each of which attracted well over 12,000 college students from throughout the country and the world, social and specifically political concerns received marked attention;[68] the People's Christian Coalition of Chicago which published the evangelical "underground" newspaper *Post-American;*[69] the Boston-based Evangelical Committee for Urban Ministries, under the leadership of Roger Dewey and Eugene Neville; and the Christian World Liberation Front, organized in the San Francisco Bay area.

To be sure, there remains a significant tension in church-state outlook in evangelical thought. In an issue of *Christianity Today* several weeks after the Congress on Evangelism, this tension was manifest in an article written by the late executive editor of the magazine, L. Nelson Bell, in which he warned against giving up "preaching the Word of God to serve tables." [70]

Thus, to some extent, a significant rift even in the main-line evangelical community (the National Association) has developed. It has been rightly asked, therefore, whether those who have become politically liberal will stay within the evangelical fold.[71] Time alone will tell but indications are that both sociopolitical activists and conservatives of historically orthodox understanding will remain theologically evangelical. This surmise can find grounding in the common biblical commitments of both groupings as well as through understanding the aims of these two diverse political attitudes. Presbyterian Dr. Francis Schaeffer, who was originally associated with evangelical social reactionaries, recoiled from identifying Christian and social conservatism and, as an American theologian and apologist living in Switzerland and with the community L'Abri (the shelter), has done much to foster understanding between these two groups of evangelicals. Because of Schaeffer and kindred thinkers, it is no longer possible to equate political and theological conservatism. Graham, at the International Congress on World Evangelization, at Lausanne, July, 1974, was himself questioned on whether he had not too facilely identified evangelical and American national interests, and he forthrightly acknowledged the cogency of this criticism.

Conclusion

In August, 1974, President Nixon resigned. His successor, Episcopalian Gerald Ford, was the first self-avowed practicing evangelical in the twentieth century to become President. He was also the first President to have a son studying in a seminary. There were signs, however, in certain statements and actions beginning the administration of President Ford, in his difficult takeover, which indicated that he himself may not have clearly distinguished what we have called an authentic evangelical faith from civil religion.

What we have seen throughout our fifty-year period, reaching back to the death of William Jennings Bryan in

239

1925, is that much of the rift in evangelical thinking concerning church and state arose through conflicting ideas on how best to preserve and advance a Christian America or better still, a strong evangelical community concerned for all of America. And when this attitude has not been present, too often evangelicals lapsed into political non-involvement, sustained by millenarian hope or into chauvinistic nationalism. In fact, as evangelical thought developed along a postmillennial line (perhaps beginning with Jonathan Edwards), it often joined in a sense of America's manifest destiny and in our own period became closely identified with political conservatism in an attempt to defend and extend the American way. As evangelical thought developed along a premillennial line (notably since the Niagara Prophetic Conferences, 1868, and thereafter, reaching a certain peak around 1925), it often became increasingly apathetic towards civic involvement, expecting an immediate Second Advent.

The challenge facing Evangelicals in 1975 is to remain or become politically alert and participant, yet always to question what is of primary importance, the nation or the faith, and to descry what is properly American political and social policy and what portends the Kingdom. The spheres of church and state can certainly no longer be seen as coterminous in this increasingly pluralistic and largely secular, but also globally aware and ecumenical, age. And grounded in a conception of the reality and importance of the faith they hold which so strongly affirms the love of mercy, the doing of justice, in the context of humility under God (Micah 6:8), a strong evangelical resurgence is needed, as we approach the final quarter of the twentieth century. To be sure, the challenge is, in essence, no different from that faced by many who have come to this land since its founding or been born here, namely to raise or keep aloft the standard of the gospel among their fellow citizens in a Republic in which church and state are constitutionally separated. For the Puritans, their faith was more important than the homeland which they dearly loved, but left. For a resurgent Christianity and a strong America in our own time the tension between faith and fatherland must be maintained on the part of evangelicals, and indeed of all Christians, without retreat from involvement in society's travail. Without a critical stance, without being ready discerningly and actively to perceive the lordship of Christ above the flag, neither the community of faith nor the democratic republic of constitutionally limited sovereignty can be winningly strong among the nations.

In the years 1925 through 1975 too often evangelicals unwittingly tried to save America at the expense of the faith or by the distortion of the faith or by the outright confusion of faith and Christian liberty with patriotism and a certain conception of economic freedom and even social exploitation.

Notes

1. The basic studies of fundamentalism and evangelicalism used in this study are those of Steward G. Cole, *The History of Fundamentalism* (New York: Richard R. Smith, Inc., 1931; reprinted in Hampden, Conn., and London, 1954); Ernest R. Sandeen, *The Roots of Fundamentalism, British and American Millenarianism 1800-1930* (Chicago: University of Chicago Press, 1970); Norman F. Furniss, *The Fundamentalist Controversy, 1918-1931* (Hampden, Conn.: Archon Books, 1963); William G. McLoughlin, ed., *The American Evangelicals, 1800-1900* (New York: Harper & Row, 1968); and, Timothy L. Smith, *Revivalism and Social Reform in Mid-Nineteenth Century America* (New York: Harper & Brothers, 1957).

2. Ray A. Abrams, *Preachers Present Arms: A Study of the War-Time Attitudes and Activities of the Churches and the Clergy in the United States, 1914-1918* (Philadelphia: Round Table Press, Inc., 1933); enlarged with the subtitle: "The Role of the American Churches and Clergy in World Wars I and II, with some observations in the War in Vietnam" (Scottsdale, Pa.: Herald Press, 1969).

3. Sydney E. Ahlstrom, *A Religious History of the American People* (New Haven: Conn.: Yale University Press, 1972); Martin Marty, *Righteous Empire* (New York: Dial Press, 1970); Ernest

Lee Tuveson, *Redeemer Nation: The Idea of America's Millennial Role* (Chicago: University of Chicago Press, 1968).

This sense of national and Christian destiny was true for all Protestant groups in the nineteeth century. See, however, Methodist Reverend Warren A. Chandler, *Great Revivals and the Great Republic*. Richard H. Niebuhr documents this in his *The Kingdom of God in America* (New York: Harper & Brothers, 1937). America, however, having been given by God a unique role to play in world affairs, was capitulating to many of the pressures which the new century began to force on her in terms of non-Anglo-Saxon Protestant immigrants (among them many radicals), new forms of knowledge which seemed to undermine formerly sacred authorities (Darwin and evolution), and new urban-agrarian causes of alienation (technology and big business). Threats to Anglo-Saxon Christian leadership seemed to grow on all fronts. See Robert T. Handy, *A Christian America: Protestant Hopes and Historical Realities* (New York: Oxford University Press, 1971).

Elton Trueblood outlines in *The Future of the Christian* (New York: Harper & Row, 1971), the civil theology that went with the idea of a Christian America: "Essential to the civil theology that has developed are these ideas: 1) that God has a purpose, 2) that finite men are called to be His instruments in the fulfillment of his purpose, and 3) that the American people are called to a special vocation for the sake of the world. (See note 11.)

4. The importance of this tension between understanding the nation as having a special role "under God" and seeing the nation as one among many before an impending Second Advent is closely related to the development of an understanding of millennialism in America. Although most Christians since St. Augustine until Joseph Priestly, a close friend of Thomas Jefferson, can be characterized as maintaining an amillennial view of history, with Priestly, who believed in the literal earthly rule of Christ in Palestine following Napoleon's victory in the Near East, one can trace an increasing belief in the literal earthly rule of Christ. Furthermore, with the publication of Jonathan Edwards' *History of the Work of Redemption* (1774), called the first postmillennial work in America, there grew the idea that the Christian millennium could be equated with American destiny.

This postmillennialism gradually developed into a premillennial understanding of the rule of Christ and felicitous thousand years as nineteenth-century optimism developed into twentieth-century pessimism. One could follow a line of thinkers on this subject from Alexander Campbell (father of the Disciples), Joseph Berg (Dutch Reformed pastor), Joseph Smith (father of the Mormons), William Miller (father of the Seventh-Day Adventists), and Charles T. Russell (father of the Jehovah's Witnesses). The increasing idea of a cataclysmic end of world history, the establishment of the rule of Christ and then thousand years of peace entered

American fundamentalist thinking and then modern evangelical thought, first through the Niagara Bible Conferences (1868) which propounded the dispensationalist theology of John Nelson Darby (d. 1882, father of the Plymouth Brethren), through the revivals of D. L. Moody and Princeton Seminary's Neo-Calvinism developed under Archibald Alexander (d. 1857), Charles Hodge (d. 1878), and J. Gresham Machen (d. 1937.)

For special studies on this subject, see C. N. Kraus, *Dispensationalism in America* (Richmond: John Knox, 1958), John F. Walvoord, *The Millennial Kingdom* (Findlay, Oh.: Dunham Publishing Co., 1959); and *The Rapture Question* (Findlay, Oh.: Dunham Publishing Co., 1957). Perhaps the most popular version of this premillennial view has been presented by Hal Lindsay, *The Late Great Planet Earth* (Grand Rapids: Zondervan Publishing House, 1970). Cf. John F. Walvoord, *Israel In Prophecy* (Grand Rapids: Zondervan Publishing House, 1962) for the importance of the new state of Israel to millennial thought.

5. On Bryan, see Lawrence W. Levine, *Defender of the Faith: William Jennings Bryan, The Last Decade, 1915-1925* (New York: Oxford University Press, 1965); Richard Challener, "William Jennings Bryan," *An Uncertain Tradition,* ed. by Norman A. Graebner (New York: McGraw-Hill Book Co., 1961); and Paul W. Glad, ed., *William Jennings Bryan, a Profile* (New York: Hill & Wang, 1968).

6. Chicago Daily *Tribune* (May 28, 1925); Willard H. Smith, "William Jennings Bryan and the Social Gospel," *The Journal of American History,* (1966) LIII, 41 ff. (The Smith article is reprinted in shortened form in Glad, *William Jennings Bryan, a Profile,* pp. 87-108.)

7. Charles R. Erdman, "The Church and Socialism," *The Fundamentals,* (Chicago: Testimony Publishing Co., 1910-15), XII, 108-19.

8. *Speeches of William Jennings Bryan: Revised and arranged by Himself,* (New York: Funk and Wagnalls Co., 1909 II, 14 ff.

9. See the life of John Roach Straton by his own son Hillyer H. Straton, "John Roach Straton: Prophet of Social Righteousness," *Foundations* (January, 1962), pp. 20 ff; Ferenc N. Szasz, "John Roach Straton and the Presidential Election of 1928," *New York History* (April, 1968), pp. 200-17; C. Allyn Russell, "John Roach Straton, Accusative Case," *Foundations* (Jan.-Mar., 1970), pp. 44-72; see also Walter Ross Peterson, "John Roach Straton: Portrait of a Fundamentalist Preacher" (Ann Arbor, Mich.: 1969), doctoral dissertation, Boston University.

10. Cf. William T. Ellis, *Billy Sunday, the Man and His Message* (New York: Winston, 1933); see also William G. McLoughlin, Jr., *Billy Sunday Was His Real Name* (Chicago: University of Chicago Press, 1955); and James F. Findlay Jr., *Dwight L. Moody;*

American Evangelist, 1837-1899 (Chicago: University of Chicago Press, 1969).

11. Compare note 4 with a variant view by Frederick A. Tatford, "The Second Coming of Christ," *Our Hope* (July, 1951), pp. 27-32; see also *The Fundamentals,* ed. by Amzi C. Dixon, Louis Mayer, and Reuben A. Torrey (Chicago: Testimony Publishing Co., 1910-15).

12. Ellis, *Billy Sunday, The Man and His Message,* pp. 77 ff. Ellis writes in this authorized biography that Billy Sunday was a "jingoistic patriot." "His loyalty to America was not hedged about by any conditions or exceptions or twilight zones. . . . His faith in America was as simple and as sincere as his faith in the Bible."

13. Ahlstrom, *A Religious History of the American People,* pp. 899, 900.

14. Of course Sunday admitted that sometimes success would not always come to a person, but he went on to add that "you might not be able to be a search light or a whistle, but you can be a cog in the machine." *Boston Herald* (Jan. 17, 19 . .), p. 9, Ahlstrom, *A Religious History of the American People,* pp. 899, 900, attributes this intolerance of nonconformist behavior to the enormous heightening of patriotic Americanism at the time of World War I.

15. McLoughlin, *Billy Sunday Was His Real Name,* pp. 225-26. Sunday voiced the feeling of the evangelical conservatives when he stated: "Some people are trying to make a religion out of social service with Jesus Christ left out. That is why your Men and Religion Forward Movement was a lamentable failure (1912). They made the Christian religion a side issue."

16. In the *Boston Herald* (March 2, 1931), p. 1, Sunday states: "Sometimes I'm glad God knocked over the heavens to put America on her knees before she became too chesty. . . . Our great depression is not economic, it is spiritual and there won't be a particle of change in the economic depression until there is a wholesale revival of the old-time religion."

17. McLoughlin, *Billy Sunday Was His Real Name,* p. 278.

18. Ralph Lord Roy, *Apostles of Discord: A Study of Organized Bigotry and Disruption on the Fringes of Protestantism* (Boston: Beacon Press, 1953) and Franklin H. Littell, *Wild Tongues, A Handbook of Social Pathology* (Toronto: Macmillan, 1969), p. 98.

19. Sunday, "Autobiography," *Ladies Home Journal* (April, 1933).

20. James Deforest Murch, *Cooperation Without Compromise* (Grand Rapids: Eerdmans Publishing Co., 1956) and *Protestant Revolt* (Arlington, Va.: Crestwood Books, 1967) should be consulted for the history of the National Association of Evangelicals.

21. Murch, *Cooperation Without Compromise,* p. 44.

22. *Ibid.,* pp. 40, 41.

23. In future references to major Supreme Court decisions on church and state, see the following collections: Mark de Wolfe Howe, ed., *Cases on Church and State in the United States* (Cambridge: Harvard University Press, 1952); John Joseph Mc-Grath, ed., *Church and State in American Law* (Milwaukee: The Bruce Publishing Co., 1962); and Joseph Tussman, ed., *The Supreme Court on Church and State* (New York: Oxford University Press, 1962). The most comprehensive account of church and state from the vantage point of the "evangelical" Lutherans (Missouri Synod) is that of Albert G. Huegli, ed., *Church and State Under God* (St. Louis: Concordia Publishing House, 1964).

24. Murch, *Cooperation Without Compromise*, p. 69.

25. Documented by Louis Gasper, *The Fundamentalist Movement* (The Hague/Paris: Mouton, 1963), pp. 52-54. For the most responsible and learned evangelical argumentation against the United Nations, see Rousas John Rushdoony, "The United Nations," *The Nature of the American System*, (Nutley, N.J.: The Craig Press, 1965), pp. 113-34.

26. Ross Y. Koen, *The China Lobby in American Politics* (New York: The Macmillan Co., 1960) and Foster Rhea Dulles, *American Policy Toward Communist China*, 1949-1969 (New York: Thomas Y. Crowell Co., 1972), pp. 85-89.

27. Murch, *Cooperation Without Compromise*, pp. 178 ff.

28. *Ibid.*, pp. 136-38, as quoted from Dr. Taylor's address "Citizens of Heaven and Earth," delivered at a Bible Conference in 1954 at Winona Lake, Indiana.

29. *Ibid.*, pp. 150-52.

30. A book documenting the growing majority-consciousness of evangelicals is that of Dean Kelley, *Why Conservative Churches Are Growing* (New York: Harper & Row, 1972).

31. "The Bricker Amendment," *Western Voice* (June 15, 1955), p. 2.

32. In January, 1954, Gallup polls showed 58 percent of Catholics supported McCarthy and 49 percent of Protestants were favorable to him. See Vincent P. De Santis, "American Catholics and Mc-Carthyism," *Catholic Historical Review*, (1965), 51, 1-30.

33. John Pollock, *Billy Graham* (Grand Rapids: Zondervan Publishing House, 1966).

34. *Ibid.*, pp. 27 ff. This cluster of schools is typical of the many fundamentalist Bible institutes begun in the early twentieth century for what was seen as the defense of the faith.

35. *Ibid.*, p. 69.

36. *Ibid.*, p. 93.

37. *Ibid.*, p. 136. The abbreviation is for *Europäische Verteidigungs Gemeinschaft*.

38. Quoted from Joseph Kamp, *The Life of John Birch* (New Haven: Constitutional Educational League, 1954) at the conclusion of Welch's own famous *The Blue Book of the John Birch Society* (Belmont, Mass.: The Society, 1958). See Benjamin R.

Epstein and Arnold Forster, *The Radical Right: Report on the John Birch Society and its Allies* (New York: Random House, 1966). Recognizing the threat to sound evangelical principles, Lester DeKoster deals with Birchism critically, *The Christian and the John Birch Society* (Grand Rapids: Eerdmans Publishing Co., 1965).

39. Roy, *Apostles of Discord*, chapter 2; Littell, *Wild Tongues;* Gasper, *The Fundamentalist Movement*, chapter 4, "The Aggravation of Militant Fundamentalism." Cf. Richard Hofstadter, "Fundamentalism and Status, Politics on the Right," *The Columbia University Forum* (Fall, 1965), pp. 18-24.

40. David Moberg, *The Great Reversal: Evangelism Versus Social Concern* (Philadelphia: J. B. Lippincott Co., 1972), pp. 228 ff.

41. In a rather uncomplimentary book, William G. McLoughlin, *Billy Graham: Revivalist in a Secularist Age* (New York: Ronald Press, 1960), predicted that Graham's revivalism had reached its apogee in 1960.

42. For details on this and related events, see Pollock's *Billy Graham*, pp. 217 ff.

43. Lowell D. Streiker and Gerald S. Strober, *Religion and the New Majority: Billy Graham, Middle American and Politics of the 70's* (New York: Association Press, 1972), p. 60.

44. This was reported in *Christianity Today* in various issues in 1960. See especially April 9, 1960. Delegates to the annual meeting of the National Association expressed doubt that a Roman Catholic President "could or would resist fully the pressures of the ecclesiastical hierarchy." At Billy Graham's alma mater, Wheaton College, the administration allowed free use of the college mail service to Nixon supporters but required Kennedy adherents to mail their literature through regular paid channels.

45. Streiker and Strober, *Religion and the New Majority*, pp. 60 ff.

46. *Ibid.*, pp. 60, 61.

47. *Ibid.*, p. 64.

48. National Association resolution approved October, 1963.

49. See National Association resolution for 1964, 1965.

50. *Religious News Service* (Dec. 14, 1970).

51. Arthur G. Gish, *The New Left and Christian Radicalism* (Grand Rapids: Eerdmans Publishing Co., 1970). An indicator of the involution of the Mennonites into mainline evangelicalism is the University of Pennsylvania doctoral thesis of Barbara Bowie Wierd, "From Separatism to Evangelism: A Case Study, 1940-1970," summarized in *Mennonite Quarterly Review*, XLVIII, 391 ff.

52. Streiker and Strober, *Religion and The New Majority*, pp. 70-73.

53. *Ibid.*, pp. 74-77. In his speech entitled "The Unfinished Dream," Graham interpreted "Honor the King" as meaning "honor

the nation." Despite the faults in the American system, belief in it is vigorously reaffirmed.

54. *Ibid.,* pp. 26-27.

55. "Is Patriotism Dead?" in *Christianity Today* (July 4, 1969). Editor Carl F. H. Henry writes in "Has Patriotism Had Its Day?" in *Christianity Today* (June 7, 1974), pp. 26-27, that "Patriotism is neither adolescent nor obsolescent."

56. Robert N. Bellah, "Civil Religion in America," *Religion in America,* ed. by William G. McLoughlin and Robert N. Bellah (Boston: Beacon Press, 1970), pp. 3-23.

57. Rushdoony, *The Nature of The American System,* p. 3. See also Will Herberg's sociological study *Protestant-Catholic-Jew* (New York: Anchor Books, 1960).

58. Sidney E. Mead, "The Post-Protestant Concept and America's Two Religions," *Religion in Life* (Spring, 1964), pp. 169-99. See also Franklin Littell, *From State Church to Pluralism* (New York: The Macmillan Co., 1962) and Harold O. J. Brown, *The Protest of a Troubled Protestant* (New Rochelle, N.Y.: Arlington House, 1969), p. 72.

59. Louis B. Wright, *Culture on the Moving Frontier* (Bloomington, Ind.: Indiana University Press, 1955) shows the Puritan roots of manifest destiny.

60. Richard V. Pierard. *The Unequal Yoke: Evangelical Christianity and Political Conservatism* (Philadelphia: J. B. Lippincott Co., 1970) pp. 131-55. Pierard points out important factors which stimulated the alliance between theological and political conservatism; a gradual erosion of social concern following the Civil War, preoccupation with issues of science, higher criticism and faith, and an attribution to liquor as the cause of all social ills.

61. *Christian Century* (April 24, 1968), p. 508. The critical evangelical editors of *The Cross and the Flag,* Robert G. Clouse, Robert D. Linder, and Richard V. Pierard, attribute much of the failure of evangelicalism to move beyond individual piety toward a critical view of America culture and politics to at least three diverse emphases, all seen developing in our fifty-year period: 1) an uncritical alliance between conservative Protestantism and conservative political interests; 2) a simplistic "Christ is the answer" approach to all social and political problems; and 3) an emphasis upon personal problems while social ones are overlooked. See also the following critical evangelical books: Vernon C. Grounds, *Revolution and the Christian Faith* (Philadelphia: J. B. Lippincott Co., 1971); Calvin Redekop, *The Free Church and the Reductive Culture* (Scottsdale, Pa.: Herald Press, 1971), and Sherwood Eliot Wirt, *The Social Conscience of the Evangelical* (New York: Harper & Row, 1968).

62. William F. Buckley in the *Boston Globe,* March 8, 1974, cites Protestant publicist Harold O. J. Brown and editor of *Christianity Today* as seeing an erosion of Protestant support of America within the United States.

63. *Christianity Today* (February 16, 1973), pp. 32-33.

64. National Association Resolutions on file in Washington, D.C., Resolutions from the Thirty-Second Annual Convention held in Boston on April 24, 1973.

65. Moberg, *The Great Reversal*, p. 164.

66. See "Does Politics Matter," by Marvin J. Van Eldeen *Reformed Journal*, (May-June, 1973), pp. 9-12.

67. See *Inside* magazine, Jan.-Feb., 1974 (published by ECUMB, 130 Warren Street, Boston; editor, Roger Dewey), p. 3.

68. For the history of the Inter-Varsity movement see Douglas Johnson, editor, *A Brief History of the International Fellowship of Evangelical Students* (Lausanne, Switzerland: The International Fellowship of Evangelical Students, 1964). In the 1973 Inter-Varsity missions conference Arthur Glasser, dean of the Fuller School of World Mission, criticized a church which sends its missionaries throughout the world to translate the Gospel of John, the Acts of the Apostles, and then leaves it to embittered nationals to translate the prophets and social teachings of Jesus into their own tongue.

69. See Jim Wallis, "Post-American Christianity," in *The Post-American*, (Fall, 1971), p. 3; and "What is the People's Coalition?" Jacques Ellul, *The Presence of the Kingdom* (Paris: Editions Roulet, 1948), p. 5, has been of tremendous influence among many of the more radical young evangelicals. This book of his should be consulted.

70. *Christianity Today*, (Oct. 24, 1969), p. 185.

71. McLoughlin and Bellah, *The American Evangelicals*, pp. 45-72. Following McLoughlin's chapter "Is There a Third Force in Christendom?" in the 1970 edition of *Religion in America* is an excellent dialogue in note 32 between McLoughlin and Professor Richard L. Millett of Southern Illinois University on the division of political and economic views among evangelicals. The nature of this debate in terms of theological implications can be followed in the controversy following the publication of Richard Quebedeaux's excellent analysis in *The Young Evangelicals: Revolution in Orthodoxy* (New York: Harper & Row, 1974). See Carl F. H. Henry's review of Quebedeaux's book in *Christianity Today*, (April 26, 1974), and the article entitled "Revolt on Evangelical Frontiers." Jim Wallis, editor for the radical Christian paper *Post-American* in the June-July, 1974, issue, p. 3 counters Henry's article in lively debate.

Evangelicals and Science:
Fifty Years After the Scopes Trial (1925–75)

V. Elving Anderson

In 1925 the Scopes Trial witnessed an important battle ostensibly over the right of John Scopes to teach evolution in a Tennessee classroom.[1] We now know that the issues were broader than that. William Jennings Bryan's futile attempt to best Clarence Darrow in verbal debate made it appear that a fundamentalist had few solid answers to give to a clever antagonist who knew something about science. This episode only confirmed in the minds of fundamentalists the opinion that science was an implacable foe of the Christian religion.

Fifty years later American evangelicals continue to wrestle with the implications of science for their faith. And yet they do not seem to be as traumatized by this investigation as were their predecessors of the twenties. In this essay, after noting some of the changes in the last half-century, we will examine the role of evangelicals in scientific endeavors and the ways in which some of them deal with the burdensome issue of evolution. We shall see that evangelicals still have divergent views on this topic. Meanwhile, other questions have arisen which deserve careful attention.

Fifty Years of Change

To begin with, let us consider some of the changes in science and technology which have taken place over the

V. Elving Anderson is Professor of Genetics at Dight Institute, University of Minnesota.

past fifty years, for evangelicals today must deal with a different scientific and cultural milieu than that faced by fundamentalists in the twenties.

In my own field of genetics, for example, we have learned that mutations can be induced by radiation and by chemicals, that genes control enzymes in biochemical pathways, that DNA is the genetic material, that genes affect behavior as well as morphology, and that the store of genetic variability in the human and other organisms is far greater than had been imagined.

The development of atomic energy has had obvious effects upon world politics, energy resource utilization, and techniques for scientific investigation. Transistors and computers have permitted miniaturization and complex data processing and control. Space flights utilized these advances and, in turn, made fundamental contributions to our understanding of the solar system.

The realization that the earth's surface is composed of about eight large plates that have been moving apart slowly has been described as a major scientific revolution. First recognized clearly in the late 1960s, the concept of "plate tectonics" has led to a thorough reevaluation of data and theories in geophysics, biology, anthropology, and other areas.

The neurosciences appear to be one of the major frontiers at the present time. A number of chemical substances serving as neurotransmitters between adjacent nerve cells have been identified, and pathways within the brain using the different neurotransmitters have been traced. The effectiveness of certain drugs in the treatment of psychotic disorders can be explained at the level of molecular structure.

There was a considerable lag period between the emergence of a new idea, however, and its introduction to science students. Furthermore, the available texts spent too much time with the results of research and not enough with the way in which scientists learn (science as inquiry).

Such questions led to an intensive collaboration between research scientists and science teachers in the preparation of the "new math," the "new biology," and counterparts in the other sciences. There have been other efforts to improve the "public understanding of science" through the mass media.

Nevertheless, the public response was one of ambivalence —an awe and appreciation for the triumphs of science, but a fear of the possible misuse of technology. The threats of atomic warfare, population explosion, environmental pollution, and declining natural resources occupied public attention for varying periods of time. Many research scientists played a leadership role in identifying the problem areas and awakening concern. If it was ever justified to accuse the scientific community of being too objective and aloof, that is no longer generally true.

Student interest in the sciences appears to have declined somewhat at the college level, partly in response to the job market, but also as part of a disenchantment with a naturalistic and impersonal scientific world view. It may be true that in some problem areas we already have enough facts and that the time has come for action, but activism that runs beyond the current store of knowledge may be harmful in itself.

To some extent the public reaction against science may reflect an overexpectation as to the nature of science. It may have been assumed that the sciences could produce "ultimate proof" for an idea, but it turns out that research is much more effective at disproof or "falsifiability." If two mutually exclusive hypotheses are being considered, the data may exclude one but cannot "prove" the second, since a third alternative (as yet untested) may be a better explanation.[2]

The impression of scientists as thoroughly objective also needs reexamination. Brush[3] claimed that there is only one established dogma in science—that scientists do not blindly accept established dogma. In his opinion, hostility to science has been intensified by the image of an "objective" robot-like scientist lacking emotions and moral values. Recent trends in the history of science stress a more realistic picture of the behavior of scientists. Brush suggested that historians should not be asked to identify ideal scientists as examples for young people, but should rather explain how certain problems came to be considered scientific and how particular standards happened to be accepted for evaluating solutions.

Evangelicals in Science

We do not know how many evangelicals were active in science fifty years ago, but at present it is clear that they are involved in all of the major areas of research and teaching. I have the impression that the proportion of evangelicals (to total scientists in a discipline) may be higher in the physical sciences, somewhat lower in the biological sciences, and lower yet in the social sciences. Nevertheless, there is no area of research considered alien or intimidating by young people with Christian presuppositions.

Pollard[4] has stressed the importance of community among scienists. For evangelical scientists in the United States and Canada this need has been met by the American Scientific Affiliation (ASA). Organized in 1941 to create a sense of identity for such a group, there are now over 2,000 members, a majority having earned doctorates. A parallel organization in the British Isles is the Research Scientists Christian Fellowship (RSCF), with members in all the major universities. In more specialized areas there are other organizations, such as the Christian Association for Psychological Studies and the Christian Medical Society.[5]

Over the years the ASA has served as a forum for discussion of theoretical issues and social problems, the emphasis shifting from time to time. The topic of population pressure, for example, was explored a few years before it began to attract national attention. Published symposia sponsored by the ASA have included books on a general overview of the sciences,[6] on evolution,[7] and on social issues involving the sciences.[8] The *Journal of the American Scientific Affiliation* maintains a vigorous exchange of letters, and book reviews in an effort to "explore any and every area relating Christian faith and science."

In 1965 the RSCF brought thirty-six scientists from ten countries to Oxford, England, for a discussion of science and Christian belief. In the international and interdisciplinary conference a number of topics at the frontiers of research were explored, with the conclusion that none of the areas presented serious obstacles to Christian faith. Malcolm Jeeves summarized and interpreted the papers and responses in a volume that remains the best statement of an evangelical perspective on this general theme.[9]

The number and diversity of topics discussed by evangelical scientists has become too large for a comprehensive review. For this reason I have chosen a more selective approach. Evolution remains an important issue, even though some may have hoped or assumed that all controversy is past. Evolution is significant, in part, because a broad understanding of the nature of science is involved, and the history of science has much to say on this point. On the other hand, many citizens and scientists are much more concerned about the effects of science upon society and the implications of work at the frontiers of research. After considering these points, I will conclude with some comments on possible strategies for the future.

Evolution

It is obvious that questions about the teaching of evolution in public schools were not resolved by the Scopes trial in 1925.[10] Similar issues have been raised in Arkansas (1965-66) and in California (1972-73), but some observations about the California controversy may suffice to indicate the current status of the problem.

253

In California, schools are expected to select textbooks from a list approved by the State Board of Education, and thus the approval process becomes important for the schools and for publishing companies. Over the past ten years several groups have been urging changes in the ways that textbooks for younger children treat the topics of evolution and origins.

The claims that have been advanced by the advocates of change include the following: (1) The teaching of science about the origins of the universe and of life has become too dogmatic.[11] (2) Evolution is as much a religious as it is a scientific concept. (3) An exclusive emphasis upon evolution represents an infringement upon the freedom of religion of students. (4) Creation is a scientific theory and thus is appropriate for inclusion in science courses. (This idea is supported by the Creation Research Society,[12] formed in 1963, which claims that a young earth and a sudden origin of life are essential for a creational view.) (5) For these reasons, science teachers should be required to give "equal time" to the teaching of creation. (Some persons would agree with only the first one or two points, while others have insisted upon all.)

In November, 1969, the *Science Framework for California Public Schools* was modified by including several paragraphs suggesting that alternative explanations for origins should be considered. In November, 1972, the State Board of Education held hearings about proposed changes in the textbooks themselves. Mr. Vernon Grose (an engineer and an evangelical) urged a moderate position—that scientific dogmatism should be reduced, but that the teaching of creation should not be required.[13] Dr. David Hubbard (a member of the State Board of Education and President of Fuller Theological Seminary) shared this general view.[14]

A number of the major scientific organizations prepared statements concerning the controversy, and one passed by the National Academy of Sciences on October 17, 1972 is representative:

Whereas the essential procedural foundations of science exclude appeal to supernatural causes as a concept not susceptible to validation by objective criteria; and whereas religion and science are, therefore, separate and mutually exclusive realms of human thought whose presentation in the same context leads to misunderstanding of both scientific theory and religious belief; and whereas, further, the proposed action would almost certainly impair the proper segregation of the teaching and understanding of science and religion nationwide, therefore we . . . urge that textbooks of the sciences, utilized in the public schools of the nation, be limited to the exposition of scientific matter.

Although much of this and other similar statements appears reasonable, the impression was given that religious issues are unimportant and that current science teaching is in fact limited to the exposition of scientific matter. In my opinion, a more satisfactory appraisal was presented by two evangelical scientists who were asked to serve as advisers to the California State Board of Education.

Commenting on the textbooks in use at the elementary level, Robert B. Fischer (Dean of the School of Natural Sciences and Mathematics at California State College, Dominguez Hills) claimed that:[15]

There are long-standing inadequacies in the teaching of the nature of science which are perpetuated in these books and these problems are brought into focus in dealing with topics of origins. First, very little attention is paid to the limits and presuppositions of science. . . . Science is permitted to come through to students (and at times to scientists, as well) with a much greater degree of certainty and finality than is warranted. Second, there is a frequent blurring of the distinctions between science and scientists and of the inevitable relationships between the two. . . . One consequence . . . is a confusing of "science" with "what scientists think" or even with "what scientists believe."
Because of both of these long-standing inadequacies in the teaching of science, there is a strong tendency to extrapolate from science to scientism—that is, from science to the philosophical view that there can be no knowledge apart from scientific knowledge. . . . There is even some ambiv-

255

alence in the use of the terms creation and evolution. The concepts of evolution are properly considered within science, insofar as the term refers to natural substances and processes and insofar as it recognizes relevant scientific limits and presuppositions. However, insofar as the term evolution refers to extrapolations into scientism, and this not infrequently is the case, evolution no longer is science and should not be presented as such.

In a parallel statement[16] Richard H. Bube (Professor of Materials Science and Electrical Engineering, Stanford University) pointed out:

A scientific theory is one that can in principle be contradicted by empirical data. . . . To the best of my knowledge current forms of "creation theory" cannot be contradicted by empirical data, even in principle. Wherever data might be thought to contradict the theory, appeal to empirical data might be thought to contradict the theory, appeal to miracle (*i.e.*, to a non-scientific descsription) is commonly made. . . . Therefore, I do not believe that the teaching of "creation theory" in a science course is appropriate.

But I also believe that "evolution theory" is all too often presented in science teaching as some kind of an absolutely infallible law free from all possibility of future contradiction. For many adherents, evolution has assumed the proportions of a religious faith and this dogmatic acceptance shows up in many texts on evolution. . . . In the teaching of evolution, what we can say about the processes going on at present is the most solidly based, what we can say about processes in the immediate past is probably largely valid, what we can say about processes in the distant past becomes increasingly speculative, and we can say nothing scientific at all about absolute origins. Yet the typical discussion of evolution starts the other way round, presenting theories about origins as if they were the foundation of our evolutionary knowledge and established beyond the shadow of a doubt. What evolution teaching needs is not the introduction of an alternative non-scientific "creation theory," but the reformation of the present courses so that they are faithful to the potentialities and limitations of the scientific method.

The decision of the Board in early 1973 was that "dogmatism be changed to conditional statements where

256

speculation is offered as explanation for origins." The proposal that science teachers be required to teach creation was denied, but teachers in the social sciences will be asked to handle the topic. It is possible, however, that the tension between more extreme points of view will continue. It should be clear that Drs. Fischer and Bube view the basic conflict as one between science and scientism, not between science and faith. Furthermore, theirs is not a compromise position (as advocates for more extreme views might argue) but one that arises from definite theological and scientific premises. In the following sections I will refer to other sources indicating that their opinions can be considered to reflect an evangelical perspective.

At this point, however, it may be helpful to review some of the reasons for rejecting proposals that would require public school teachers to teach creation as a scientific alternative to evolution. (1) When a whole view of the biblical record is taken, the doctrines of creation and providence deal primarily with relationship and meaning and purpose and responsibility, rather than with mechanisms or time. The doctrines of creation and providence are significant affirmations of faith in God as Creator and Sustainer, not empirically testable theories or hypotheses subject to disproof. (2) A serious problem in terminology would arise. Alternative scientific hypotheses should be stated in testable terms. Thus it would seem preferable to discuss a "young earth" hypothesis or a "sudden origin of life" hypothesis, reserving the term "creation" for the broader doctrine. (3) A Christian view of Creation cannot be considered fairly without extensive reference to the biblical data, and this might be considered inappropriate in the religiously pluralistic classroom setting in public schools in the United States.

The Nature of Science

It is obvious that a constructive approach toward a problem like that of evolution requires an adequate under-

257

standing of the nature and limitations of science. Some of the public antipathy toward science arises from a basic misperception at this level, and some Christians unnecessarily reject science for the same reason.

The debt of evangelicals to Bernard Ramm must be acknowledged. His 1954 book[17] helped many young people to maintain a vigorous interest in both science and Scripture, and he continues to write in a provocative and constructive manner.

More recently we have the symposium by members of the RSCF with the intriguing title of *Christianity in a Mechanistic Universe*. The authors agree that "it is in the biblical theistic view of the natural world, in all its fullness, that we see the strongest ultimate grounds for the confidence we have as scientists in the scientific enterprise." [18] A shorter booklet by Donald MacKay remains a classic treatment of the same position.[19]

Richard Bube has drawn upon his experience in talking with those who reject science without knowing what it means and with those who reject Christian faith without understanding it.[20] He has found that certain types of parallelism aid in communication. Thus, the meanings of revelation, evidence, and objectivity are examined for science and then for Christian faith. The use of models to simplify complex systems is described, both for science and for theology. But there are differences as well. Science must strive to be objective, but faith in Christ must involve a personal response toward God. Christian faith is based on the reality of an absolute, while science is by nature relative.

An important point stressed by many evangelicals in science is that scientific explanations do not exclude or replace religious interpretations. "According to the Bible, creation is not 'explanation' of the world around us, but it relates this world, and the things in this world to God, 'Explanations' can be quietly left to the domain of science,

258

but the relationship between God and this world is eminently the domain of theology." [21]

But scientific explanations by themselves are not completely satisfying. In a consideration of the reasons why
people are turning away from science Denis Alexander
suggested that scientific thinking has appeared to create a
closed-system mechanistic universe with no ultimate meaning.[22] He then argued that meaning and mechanism are
two aspects of one and the same reality. A biblical view
of the creator relationship between God and the universe
provides meaning as well as mechanism and thus heals the
breach between man's reason and humanness.

The History of Science

The nature of science can be seen more clearly when
viewed from the perspective of history. Only thus is it possible to understand how our views are influenced by ideas
in the surrounding culture.

Professor R. Hooykaas is well known among historians
of science, but his work is not appreciated sufficiently by
evangelicals. In a recent volume (perhaps the most significant recent book about science written by an evangelical)
he has reviewed the effect of Christian faith on the emergence of modern science.[23] Many have assumed that the
Christian faith has restricted and inhibited research and
teaching in the sciences. Prof. Hooykaas counters by showing how Christian faith provided the freedom essential for
the development of science. It helped to de-deify nature
and to counterbalance the rationalistic approach of some
elements in the Greek heritage. De-deifying nature made it
possible to accept mechanistic interpretations. (Evangelicals
do not deny mechanistic views, but assert their limitations.) He concluded that "for the building material of
science we have to look to the Greeks; but the vitamins
indispensable for healthy growth came from the biblical
concept of creation." [24]

259

There are two important consequences of this point of view: (1) Since God is free and nature is contingent upon his will, research is essential for an understanding of nature. This provides for freedom in science and rejects attempts to build science upon special texts from the Bible. Efforts to present creation as a scientific theory, for example, often are linked with an insistence that a young earth and a sudden origin of forms of life are the *only* acceptable interpretations of the Bible. In my own opinion, such a view cannot be considered to lie historically in the mainstream of evangelical thought. In fact, there is a strong resemblance to the Protestant scholasticism that developed in the seventeenth century with a heavy influence from Greek philosophy.[25] (2) The de-deification of nature prevents the elevation of aspects of nature to a central world-view role. Hooykaas has claimed that "our silence about God in nature will end in the deification of nature . . . and materialism, evolutionism, scientism—that is, pseudo-religion under the disguise of science—will take the place of religion. . . . For when religion is thrown out, idolatry inevitably creeps in; the religious *functions* cannot be eradicated."[26]

In a similar manner Toulmin described "Evolution with a capital E" as a scientific myth. "If we think ourselves myth-free, when we are not, that is largely because the material from which we take our myths is taken from the sciences themselves. . . . The myths of the twentieth century are not so much anthropomorphic as mechanomorphic." [27] In the same set of essays Toulmin was critical of efforts to use evolution as a "cosmic sanction for ethics."

Science and Social Concerns

The current disenchantment with science has arisen in part from fear of the misuse of science and technology and in part from the belief that scientists have not shown sufficient concern for the effect of their research work upon the broader society. As Alexander has suggested, science has become the "God that failed." It is precisely at the points where science has been elevated to a god-like status that the sense of disillusionment has been most marked.[28]

There is the further charge that Christian beliefs have contributed significantly to the misuse of technology. White, for example, claimed that "we shall continue to have a worsening crisis until we reject the Christian axiom that nature has no reason for existence save to serve man." [29] His paper at least made it clear that what we do about the environment depends upon our beliefs about human nature and destiny, and thus provided a basis for legitimate discussion of religious ideas in the science classroom. Subsequent discussions, however, have shown that environmental problems are not limited to Christian nations, but appear to be more directly related to the state of technology. Adequate solutions for environmental concerns are complex and should recognize economic as well as biological factors. Individual life-styles would be affected, and it is likely that changes in personal priorities and in world view may be required.

The point of interest here is that evangelical scientists have been concerned about issues of this type for some time.[30] They understand that belief in God as Creator and Sustainer includes a deep and persisting concern for the welfare of others and for the stewardship of God's handiwork.

Public interest in the environment appears to be transitory and it is displaced easily by new issues. There is an obligation for those whose interest arises from basic convictions to help maintain the concern that will be needed for any effective change. Evangelicals can share in this obligation.

Human Origins and Behavior

An understanding of human origins obviously is important for our view of human nature. Within the past few decades much new information concerning the fossil record has become available, and interpretations of the evidence have been undergoing some revision. Evangelical writers have reviewed the Genesis record together with modern anthropological theories and find a general agreement about a unitary origin of mankind from a single group. On some other points there is no clear consensus.

Pearce summarized the arguments for a late-date Genesis man.[31] He held that the descriptions of culture in Genesis 2-4 portray Adam as a New Stone Age (Proto-Neolithic) farmer living about 10,000 to 12,000 years ago. On this view most fossil forms would have preceded Adam and might represent a separate creative activity by God.

Other evangelical anthropologists prefer an early-date Genesis man (perhaps 50,000 years ago). Kornfield, for example, discussed Neanderthal and Cro-Magnon man[32] and concluded: "I find it most difficult to believe that God would make a being so very much like us physically and mentally, with a definite cultural tradition, along with a capacity to bury the dead in a carefully planned ritual manner, that yet wasn't created in His image."

When we turn attention to the current scene, the possibility of tension between science and faith appears particularly acute with reference to human behavior. Mechanistic explanations of behavior, particularly as described by B. F. Skinner,[33] might seem to conflict with views of human free-will and responsibility.

A different perspective was presented by Underwager[34] who claimed that "it cannot be denied that Skinner is able to explain, predict, and control a great deal of outcome variance in human behavior by means of operant conditioning." He then considered how Skinner's research findings "can be gracefully integrated with a biblical conception of man as a significant, free, choosing being."

Perhaps the most comprehensive discussion of this problem by an evangelical scientist appears in the writings of Donald M. MacKay.[35] In his opinion, "we have no 'battle' on our hands as Christians to prove that man's brain somehow or other will defy physical explanation, or disobey physical laws; nor have we any 'battle' to prove that some kind of non-physical forces act upon the matter in man's brain." [36]

After reviewing his own and other research studies MacKay continued:

> What we have seen indicates that we have in human nature a "unity" which demands, to do justice to it, at least two levels of discussion: the level of the mechanical, appropriate for an outside observer, and the level of the personal, appropriate from the inside standpoint of the agent himself. . . . The level of the mechanical rightly finds no place for such concepts as "freedom" and "responsibility," for they do not belong there. They belong to the level of the personal and there is, as we have seen, no incompatibility between them and the mechanistic view of brain function which we have been assuming. . . . In summary, then, I would suggest not only that I see harmony between the study of man as a psychological being and the study of man as a mechanism, but that in some doubtless crude and imperfect way this even throws a little light on the relation between the spiritual life which is offered to man and the psychological structure in which that spiritual life must, by God's grace, be embodied." [37]

Here, then, is further indication that evangelicals need not fear mechanistic explanations, so long as they are not claimed to be exhaustive. The possibility that methods of behavior control might be used in an authoritarian manner to restrict freedoms, however, remains an important topic for continuing attention.

Some Future Needs

In this brief review it has been possible to consider only the broader scientific and theological issues. A detailed record of evidence, a consideration of specific points, and an indication of diversity in opinion can be obtained from the references cited. Nevertheless, in my opinion, there are sufficient grounds for claiming that the role of science is not strengthened by scientism and that belief in the Bible is not aided by denials or caricatures of science. Evangelicals have shown that faith in God as Creator and Sustainer can support freedom for science and also give meaning to personal existence. How can they serve in the future?

Thoughtful scientists realize their own need for a world-view that satisfies the whole person. Jacques Monod (molecular biologist and Nobel prize winner) has reflected on the human need for a complete explanation, which he considers to be universal and innate. He has found his own answer in accepting the "principle of objectivity" as the condition of true knowledge, but acknowledges that this "constitutes an ethical choice and not a judgment arrived at from knowledge."[38] Although Monod's choice is not convincing,[39] a discussion of his book can provide an opportunity for explaining to our colleagues Christian faith as a lively option.

The California controversy has raised some important issues about a philosophy for teaching sciences in the lower grades. Unfortunately, some professional groups may merely wait for a change in the membership on controlling boards, and then press for a return to the original status. Evangelicals in science are in a good position to explain why some changes are indeed desirable and can be carried out without the fear that science will be damaged in the process. Meanwhile teachers might welcome additional resource materials that explain religious issues related to the sciences in a manner that will be useful in public school science classrooms.

The possibilities for scientific control of human genetic material or of human behavior appear awesome. It is unreasonable, however, to give the impression (as some writers have done) that future events will be so unique that the general public will be completely unable to cope with them. We need a comprehensive theological view that will help us to deal with "technological shock,"[40] and we also need the sense of humility that should arise from a thorough grasp of the history of science.

A final point has to do with science in the third world. In professional journals I have read how UNESCO and other organizations are encouraging science activities among young people in many countries. Through our churches we have learned about the growing influence of third world leaders in evangelism and mission. But I have little acquaintance with evangelicals in such countries who are trained in the sciences. The changes in developing nations caused by the introduction of Western science, technology, and industry may lead to a total secularization and then to a worship of science and technology themselves.[41] If we are truly concerned about the implications of Christian faith for the total culture, then evangelicals in science around the world have much to learn from each other.

Since the Scopes Trial of 1925 the relationships between science and faith have been reassessed in a manner which has a special bearing on the issue of evolution. It is true that probably the majority of evangelical laymen and pastors still maintain a firm stance against evolution, regardless of what way it is defined. On the other hand, among evangelical scientists several positions are now evident; some adhere to a "young earth" hypothesis and the "sudden origin of life" (or as an alternative, the sudden origin of life in the far distant past); others lean towards a belief in evolution with a small "e" which they affirm does not contradict a belief in creation with a capital "C." It is also true that there are scientists for whom scientific methods are not merely ways of acquiring knowledge about nature but have become the basis for quasireligious world views. Increasingly, however, it is being realized that the extreme stances on either side of today's discussions are not the only options. It is entirely possible to be honestly and comprehensively scientific while remaining thoroughly and uncompromisingly Christian. And that is what should have been evident from the beginning.

Notes

1. Willard B. Gatewood, Jr., ed., *Controversy in the Twenties: Fundamentalism, Moderism and Evolution* (Nashville: Vanderbilt University Press, 1969).

2. A short, clear exposition of the current role of science can be found in Robert B. Fischer, *Science, Man and Society* (Philadelphia: W. B. Saunders Co., 1971).

3. Stephen G. Brush, "Should the History of Science be Rated X?" *Science*, (1974), 183, 1164-72.

4. William G. Pollard, *Physicist and Christian. A Dialogue Between the Communities* (New York: The Seabury Press, 1961).

5. One of the symposia sponsored by the Christian Medical Society is Walter O. Spitzer and Carlyle L. Saylor, ed., *Birth Control and the Christian* (Wheaton, Ill.: Tyndale House Publishers, 1969).

6. The American Scientific Affiliation, *Modern Science and Christian Faith* (Wheaton, Ill.: Van Kampen Press, 1948).

7. Russell L. Mixter, ed., *Evolution and Christian Thought Today* (Grand Rapids: Eerdmans Publishing Company, 1959).

8. Gary R. Collins, ed., *Our Society in Turmoil* (Carol Stream. Ill.: Creation House, 1970).

9. Malcolm A. Jeeves, *The Scientific Enterprise and Christian Faith* (London: Tyndale Press, 1969).

10. Judith Grabiner and Peter D. Miller, "Effects of the Scopes Trial, Was It a Victory for Evolutionists?" *Science* (1974), 185, 832-37.

11. John W. Klotz, *Genes Genesis and Evolution* (St. Louis: Concordia Publishing House, 1970), provides a fair-minded interpretation of this point from a "creationist" view.

12. Some papers from the Creation Research Society are reprinted in Walter E. Lammerts, ed., *Why Not Creation?* (Grand Rapids: Baker Book House, 1970). The Society also has prepared a textbook: John N. Moore and Harold S. Slusher, ed., *Biology: A Search for Order in Complexity* (Grand Rapids: Zondervan Publishing House, 1970).

13. Harald Bredesen, "Anatomy of a Confrontation. An Interview with Vernon L. Grose," *Journal of the American Scientific Affiliation,* (1971), 23, 146-49.

14. David A. Hubbard, "Should Evolution be Taught as Fact or Theory?" *Eternity,* (May, 1973), p. 23.

15. Robert B. Fischer, "The Evolution of a Policy on Textbooks," *Los Angeles Times,* (Apr. 15, 1973).

16. Richard H. Bube, "Creation and Evolution in Science Edu-

cation," *Journal of the American Scientific Affiliation,* (1973), 25, 69-70.

17. Bernard Ramm, *The Christian View of Science and Scripture* (Grand Rapids: Eerdmans Publishing Company, 1954). An evaluation of the positions held by Ramm and other theologians can be found in Carl F. H. Henry, "Science and Religion," *Contemporary Evangelical Thought,* ed. by Carl F. H. Henry (Great Neck, N. Y.: Channel Press, 1957), pp. 247 ff.

18. Donald M. MacKay, ed., *Christianity in a Mechanistic Universe and Other Essays* (Chicago: Inter-Varsity Press, 1965).

19. Donald M. MacKay, *Science and Christian Faith Today* (London: Falcon Booklets, 1960).

20. Richard H. Bube, *The Human Quest: A New Look at Science and Christian Faith* (Waco, Texas: Word Books, 1971).

21. Aldert van der Ziel, *Genesis and Scientific Inquiry* (Minneapolis: T. S. Denison & Co., 1965), p. 201.

22. Denis Alexander, *Beyond Science* (Philadelphia, A. J. Holman Co., 1972).

23. R. Hooykaas, *Religion and the Rise of Modern Science* (Edinburgh: Scottish Academic Press, 1972).

24. *Ibid.,* p. 85.

25. R. Hooykaas, *Philosophia Libera: Christian Faith and the Freedom of Science* (London: The Tyndale Press, 1957).

26. R. Hooykaas, *The Christian Approach in Teaching Science* (London: The Tyndale Press, 1966), p. 9.

27. Stephen Toulmin, *Metaphysical Beliefs, Three Essays* (London: SCM Press Ltd., 1957), p. 16.

28. Alexander, *Beyond Science.*

29. Lynn White, Jr., "The Historic Roots of Our Ecologic Crisis," *Science,* (1967), 155, 1203-7.

30. R. J. Berry, *Ecology and Ethics* (London: Inter-Varsity Press, 1972); Collins, *Our Society in Turmoil;* John W. Klotz, *Ecology Crisis* (St. Louis: Concordia Publishing House, 1971); articles in the *Journal of the American Scientific Affiliation* (Mar., 1973).

31. E. K. Victor Pearce, *Who Was Adam?* (Exeter, Devon: The Paternoster Press, 1969). See also his article, "Proto-neolithic Adam and Recent Anthropology," and critiques by Paul H. Seeley and George J. Jennings in the *Journal of the American Scientific Affiliation* (Dec. 1971).

32. William J. Kornfield, "The Early-Date Genesis Man," *Christianity Today,* (June 8, 1973), p. 7. See also James M. Murk, "Evidence for a Late Pleistocene Creation of Man," *Journal of the American Scientific Affiliation* (1965), 17, 37-49.

33. B. F. Skinner, *Beyond Freedom and Dignity* (New York: Alfred A. Knopf, 1971.

34. Ralph C. Underwager, "What's Beyond Freedom and Dignity?" *The Scientist and Ethical Decision,* ed. by Charles Hatfield (Downers Grove, Ill.: Inter-Varsity Press, 1973), pp. 131-46.

35. Summarized in Jeeves, *The Scientific Enterprise and Christian Faith,* pp. 132 ff.

36. Donald M. MacKay, "Man as a Mechanism," in *Christianity in a Mechanistic Universe,* ed. by Donald M. MacKay (Chicago: Inter-Varsity Press, 1965), p. 52.

37. *Ibid.,* pp. 66, 69.

38. Jacques Monod, *Chance and Necessity. An Essay on the Natural Philosophy of Modern Biology* (New York: Alfred A. Knopf, 1971), p. 176.

39. Alexander, *Beyond Science,* p. 138.

40. Bernard Ramm, "Evangelical Theology and Technological Shock," *Journal of the American Scientific Affiliation* (1971), 23, 52-56.

41. R. Hooykaas, *The Christian Approach in Teaching Science* (London: The Tyndale Press, 1966), p. 17.

From Puritanism to Evangelicalism: A Critical Perspective

Sydney E. Ahlstrom

"Evangelicalism" is a battle-torn flag that has waved over many different Protestant encampments ever since the Reformation, sometimes over more than one at the same time. Usually it has been a signal of militancy with implications of exclusiveness. Yet the persistent presence of this defensive-aggressive spirit is both odd and unfortunate, for the Evangel issues from very high ground indeed. According to an old Puritan formulation of Christian doctrine which has had an immense impact on American religion and life, the proclamation that there is good news in the universe has its origins in the Covenant of Redemption, whereby "it pleased God in his eternal purpose to choose and ordain the Lord Jesus Christ to . . . be the savior of his church, . . . unto whom he did from all eternity give a people to be his seed" (Westminster Confession, chapter VIII). Those who were by him in time redeemed were presumably evangelicals.

Yet it has not pleased God to establish any uniformity of usage for this sacred and solemn term. For Lutherans, who have probably used the word longer and more tenaciously than any other communion, it became in effect a synonym for Christian, that is, for one who lived by faith alone,

Sydney E. Ahlstrom is Professor of American History and Modern Church History at Yale University.

rejoiced in the gospel, and relied not on "works of the law" in either Catholic or Reformed terms. Perhaps most decisive in giving content to the term in English-speaking Protestantism was the great eighteenth-century revival of experiential religion inspired by the Wesleys and Whitefield. Among Anglicans especially "evangelicalism" became the name of a major ecclesiastical party. No single usage, however, has been normative in subsequent discussions. And historians who sail these seas have been as helplessly caught in the currents of popular usage as the humblest fisherman. For present purposes, however, it is probably best to establish a working definition that arises out of the beliefs, piety, and institutional life of the American tradition. If this seems to beg the question, let us remember that a circle is the most perfect of forms and that a tautological argument can reveal much about the essential unity of a tradition.

In contemporary American parlance the noun *evangelical,* when not being used simply as a noncontroversial reference to all Christians or all Protestants who regard *sola gratia* as a cardinal doctrine, refers to those Protestants who:

(1) repudiate Roman Catholic polity, liturgics, piety, and doctrine, and at least used to regard the Roman Catholic Church as the Anti-Christ;

(2) insist upon verbal inerrancy of the received biblical text, tend to interpret revelation in strict propositiona. terms, and question the value of historico-critical studies of biblical religion;

(3) regard the doctrine of *sola scriptura* as having very serious import for the devotional life of every Christian;

(4) emphasize the experiential dimensions of being or becoming a Christian and hence tend to diminish the significance of the sacraments, a sacerdotal clergy, authoritative hierarchical structures, and doctrinal complexities;

270

(5) understand the ethical teachings of the Bible in a precisionistic or legalistic manner and oppose utilitarian or situational approaches;

(6) resist the extension of fellowship or even the name of Christian to persons and churches that do not share these convictions.

This is, I believe, an uncontrived and untendentious definition of a movement which includes Christians who belong to several quite diverse confessional families. It says nothing of social or political attitudes or of philosophical positions that many evangelicals might regard as extrinsic to their theological position.[1]

My argument in this essay will be that the term evangelicalism (in the above described sense) does in fact refer to a fairly unified tradition. Though it has over the centuries undergone considerable change, it has nevertheless maintained its identity and looked back to its origins with considerable sympathy and respect. Its origins lie in that revolution in Christendom which the English Puritan movement intended to accomplish. Only in North America, however, where ancient traditions had very little social and economic footing, were the full implications of this revolution borne out. But certain theological matters are essential to an understanding of this momentous process.

Puritan churches gained their most fundamental character from their confident belief that they were in covenant with the Lord God of Israel who had called them out of the world as an "elect nation" and laid upon them the burden of establishing in these latter days a true church of visible saints and a civil order that would exemplify its ethical implications. In this sense they intended to bring about a decisive abrogation of those forms of ecclesiastical corruption and superstition which had dominated the Middle Ages and a breaking of those political fetters that had been hindering the true church since the age of Constantine. They wished to revive the church of the New Testament. The abominations of Rome, therefore, stood

271

in the forefront of Puritan thinking, from the papacy to the sign of the cross to the mere repetition of printed or "stinted" prayer. The church, they insisted, was not to be shaped by the customs of mankind but by the law of God as set forth in the Scriptures.

Although they revered the theology of Calvin and Bullinger, it was the general consensus of Reformed thinking as summarized at the Synod of Dort (1618-19) and fully elaborated in the Westminster formularies which was accepted as the norm for what the Bible actually taught. At the center of this theology was the idea of divine sovereignty and the subsidiary doctrines which this entails: total depravity, unconditional election, limited atonement, and irresistible grace.

When we look for the religious results of this awesome body of doctrine and of these fiercely held convictions, and when we do this with the particular purpose of forging the links between Puritanism and latter-day evangelicalism, the development of overwhelming importance is the new kind of Christian piety that grew out of the anxieties produced by the doctrine of election. The problem of assurance became existentially central. When neither professions of faith, nor attendance on the ordinances, nor outward evidences of sanctified living could assuage this concern, only an inward experience of God's redeeming grace would suffice. And in the tradition of pastoral care that shaped this accent on conversion and in the vast devotional literature that arose to sustain it one discerns an emphasis on a subjective criterion of salvation that is unmistakably modern—and proleptically "evangelical."

Of almost equal importance was the fact that this stress on inward experience laid bare the distinction between the visible and invisible church. Roger Williams first and the Baptists later were to insist on institutional recognition of this cleavage with special force; and the result was an enduring tendency to separatism and to controversies on the question of fellowship. It is hardly a coincidence, therefore, that in due course the Baptists became the most numerous and active bearers of the Puritan impulse.

A third result flowed from the Puritan's desire for specific biblical warrant not only in ethical matters but on detailed questions of church order. Because so many of the matters in question, such as whether to kneel or not for prayer or how and when to observe the Sabbath, were open to public scrutiny and debate, the road to picayune debate, censoriousness, and divisive controversy was opened wide —and heavily traveled.

Finally, Puritans developed a set of new attitudes toward the secular order which Max Weber and many other scholars have seen as constituting a "Puritan Ethic." Perhaps most important for this reorientation were their views on vocation, election, and eschatology; but it was strengthened by their pronounced objections to indolence, vain, display, and pleasure seeking in general. Partly because they laid so large a stress on individual moral decision and partly because of their opposition to the arbitrariness of kings and the profligacy of court life, they objected to monopolies and economic privileges. They sought to bring the economic order into the realm of personal ethics. For these same reasons and because they also tended to enlarge the laity's role in their churches, the Puritans turned their efforts toward larger measures of personal freedom, political liberty, and economic individualism. It was this "worldly asceticism" that was leading them inexorably into a social revolution.[2] During the whole course of the seventeenth century, moreover, this dynamic movement, in nearly all of its multiple variegations, would be transplanting itself on American soil, where in time still other circumstances would lead it on to yet another more complete revolution.

The establishment of Puritanism in the various British colonies, however, brought to light divergent ideas within it. It is a mistake to imagine that Reformed theology was a monolithic structure which allowed no exceptions and

273

tolerated no innovations. Many good historians have argued that Calvin would have disapproved of the Dort decrees and the Westminster Confession; and with the passing decades one may note a transition not merely in world-view but in theology as well. This development was not to cease. The Antinomian controversy of the 1630s exposed some of these tensions. Edwards, in one of his most effective sermon series, was to complain of widespread Arminian tendencies. Ultimately at least two thirds of the hundred oldest Puritan churches in Massachusetts became frankly Arminian and then forthrightly Unitarian. Still others moved on, in considerable numbers, to Universalism and various degrees of Transcendentalism.

While some of these later movements were clearly departures from Puritanism, it would be wrong not to see them as infused with much of its spirit. As for the rise of Wesleyan Arminianism, it must be understood as an almost immanent development. Most Anglo-American Puritans of the seventeenth century agreed with the basic doctrinal content of the chief Reformed confessions, but consensus of interpretation on the doctrine of election did not come easily; indeed, tension on the subject is almost intrinsic to the Reformed tradition—if not to all Christian theology. Not even Edwards was able to convince more than a minority of the best minds who wrestled with his argument; and in almost every Protestant land and communion a broader view of Christ's atoning work emerged. Teaching akin to Wesley's on sin, contrition, penitence, and free grace reached far and wide. Nowhere was it more widely received than among Americans.

In time, of course, the intense fervency that had attended the early decades of the Holy Commonwealth waned, but growth was steady, and an independent and self-sufficient establishment was widely supported. Two colleges supplied the churches with a well educated ministry. In response to unforeseen problems a "half-way covenant" had to be authorized so that the children of baptized but unawakened

274

parents could also be baptized, but the basic principle that only visible saints would be admitted to full membership was in most places respected. There was considerable lamentation among the clergy, and in 1689 Massachusetts even convened a synod to seek means of rejuvenating the churches. Then toward the end of the century signs of revival appeared. Solomon Stoddard's parish in Northampton experienced several revivalistic "harvests," as did Timothy Edwards' parish in East Windsor. But before the greatest of all harvests came to Northampton, there were stirrings in New Jersey among the Dutch Reformed, the Congregational, and Presbyterian churches; these were followed by a great revival in the middle states where Dutch and English congregations had significantly affected each other.[3]

The Great Awakening, customarily traced to Edwards' Sermons on Justification by Faith and pursued through the "Frontier Revival" and into its main phase under Whitefield and Tennent, represented a reassertion of this Puritan tradition. It rested firmly on the Puritan emphasis on an inward experience of regeneration, and Edwards drew much of his theological sustenance and substance from his Puritan forefathers, notably Stoddard and Thomas Shepard. His methods of preaching following the old pattern, and his way of interpreting the religious phenomena of his day revealed the force of his heritage.

In due time he would depart from Stoddardean understanding of church membership and the qualifications for partaking of the Lord's Supper; but these were old Puritan arguments in which Edward Taylor and Cotton Mather had taken similar positions. Of course Edwards knew from early youth that his philosophical theology was boldly innovative, but this in no way weakened his allegiance to the Westminster Confession. And as President of Princeton he belongs to an essentially Puritan sequence of Presidents that was not broken until Witherspoon's arrival, and even Witherspoon, as a high-flying Scottish evangelical with books on *Justification* and *Regeneration* to his credit, was by no means outside of a circle that appreciated the old Puritan authors.

Yet when all has been said in this vein, it must be insisted upon that Edwards himself saw the first great events in Northampton as singular. Benjamin Coleman in Boston thought likewise and asked for a fuller account so that certain eminent divines in Great Britain could be apprised of these spiritual events in an obscure corner of the New World. And *they* were astounded by what they heard. The great Isaac Watts wondered if anything so portentous had happened "since the days of the apostles." To these Englishmen as well as to many American divines and searchers of Scripture the events were not only newsworthy— they were signs of the times with momentous eschatological significance. New England seemed to be taking a role in *Heilsgeschichte.* Nor did Edwards back off from such an interpretation; to the contrary in *Some Thoughts Concerning the Revival* (1743) he was willing to suggest that the Kingdom of God would be manifested first in America.[4] This statement and others appearing elsewhere in Edwards' writings do in fact instantiate (though it probably cannot be said that he inaugurates) a new postmillennialist eschatology—a tendency which at that time added fuel to the American's national self-consciousness and hence gave further impetus to the movement for independence. In later years it would also lend itself to extreme forms of chauvinism and claims to America's manifest destiny as well as to a liberal doctrine of inevitable progress. Later premillennialistis would thus always be embarrassed to have Edwards in the tradition they anathematized. But the Awakening was also revolutionary in several other ways.

First, the heirs of Edwards, such as Bellamy, Hopkins, and Nathaniel William Taylor, were also the architects of the New Divinity which in responding to modern scientific and philosophical thought, modified the Westminster doctrines of imputation, original sin, atonement, and the Trinity.

Second, the religious excitement generated widespread distrust of formal education. In New London revival leaders even founded a seminary, the "Shepherd's Tent," where the courses consisted in testimonies, prayer meetings and Bible reading. There was also an extramural burning of books. Since this was no passing absurdity but representative of a prevailing attitude, Richard Hofstadter was correct in naming revivalism as one of the major sources of American antiintellectualism—business and politics being the other two.[5] On the other hand, some denominations noted for their evangelical fervor paradoxically were at the same time founding colleges and universities such as Princeton and Dartmouth.

Third, the tendency to separatism inherent in Puritanism was again given tangible expression, with the Baptists peeling off in especially large numbers. Given the fact of numerous religious establishments, the more radical revivalists were also led into a long political struggle that would eventually issue in disestablishment and religious freedom both in New England and elsewhere.

Fourth, the Awakening made the revival an accepted phenomenon of the parish ministry, thus inaugurating the age of planned or concerted revivalism in American religious life.

Finally, it fostered an ecumenism amongst evangelicals by which they were able to discover fellow spirits and to think in more ambitious terms of "national accomplishments." This new sense of confidence would in due course lead into the multiple interinvolvements of the Evangelical United Front in the antebellum period. Thus, the Great Awakening was at its center a recrudescence of Puritanism, but in its outworkings it transcended and modified the earlier movement out of which it sprang.

In time, it was to be followed by the Second Great Awakening whose origins could perhaps be placed to the

277

series of revivals that began between 1763 and 1765, but which have been more commonly traced to the Connecticut village revivals of the 1790s. With minor recessions and undulations, it was to flow on so continuously that it can hardly be considered a discrete event. Joining forces with the revivalism was an awakening of missionary interest located in the period from 1790 to 1810; and out of this combination there would issue a mighty resurgence of evangelicalism such as has been experienced at no other time. The American Board of Commissioners for Foreign Missions awakened new and rapidly expanding concerns for evangelism beyond the sea; while a host of other associations turned their efforts to domestic missions, especially in the trans-Appalachian regions into which a vast unchurched population was moving.

Almost simultaneously with this campaign came a powerful and immensely variegated movement of moral and social reform in which many of the revivalistic missionaries became deeply involved. And perhaps nobody embodied these multiple concerns more energetically than Lyman Beecher, who won his spurs in the antiduelling protest that was stimulated by Aaron Burr's killing of Alexander Hamilton but who really hit his stride only with the Temperance movement, for which he sounded the keynote in 1810 and produced his magnum opus in 1826, *Six Sermons . . . On Temperance.* Due to its unpopularity among the "better people," this campaign broke ground for the antislavery crusade which opened with striking suddenness in the early 1830s and was borne forward by the great revivals which had Charles Grandison Finney (1792-1875) as their leading figure.

Here again there were innovations—Finney and his many critics alike called them the "New Measures," which is to say that he developed nearly all of the major features of what has become familiar in the Billy Graham campaigns, emphatically including a concentration on the large urban Babylons of America, but doing far more than Graham has ever done to challenge the cultural acceptances of his time and to lead his converts down a road to sanctification that required socially relevant activism.

With regard to the dominant tradition of preaching and church practice, the most impressive characteristic of this period is its continuity with Puritanism and with the Great Awakening. It was these very characteristics that led its critics (like John Williamson Nevin) to identify the prevailing evangelicalism as "Modern Puritanism" [6] and to denounce its subjectivism, its antiintellectualism, its disinclination for philosophical clarity, its disinterest in historical tradition, and its depreciation of catechetics and the sacraments. Nevin, in fact, would see in these sectarian trends the awful mark of the Anti-Christ. In very much the same spirit the Old School Presbyterians in 1838 extruded four-fifths of the denomination for their doctrinal subjectivism, congregational tendencies, laxity on the decrees, and their addiction to the New School theologies stemming from New England, in particular from Nathaniel William Taylor's podium at Yale.

The Protestant quasiestablishment of the antebellum period was, of course, constituted by many denominations and each of these had certain "distinctives" whether of piety, polity, or doctrine; yet to a remarkable degree this "land of the Pilgrim's pride" had provided them a common heritage and instilled in them objectives that were compatible with denominational rivalries. Thus when Beecher invoked the memory of the nation's Puritan founders (as he did repeatedly) or when he expounded his "Evangelical System" of theology, he was very widely regarded as the age's most effective spokesman.[7] Even Old School Presbyterians and low-church Episcopalians shared many of these views and contributed leadership to the countless voluntary associations (local, regional, and national) that advanced the common cause, which was to shape a pious, productive, prosperous, prolific, and above all a Protestant republic that would carry out the mission that God had entrusted to it.

279

When one asks the major question as to the distinctive character of antebellum evangelicalism, a nativistic defensiveness against immigrant Catholics is no doubt a large factor, but it is not the chief one. That honor must go, rather, to the vast missionary challenge produced by the westward movement and the great vision of national greatness it aroused. Yet the underlying dilemma, the cloud on the horizon, the fearful contradiction in the American consciousness, north and south, was the whole nation's implication in the dark crimes of chattel slavery—and the impossibility of incorporating that fact in the vision of God's New Israel.

It was because of "a peculiar and powerful interest" in slavery, Lincoln said, that the nation went to war against itself. But the nation which emerged from the carnage was unable to dedicate itself to the unfinished work which had been so nobly advanced by all those who had given their last full measure of devotion. After a decade the strenuous efforts of Radical Republicans to accomplish a genuine reconstruction were lost amid the scandals of Grantism. The robber barons took the reins as an almost anarchic country struggled with the disorienting experiences of industrial expansion, tumultuous urban growth, a vast tide of immigrants, and a resurgence of nativism and discrimination.

In this new environment the great Protestant phalanx of antebellum days fell into disarray. The chief leaders of government and business, like the people generally, continued to support the institutions of religion. Between the war's end and 1900 the proportion of Americans with church membership seems to have doubled; but the old evangelical system which Lyman Beecher had so confidently expounded now lost its force. Why it happened no one will ever know—because the whole past of America and even of Christendom is implicated in the event. But it is our obligation to speculate on the more immediate sources of this great transformation of spirit.

Most obvious to any beholder of that day would have been the kinds of radical social change that have led Robert Wiebe to describe the age in terms of "a distended society" in the midst of "a search for order." Old ways of life were becoming obsolete; the agrarian ideal was losing its relevance; patterns of church organization and evangelism that had been shaped by steady westward expansion were becoming inoperative in the new urban context; and where this was not the case, many church members came to feel themselves to be living at cross-purposes with the age's forward movements. In the South and the North alike there were vast constituencies yearning for the old time religion at just the moment when America was leading the world into a new machine age.

Far more serious than this kind of social and institutional bewilderment were a whole series of scientific, scholarly, and philosophical developments that literally changed the entire religious landscape of Christendom, but which struck American Protestants with special force because the Evangelical tradition for over a century had been paying very little attention to these troublesome intellectual developments and because the institutions of learning which it had founded had, with very few exceptions, given very little encouragement to the advancement of science and had often intimidated those who took these problems seriously. What it came down to in the most basic sense was the fact that American Protestants in large numbers had to deal very belatedly with the implications of the scientific temperament as it had been applied, in a fundamentally historical mode, to matters that impinged directly or indirectly on virtually the whole range of religious belief, from the birth and death of the sun and the biography of the earth through the development of all forms of life, to the nature of Holy Scripture and the history of every aspect of mankind's religion in all times and places. The impact of all this was understandably staggering.[8]

Most disturbing of all was the fact that the churches

281

and their complex structures of theology and ethics rested on biblical foundations which were called in question by this intellectual revolution, at least to the extent that they required rethinking. And such rethinking was not easy even for those who had long been wrestling with the emerging problems. It was an excruciating experience for the average Christian, whether clerical or lay, and it is not difficult to understand why people in their situation responded with anger and a sense of betrayal. Nor should it surprise us that their rage was turned with equal force against both those who created these unsettling problems and the liberal theologians who tried to respond with creative and religiously satisfying responses.

The impact of these several developments was, of course, uneven. The social and intellectual change experienced in the rural South (or in rural areas generally) was very different from that in the industrial and urban North. Educational levels were also a vital factor, and the South's lack of universities and seminaries which had become independent of church control through the philanthropies of the wealthy had a delaying effect on the outbreak of controversy in that region.

The general effect of these various developments, nevertheless, was to bring about a gradual but drastic change in the mood and spirit of evangelicals. And nothing reveals the nature of this better than the changed tone of the great revivals of this period which were led by Dwight Lyman Moody and then, after his passing, by Billy Sunday and his many competitors. The huge Protestant audiences to whom Moody and his successors conveyed a new sense of evangelical solidarity were in fact a sign of an inner schism in the churches. Gone was the millennial vision of American that had fired prewar evangelicals. That kind of advocacy now shifted to the more liberal and forward-looking constituencies, who accepted Josiah Strong's nationalistic and imperialistic vision of the coming kingdom.

Moody took the opposite position:

I don't find any place [in the Bible] where God says the world is to grow better and better, and that Christ is to have a spiritual reign on earth of a thousand years. I find that the earth is to grow worse and worse, and that at length there is to be a separation. . . . I look on this world as a wrecked vessel. God has given me a life-boat, and said to Moody, Save all you can.[9]

Clearly evident in such preaching are the new forms of eschatological teaching that were rapidly gaining ground among those Protestants who were alarmed by theological liberalism and the more routine conceptions of church membership that were gaining ground in the churches. This new line of conservative thought owed much to England's Plymouth Brethren and considerably more to the refinements that were being formulated by a growing American movement of dispensational premillennialism. Its basic component was a rigid doctrine of biblical inspiration which insisted on the verbal inerrancy of the Bible and the unity of the Old and New Testaments. The result was a vigorous new conservative impulse that would soon constitute itself as the militant core of the fundamentalist movement. During the ensuing century it would lead an organized resistance to the advance of modern religious ideas, including evolutionary theories and many types of historical study, in seminaries and churches as well as in public schools and universities.[10] Its rapid growth and continued vitality as a movement is no doubt a function of the comfort it brought to many people who were disturbed by the growing worldliness of American society and the increasing strength of liberalism.

These same fears naturally took other forms, depending on the circumstances. Among the Presbyterians they led to the formulation of the famous (or infamous) Hodge-Warfield doctrine of scriptural inerrancy, which between 1892 and 1910 was given official status by several deliverances of the General Assembly, including one that made

283

subscription to the "five points" of fundamentalism a condition of ordination.

In Methodist constituencies, where doctrinal rigor was less prominent, a similar response to the times led to a new surge of holiness associations, and then beyond that to the emergence and rapid growth of Pentecostalism— both of which movements also tended toward strict views of biblical inerrancy and strong apocalyptic interests. In all of these and many other churches there was great restiveness about liberal inroads on the foreign mission fields, which led to the foundation of many new independent or faith missions. This interest in world evangelism also received much encouragement from Moody and from the Student Volunteer Movement. So great was the success of these new enterprises that by 1917 a national association of independent missions was organized. Missions controversy was also prominent among the northern Baptists; but not until after 1920 did formal conservative secessions occur.

The continuing story cannot be reviewed here except to says that these rifts deepened and widened during the ensuing decades and that during the 1920s, when many of the issues of the Gilded Age returned in much intensified forms, the rift became a clear and permanent aspect of American Protestantism. After 1942 there was a National Association of Evangelicals to counterbalance the National Council of Churches. By this time there also existed a large network of Bible institutes and colleges (also inspired by Moody's example) and a considerable number of conservative seminaries, which taken together constituted a large self-enclosed educational system. And this school system may serve as well as anything to symbolize what had been happening within the Protestant establishment during the Gilded Age and the decades which followed. In the face of profound intellectual and social challenges, evangelicals began to lose confidence in America as well as in modern thought and hence surrendered their culture shaping role. They began to separate themselves from the main body of denominational Protestants, middleclass and middle-of-the-road, who made do with a benign mixture of a little evangelicalism, a little liberalism, much patriotism, too much ethnic pride, and a heavy commitment to the Puritan ethic. Still more remote from evangelicalism was a smaller but rapidly growing group of liberals, future-oriented and optimistic, who had in their midst a more realistic social gospel group which qualified its optimism with demands for drastic kinds of social reform. Hereafter the term evangelicalism would no longer designate a confident Protestant majority but an increasingly embattled minority.

The dilemma in which contemporary evangelicalism finds itself then, is deeply rooted in its historical heritage. On the one hand, it has direct links with the Protestant Reformation and earnestly seeks to retain these. Decisive modulations in this tradition's outlook have taken place. In the Great Awakening, the dimensions of enthusiasm in Puritanism were heightened, revivalism was institutionalised, and an open rift in the church was produced. The "New Lights" supported the revivals, deemphasized higher learning and attacked rationalism; the "Old Lights" were cool towards the revivals, hostile to religious experientialism, and more sympathetic toward rationalistic orthodox dogmatics. The Edwardsean tradition that ended in the New Divinity sought to mediate between the factions, but pleased neither side, being too orthodox for the one and too metaphysical for the other. The Puritan current, therefore, divided in the nineteenth century, one side calling itself evangelical and the other liberal. A powerful reconsolidation of "Modern Puritanism" took place, however, in the Second Great Awakening. Despite denominational rivalries, a large interlocking network of voluntary associations became a remarkably dynamic factor in American life. Great campaigns of evangelism and reform were carried on, despite the deep regional divisions over the slavery question. Thus the Puritan outlook, though gradually modified by the challenges to evangelism of nineteenth-century America, was in its essential features maintained.

On the other hand most evangelicals, unlike Jonathan Edwards, had allowed these very challenges to divert them from those forms of social and, above all intellectual and spiritual change, that had been a constant feature of the Western world ever since the days of Isaac Newton and John Locke. The result was a deepening theological crisis that became especially acute during the decades after the Civil War. The basic nature of this crisis had been exposed by various proponents of "Progressive Orthodoxy" such as James Marsh and Horace Bushnell who tried to mediate between the older Puritan heritage and the more critical currents of romantic and transcendental thought. Except for a few isolated intellectuals and a few embattled professors, however, America's countless colleges and seminaries were at this time closed to the critical spirit; academic freedom was almost unknown. America's vast Protestant constituency remained relatively unprepared for the avalanche of issues that the postbellum era would bring down upon them.

By the end of the century Baptists and Presbyterians were seriously divided internally, the Disciples of Christ were torn, the revivals initiated by Moody became more sectarian, dispensational, and militantly conservative. The movement was headed into fundamentalism, the Scofield Bible, the Monkey Trial, and multiple ecclesiastical divisions.

It is true that late in the 1940s this embattled and amorphous evangelicalism, consisting variously of individuals, congregations, sects, and denominations found a symbolic leader in Billy Graham and a measure of cohesion with the founding of *Christianity Today*. During the Eisenhower years, too, it found some solace in the vague approbation of conservative views which the president and many other public leaders encouraged. The soporific fifties, however, could not really soften the harsh reality for evangelicals of having to sustain their Puritanism in a world that was markedly secular, which was soon to explode in the violence of the 1960s and then be caught up in the whole shifting structure of Western moral and religious values of the 1970s.

In its present state, therefore, American evangelicalism demonstrates the amazing vitality and profound human significance of that religious revolution which the Puritans carried out and conveyed to the world. Its very durability constitutes an apologetical argument of considerable power.

On the other hand, the cost of a sharp silhouette has been great, for it has tended to bring the movement as a whole into a kind of "cognitive deviancy." [11] Most unfortunate are the types of intellectual nihilism that Elmer Towns of the Baptist Bible Fellowship celebrates in his books on the country's fastest growing congregations and Sunday schools. Here we have the frank and explicit appeal to dictatorial methods, the serving up of "simple formulae" to alienated people, charismatic preachers who are to be unhindered by church boards, and Sunday schools which are to be unspoiled by religious education.[12] Less unfortunate but still costly in the long run are those efforts to create a self-sufficient educational system, wherein learners will be spared a direct acquaintance with the difficult implications of modern science and learning. Even now it would seem to be the case that evangelicals have almost by definition resisted modern learning as it is prosecuted in both the natural and the behavioral sciences of any genuinely free university. To the extent that this is the case, evangelicalism has become a subculture that, in effect, maintains itself after the end of the Puritan epoch. As a result, the movement as a whole tends to support conservative causes in the social and political spheres as well as in the moral, religious, and intellectual spheres. Its norms tend to be drawn from the past; its critiques tend to be directed against the modern.

287

Puritanism in its flowering time was a revolution. Evangelicalism is a counterrevolution; it does not joyfully reap the harvest of the Puritan quadricentennium and then turn those riches to solution of the frightening problems, the profound moral issues, and the terrible suffering of the post-Puritan world. It tries instead to harvest the past on the assumption that the modern is the chaff which the wind driveth away. This may be a very risky strategy. And one may doubt that it is the best way to convey the riches of a great tradition to a needy world.

Notes

1. Three recent studies, not to mention innumerable others, illustrate the difficulties of definition as well as a tendency toward consensus: Bruce L. Shelley, *Evangelicalism in America* (Grand Rapids: Eerdmans Publishing Co., 1967); Donald G. Bloesch, *The Evangelical Renaissance* (Grand Rapids: Eerdmans Publishing Co., 1973); and Bernard L. Ramm, *The Evangelical Heritage* (Waco, Tex.: Word Books, 1973). Ramm praises Scholastic Orthodoxy, tends to reject modern thought (chap. 5) and yet speaks of 35 to 40 million evangelicals located almost everywhere. Bloesch calls evangelicalism a "mood," yet names nine hallmarks and then undoes that sign of precision by throwing out dozens of names from St. Theresa of Avila to Bonhoeffer. Shelley, as an historian of the National Association of Evangelicals, is more inclusive than Ramm, less eclectic than Bloesch, and more inclined to stress "a true decision for Christ." Bloesch somewhat confusingly speaks of a new evangelicalism replacing the old "Neo-Evangelicalism" of the forties and fifties (p. 30). All three distance themselves to varying degrees from fundamentalism, but do not exclude it. These works tend to confirm my view that evangelicals belong to that branch of Puritan tradition which was profoundly modified by Eighteenth- and Nineteenth-century revivalism, but which, perhaps for that reason, has only very reluctantly participated in the great intellectual revolutions of the last two or three centuries.

2. See the comments of R. H. Tawney, *Religion and Rise of Capitalism* (New York: Harcourt, Brace, 1926), p. 165; Karl Marx, *The 18th Brumaire of Louis Napoleon* (New York: International Publishers, 1963), pp. 15-17; and David Little, *Religion, Order, and Law* (New York: Harper & Row, 1969). Little's discussion of Weber's thesis and several major contributors to the ensuing debate is extremely valuable.

3. See F. Ernest Stoeffler, *The Rise of Evangelical Pietism* (Leiden: E. J. Brill, 1971); James R. Tanis, *Theodorus Jacobus Frelinghuysen* (The Hague: M. Nijhof, 1967).

4. Jonathan Edwards, *The Great Awakening;* Vol. IV: *The Works of Jonathan Edwards* (New Haven: Yale University Press, 1972).

5. Richard Hofstadter, *Anti-Intellectualism in American Life* (New York: Alfred A. Knopf, 1963). Richard Warch in a forthcoming article greatly clarifies the nature and significance of the Shepherd's Tent.

6. Nevin's most detailed indictments of "Modern Puritanism" were his studies entitled *The Anxious Bench* (1843) and *The Mystical Presence* (1846). See James H. Nichols, *Romanticism in American Theology* (Chicago: University of Chicago Press, 1961); John Williamson Nevin, ed., *The Mercersburg Theology* (New York: Oxford University Press, 1966).

7. See Stuart C. Henry's recent biography of Beecher, *Unvanquished Puritan* (Grand Rapids: Eerdmans Publishing Co., 1973), and George M. Marsden, *The Evangelical Mind and the New School Presbyterian Experience* (New Haven: Yale University Press, 1970).

8. *Robert H. Wiebe, The Search for Order 1877-1920* (New York: Hill & Wang, 1967). Cf. Gilman M. Ostrander, *American Civilisation in the First Machine Age: 1890-1940* (New York: Harper & Row, 1970); Sigmund Diamond, *The Nation Transformed: The Creation of an Industrial Society* (New York: George Braziller, 1963); and Paul A. Carter, *The Spiritual Crisis of the Gilded Age* (Dekalb: University of Northern Illinois Press, 1971).

9. Dwight Lyman Moody, "The Return of the Lord," quoted in William G. McLoughlin, ed., *The American Evangelicals, 1800-1900* (New York: Harper & Row, 1968).

10. Cf. Millard B. Gatewood, ed., *Controversy in the Twenties: Fundamentalism, Modernism, and Evolution* (Nashville: Vanderbilt University Press, 1969).

11. Peter Berger defines and applies this valuable concept in *The Sacred Canopy* (New York: Doubleday & Co., 1967).

12. Elmer L. Towns, *America's Fastest Growing Churches* (Nashville: Impact Books, 1972), pp. 193-218; Dean M. Kelley, *Why Conservative Churches are Growing* (New York: Harper & Row, 1972).

Part IV A Guide to Further Reading

Donald Tinder

Although it should be obvious, it is necessary to state that the best way to begin to learn more about American evangelicalism is through personal exposure to a wide range of evangelical individuals, congregations, and other kinds of organizations. Exposure to only a narrow range leads to results as misleading as if the cat family were described on the basis of a study of only lions or cheetahs or domestic cats. Regrettably, generalizations based on just such limited observation are all too common. To make such perceptions even less excusable is obviously a chief concern of this book.

Of course, in addition to first-hand exposure to flesh-and-blood evangelicals, careful reading of primary and secondary works is essential not only to gain historical perspective but also to learn of even greater diversity within the movement that personal encounters alone could provide.

By far the best book in which to read about the setting for American evangelicalism is *A Religious History of the American People* by Sydney E. Ahlstrom (New Haven: Yale University Press, 1972), who also wrote a chapter in this book. Although in his chapter Ahlstrom obviously questions contemporary evangelicalism's stewardship of its Puritan heritage, in his *magnum opus* he seeks to be, and

Donald Tinder is Associate Editor of Christianity Today.

largely succeeds in being, scrupulously fair, not only to evangelicalism but to the multitude of other American religious movements as well. Martin Marty sets a wider stage but with considerably less detail in what is more a phenomenological than an historical study covering the whole sweep in *Protestantism* (New York: Holt, Rinehart and Winston, 1972). Of special value are the hundred pages of annotated bibliography.

The New International Dictionary of the Christian Church, edited by J. D. Douglas (Grand Rapids: Zondervan Publishing House, 1974), has the dual advantage of briefly speaking on just about every major person, place, doctrine, or movement in the whole history of Christianity and of having been done by evangelicals from a broad range of denominational traditions. The result is not only an indispensable reference work on its subject, but a good demonstration of the maturity of evangelical scholarship. Its articles and their bibliographies should be consulted, especially for the branches of evangelicalism underemphasized in this book.

A comparable presentation of evangelical biblical scholarship on a much larger scale is the five-volume set, *The Zondervan Pictorial Encyclopedia of the Bible,* edited by Merrill C. Tenney (Grand Rapids: Zondervan Publishing House, 1975). A one-volume work serving the same purpose of illuminating both the Bible and how academically qualified evangelicals understand it is *The New Bible Dictionary,* edited by J. D. Douglas (Grand Rapids: Eerdmans Publishing Co., 1962).

Evangelical reflections on hundreds of aspects of behavior are provided in *Baker's Dictionary of Christian Ethics,* edited by Carl F. H. Henry (Grand Rapids: Baker Book House, 1973). The same is done for doctrinal themes in *Baker's Dictionary of Theology,* edited by Everett F. Harrison (Grand Rapids: Baker Book House, 1960). The notes following many of the chapters in the preceding pages will direct the student to almost all of the significant recent books by evangelicals on specific ethical and apologetical issues.

As the name of the movement implies, evangelism, sharing the *evangel*—the good news—is at the heart of evangelicalism. The papers and reports of three major congresses (Berlin, 1966; Minneapolis, 1969; and Lausanne, 1974) represent about as wide a range of evangelical leaders as is likely to be assembled together. Theological as well as practical reflections on the gospel itself, on the various ways of communicating it, and on its implications for society were presented. The first and third of these congresses were worldwide in scope, the second being American. The three reports were all published by World Wide Publications and are, respectively: *One Race, One Gospel, One Task,* edited by Carl F. H. Henry and W. Stanley Mooneyham (two volumes, 1967): *Evangelism Now,* edited by George M. Wilson (1970; and *Let the Earth Hear His Voice,* edited by J. D. Douglas (1975).

The notes following many of the chapters in this book refer to numerous articles and books *about* evangelicals (without reference to the personal faiths of the authors) as distinct from the basic reference works *by* evangelicals just mentioned. There are three warnings concerning books on evangelicalism which the student must keep in mind.

First, many, perhaps most, writings about evangelicalism are partisan. Some writers seek to discredit subtly the movement as a whole by stressing its most unattractive parts; others seek to advance only one segment of the movement while belittling and misrepresenting other segments as corollary. Some of these writings frankly admit such intentions. The ones that conceal them require even more cautious use.

Second, a problem common to many books is that their titles promise a far more general scope than their contents actually provide. The almost total exclusion of black evangelicalism from customary purview has been noted in these pages and an attempt made to correct it. However, the very large Lutheran, Wesleyan, Campbellite (Christian Churches and Churches of Christ), and Pentecostal expressions of evangelicalism have been almost as ignored in most putatively general treatments, not to mention the overlooking of smaller movements such as the Mennonites. Various explanations and excuses may be made for these omissions. What is pertinent now is to recognize that just as humanity consists of women as well as men, so American evangelicalism includes considerably more than certain white Baptists, Congregationalists, and Presbyterians.

Third, for the past half-century "fundamentalism" has been and continues to be used by many scholars, journalists, and others to refer to the whole of the movement which this book has designated "evangelicalism." On the other hand, in the past two decades a self-styled fundamentalist movement has emerged which is clearly a subdivision of evangelicalism and only partially the successor of the fundamentalist movement of the twenties. The basic point is that the contents of the book or article, not the title or terminology, have to be consulted to see about whom the author is speaking.

The History of Fundamentalism by Stewart G. Cole (1931, now published by Greenwood Press in Westport, Connecticut) and *The Fundamentalist Controversy, 1918-1931* by Norman F. Furniss (1954, now published by Archon) were written by scholars with little sympathy for or understanding of the evangelical movement. Their focus was on the controversies of the 1920s in several major denominations. Furniss explicitly disavows any intention of theological analysis. It is useful for the references to countless men and organizations and to primary sources, but the value judgments and feeble attempts at contextual understanding should be ignored. Much the same can be said for Cole who, unfortunately, was long regarded as the "standard" historian. He is the source for the often cited but mythical "five points of fundamentalism." An insufficiently noticed book is *Fundamentalism and the Mis-*

293

souri Synod by Milton L. Rudnick (St. Louis: Concordia Publishing House, 1966). The author surveys the controversies of the twenties and their precursors, and then his own Lutheran denomination. Contrary to what he expected to find when he started, his studies convinced him that the two movements, though they have many parallels, were essentially independent expressions of historic Protestantism.

Even in the twenties, and much more today, many who are called "fundamentalists" prefer the designation "evangelicals." Increasingly, those who still prefer the fundamentalist label reciprocate by disavowing the term evangelical. Generally speaking, today's fundamentalists regard evangelicals as fellow Christians who have lamentably compromised biblical standards of doctrine and practice and with whom they cannot therefore engage in cooperative endeavors. These aggressive, contemporary fundamentalists are least represented in the evangelical reference works and evangelistic congresses referred to earlier. To offset this, one should study *A History of Fundamentalism in America* by George W. Dollar (Greenville, S.C.: Bob Jones University, 1973). Dollar makes no attempt to conceal his identification with contemporary militant fundamentalism, from which he distinguishes moderate and modified fundamentalism, both of which generally prefer the evangelical designation. Moreover, Dollar recognizes that many who were looked upon as fundamentalist leaders a generation ago would not deserve that label by contemporary standards. On the other hand, Dollar is also able to fault various excesses of certain "prima donna" fundamentalist leaders. His descriptions of countless denominations, individuals, and specialized organizations make this work invaluable. Dollar's own stance is so evident that no reader will have difficulty detecting where facts fade into (usually critical) evaluations. It should be added that Dollar concentrates very heavily on Baptists. Moreover, he insists more strongly on the pretribulational rapture of the church

294

than even many militant fundamentalists would do. (And it should be added that many pretribulationists are placed both by Dollar and themselves in the evangelical camp.)

The beginnings of the split within evangelicalism into the militant fundamentalist and the self-styled evangelical subdivisions are dispassionately and fairly accurately portrayed by Louis Gasper in *The Fundamentalist Movement* (The Hague: Mouton, 1963). Gasper concentrates on the transdenominational expressions of evangelicalism since 1930. He rightly sees the emergence of Billy Graham to national prominence as being the decisive culmination of the split begun a few years earlier. As a rough rule of thumb, those who continue to use the fundamentalist label are strongly opposed to Graham's principles of operation (comparatively little exception is taken to his message otherwise), while evangelicals are generally supportive of him.

The historical background to twentieth-century evangelicalism is briefly summarized in the first half of *Evangelicalism in America* by Bruce L. Shelley (Grand Rapids: Eerdmans Publishing Co., 1967). The second half deals essentially with the National Association of Evangelicals (founded in 1942) which brings together Wesleyans and Pentecostals with the Baptists and Presbyterians who were more in the limelight in the fundamentalist controversies. (On the other hand, blacks, Lutherans, and Campbellites have not been nearly so active in the N.A.E., and militant fundamentalists have been opposed to it.)

A slightly longer overview is provided by Bernard Ramm in *The Evangelical Heritage* (Waco, Tex.: Word Books, 1973). His method is to trace broadly the history of theology rather than the histories of the various component traditions within evangelicalism. Consequently, Ramm has been faulted for minimizing the pietistic and revivalistic aspects of the heritage and the accompanying Wesleyan way of "doing" theology in favor of more "scholastic" and Calvinistic approaches. Read as a statement by one of the leading evangelical theologians, this is helpful and thought-provoking, but the students should recognize that there are other ways of telling about the heritage of evangelicalism.

One final book on historical origins is *The Roots of Fundamentalism: British and American Millenarianism, 1800-1930* by Ernest R. Sandeen (Chicago: University of Chicago Press, 1970). The consensus of reviewers is that the subtitle should have been featured rather than the title. Sandeen has done an excellent study of the rise of pre-millennialism amid a once overwhelming postmillennial milieu. However, this is only one aspect, and that not the most important, of one portion, largely Baptist and Presbyterian, of the fundamentalist or evangelical movement. Although Sandeen includes occasional qualifications, the general thrust of his work is to equate premillennalism with fundamentalism. George Dollar would agree with him on this, but most other recent students of the movement do not. Nevertheless, Sandeen's work is extremely useful if studied for what the subtitle denotes. Moreover, Sandeen has demolished the "five points of fundamentalism" myth and demonstrated the basically theological and religious nature of fundamentalism as distinct from the agrarian and antiintellectual protest movement which so many secular scholars have deemed it to be.

Finally, four books should be mentioned which reflect slightly differing postures within the wing of evangelicalism furthest removed from the militant fundamentalism advocated by George Dollar. The four all seek to distinguish a "new" evangelicalism from fundamentalism, but they by no means represent all nonfundamentalist evangelicals. They are *The New Evangelicalism* by Ronald Nash (Grand Rapids: Zondervan Publishing House, 1963), *The New Evangelical Theology* by Millard Erickson (Old Tappan, N.J.; Fleming H. Revell, 1968), *The Evangelical Renaissance* by Donald G. Bloesch (Grand Rapids: Eerdmans

Publishing Co., 1973), and *The Young Evangelicals* by Richard Quebedeaux (New York: Harper & Row, 1974). Bloesch has a long, appreciative chapter on the Pietist heritage. Quebedeaux distinguishes older and younger forms within new evangelicalism.

Index

299

301

DATE DUE